"*Visions of Vocation* is a feast for the heart, mind and soul. A master teacher, story-teller and writer, Steve Garber has woven together a lifetime of stories, insights and wisdom, vividly—and at times emotionally—showing how our vocations are at the heart of our love and service to God. I have never known anyone who teaches through story, literature and movies better than Steve. His narratives not only pull me in but they hit me right in the heart—and mind—time and time again, shaping my imagination so that when I have finished I see the world differently. And I act differently. Teachers, professors, students, parents, those in the marketplace, and all who want their lives to matter should read this book. This is a very important book for the church and Christians today."
Jim Belcher, author of *In Search of Deep Faith*

"We are known by the questions we ask, the lives we lead and the company we keep. In this wise and wonderful book, Steve Garber engages us with important and big questions, narrates stories of remarkable people and keeps great company. And along the way, we see God and the world—and ourselves—more clearly and deeply."
L. Gregory Jones, professor of theology, Duke Divinity School, and strategic director, Laity Lodge Leadership Initiative

"Few have thought as long, hard or well about vocation as Steve Garber. With his characteristically accessible and pastoral prose, in *Visions of Vocation* Garber sheds light upon the dilemmas of working well in this broken-yet-beautiful world. He equips us to fight against our tendencies toward cynicism, stoicism and distraction with biblical truth and insights from the best of philosophy and literature. His real-life stories of Christians living for the common good make vocational faithfulness—the willingness to be implicated in the pain of this world—plausible and attractive. Read this and see afresh how the Great Christian Story, and especially the innumerable wonders of the incarnation, empower us to 'tear off a corner of the darkness' in the particular places and roles we daily inhabit."
Amy L. Sherman, author of *Kingdom Calling*

"Steve Garber is a sensitive, passionate, thoughtful and wise man. This book accurately captures his concerns and hopes as he battles to make sense of a world that is simultaneously ugly and glorious. You're happy to make the journey with him because of the love and vulnerability which exude from every page."
Steve Turner, poet and author of *Popcultured*

"Reading Steve Garber on the subject of vocation and the mission of God is essential for anyone attempting to see what God is saying to the church in our day. Too many of us give lip service to the concept of the ministry of all believers, but few have truly pondered this notion as has Steve. I have found this book to be not just helpful and challenging but compelling and riveting."
John Yates, rector, The Falls Church Anglican

"Steve Garber is one of the few consistent sources of wisdom that I rely on personally for my journey as an artist and as a Christ-follower. Like Magi's stars to the weary travelers in faith and culture, *Visions of Vocation* is a clear manifestation in the dark skies of our complex times to point to an integrated source of wisdom, delight and hope."
Makoto Fujimura, artist

"*Visions of Vocation* asks the most compelling and human questions about how to love the world once you come to truly know it. These pages are packed with stories of wisdom and grace, serving as a vocational compass for anyone seeking true guidance in the midst of a complex world. I am grateful for the mentorship of Steve Garber's words, and I know you will be too."
Jena Lee Nardella, cofounder, Blood:Water Mission

"Good books tell the truest truths about the human condition, and this is truly a great book. Artfully weaving together stories, literature and his own experience, Steve has shaped the best book on vocation we have ever read. He has beautifully articulated a vision of work that we think is a must-read for everyone who wants to live with eyes wide open to the kingdom of God and the common good. This book will help you 'crush it' for the glory of God!"
Evan Loomis and Jason Ballard, entrepreneurs and cofounders of TreeHouse

"*Visions of Vocation* was not birthed in the dusty stacks of libraries, nor is it dryly academic. Steven Garber is a scholar, but also a storyteller. It is passionate and accessible, a life-affirming exploration of a question we all must face: do my life and work matter, and how can I know? Garber takes us with him into conversations with people whose daily life is in politics, business, art, homemaking and hamburgers, all for the common good. By bringing the ancient wisdom of seers and apostles together with the stories of contemporary people Garber illuminates the meaning of vocation—yours and mine—so that we can see and move beyond the restrictive confines of mere career, job and duty."
Denis Haack, editor of *Critique* and cofounder of Ransom Fellowship

"The conversation on calling has been animated by many voices, and never far from these important dialogues you will find Dr. Garber, asking the questions that have shaped and informed the trajectory of his work: What does it mean to be human? How are we to live? What truly matters? God calls us to engage this world in all its brokenness. *Visions of Vocation* is a gracious and faithful companion for this journey, much like its author."

Lisa Park Slayton, president, Pittsburgh Leadership Foundation

"*Visions of Vocation* will be considered a classic of our time, inspiring many to care more deeply and live out their own passions with vitality and integrity."

Byron Borger, Hearts & Minds Bookstore, Dallastown, Pennsylvania

"*Visions of Vocation* draws us into conversation not only with Steven Garber but also with his many and varied friends, mentors and students. The result is a rich and deep engagement with life in all its ordinariness, adventure, disappointment and mystery. At the heart of this conversation is the challenge and power of living responsibly—of taking life seriously, or paying attention, of learning and suffering, and above all, of choosing to put love into action. The result is not guaranteed, but it puts us in a place where hope is sustained and, however partially, often satisfied."

Paul S. Williams, Regent College, Vancouver

"Steven Garber's lovely and poignant book *Visions of Vocation* is a moving testament to the truth that purpose and meaning come from taking responsibility for acting upon what we know, and not hiding behind the lie that our beliefs have no real relevance in the secular marketplace. His chapter on my ancestral village of Le Chambon-sur-Lignon, where Protestant Huguenot villagers shielded 5,000 Jews from Nazi persecution during World War II—at great personal risk and without a second thought—was a reminder that like the Hebrew expression, knowing and doing are indeed inseparable aspects of a life worth living. This book should and will influence many for the good."

Bruno Roche, chief economist, Mars, Incorporated

"Steve Garber has a way of making me feel spiritually rich. What he thinks and says is what I need. I realize this because he does both so well. His exceptional biblical insight and profound humanity increase my hunger for God and the ways of God. I am left seeking God's calling into a more genuine life and believing God intends this as part of the common good for which we are made and redeemed. Feast on this book and be fed."

Mark Labberton, president, Fuller Theological Seminary, and author of *The Dangerous Act of Loving Your Neighbor*

"Steve Garber is fond of quoting Walker Percy's articulate summary of novel crafting: 'Bad books lie. They lie most of all about the human condition.' *Visions of Vocation* is precisely the opposite of a bad book—this is a good book that tells the truth about the human condition as well as so many other truths."

Donald C. Guthrie, professor of educational ministries, Trinity Evangelical Divinity School

"*Visions of Vocation* is a thoughtful meditation on human brokenness and our failure to be honest in recognizing Thoreau's insight that most of us live lives of quiet desperation. Rather than preach despair, Garber points us to Scripture, literature, music and film to illustrate the simple truth that the examined life is the only one worth living. . . . How fitting that in a book about vocation, Steven Garber has winsomely achieved his life's greatest work."

Micheal Flaherty, cofounder and president, Walden Media

"*Visions of Vocation* touches a deep place within us, which is not surprising because Steve Garber is part storyteller and sage, part prophet and soul doctor. His unique ability to guide, encourage, challenge and nurture the reader is a gift of grace and wisdom. Drawing on his years as professor and friend, Steve weaves a vision for a purposeful life, introducing us to the traveling mercies of companions who help illumine our way."

Steven Moore, president, Murdock Trust

"If I could sit at the feet of anyone to learn about vocation, it would be Steven Garber. Tuck yourself away in a corner with these pages and prepare your heart and soul to dream again. In a culture where imaginations are running dry, Garber floods your mind with the possibilities of what your role might be in putting the world back together, one vocation at a time."

Gabe Lyons, author of *The Next Christians* and founder, Q Ideas

"Garber asks the big questions in the context of today's world, artfully and compellingly opening into a conversation that moves beyond cynicism and explores more life-bearing ways of being and doing in the vast, soul-stretching space between is and ought, knowing and yet still loving."

Sharon Daloz Parks, coauthor of *Common Fire: Leading Lives of Commitment in a Complex World*

VISIONS *of* VOCATION

Common Grace for the Common Good

STEVEN GARBER

An imprint of InterVarsity Press
Downers Grove, Illinois

InterVarsity Press
P.O. Box 1400, Downers Grove, IL 60515-1426
World Wide Web: www.ivpress.com
Email: email@ivpress.com

InterVarsity Press® is the book-publishing division of InterVarsity Christian Fellowship/USA®, a movement of students and faculty active on campus at hundreds of universities, colleges and schools of nursing in the United States of America, and a member movement of the International Fellowship of Evangelical Students. For information about local and regional activities, write Public Relations Dept., InterVarsity Christian Fellowship/USA, 6400 Schroeder Rd., P.O. Box 7895, Madison, WI 53707-7895, or visit the IVCF website at www.intervarsity.org.

All Scripture quotations, unless otherwise indicated, are taken from THE HOLY BIBLE, NEW INTERNATIONAL VERSION®, NIV® Copyright © 1973, 1978, 1984, 2011 by Biblica, Inc.™ Used by permission. All rights reserved worldwide.

While all stories in this book are true, some names and identifying information in this book have been changed to protect the privacy of the individuals involved.

Excerpt from "To Tanya, on My Sixtieth Birthday," Copyright © 2005 by Wendell Berry from New Collected Email. Reprinted by permission of Counterpoint.

"To a Long Loved Love: 7" from THE WEATHER OF THE HEART by Madeleine L'Engle, copyright © 1978 by Crosswicks, Ltd. Used by permission of WaterBrook Multnomah, an imprint of the Crown Publishing Group, a division of Random House LLC. All rights reserved. Any third party use of this material, outside of this publication, is prohibited. Interested parties must apply directly to Random House LLC for permission.

Cover design: Cindy Kiple
Interior design: Beth Hagenberg
Image: The Reaper: Le moissonneur by Vincent van Gogh, Private Collection, Photo © Christie's
        Images/The Bridgeman Art Library

ISBN 978-0-8308-3666-6 (print)
ISBN 978-0-8308-9626-4 (digital)

Printed in the United States of America ∞

Library of Congress Cataloging-in-Publication Data
Garber, Steven.
   Visions of vocation : common grace for the common good / Steve Garber.
      pages cm
   Includes bibliographical references.
   ISBN 978-0-8308-3666-6 (pbk. : alk. paper)
1. Vocation—Christianity. I. Title.
   BV4740.G365 2014
   248.8'8—dc23
                                                                 2013047718

| P | 18 | 17 | 16 | 15 | 14 | 13 | 12 | 11 | 10 | 9 | 8 | 7 | 6 | 5 | 4 | 3 | 2 |
| Y | 29 | 28 | 27 | 26 | 25 | 24 | 23 | 22 | 21 | 20 | 19 | 18 | 17 | 16 | 15 | 14 |

For Meg,

who has shown that the world can be fully known

and still loved.

Contents

On Vocation

The word *vocation* is a rich one, having to address the wholeness of life, the range of relationships and responsibilities. Work, yes, but also families, and neighbors, and citizenship, locally and globally—all of this and more is seen as vocation, that to which I am called as a human being, living my life before the face of God. It is never the same word as *occupation*, just as *calling* is never the same word as *career*. Sometimes, by grace, the words and the realities they represent do overlap, even significantly; sometimes, in the incompleteness of life in a fallen world, there is not much overlap at all.

Introduction

On Learning to Be Implicated

Whenever I have encountered any kind of deep problem with civilization anywhere in the world—be it the logging of rain forests, ethnic or religious intolerance or the brutal destruction of a cultural landscape that has taken centuries to develop—somewhere at the end of the long chain of events that gave rise to the problem at issue I have always found one and the same cause: a lack of accountability to and responsibility for the world.

VÁCLAV HAVEL, IN *CIVILIZATION*

*I*t began with a phone call from the State Department. "Would you come spend an evening with the leaders of the Tiananmen Square protest? They are going to be in Washington and have some questions to ask."[1]

That was at least fifteen years ago now, but I have not forgotten that night—and I will not. Sometimes we meet people, sometimes we have conversations, that change us forever.

The questions they asked all focused on their desire to return to China someday, because—in their own words—"We love China." Politically *personas non grata* in China, they wanted a good reason to go home, one that could be sustained even in the face of suffering, of prison, of death. They were willing to do anything that might be required of them, but they wanted a reason to care about their culture.

After many questions, there was one that mattered most. In various ways they put it like this: "We have been reading the philosophers of the world, asking each, 'Do you have a good reason to be responsible for history? And is your reason sustainable, philosophically and politically?' We have not been satisfied, and we wonder whether the Christian vision is different. Does it have a better answer? We wonder what you think."

That one night turned into another a year later, and it only added to the weight on my heart. Though much of my life is conversation, I have rarely had a more intense three hours than I had with one man that second night. He had been one of the principal leaders of the protest and had finally made it out two years after Tiananmen, as he put it, "crawling from Beijing to the border." A very thoughtful and articulate person, he had the most heart-searching questions about guilt and grace—and he wanted answers.

Over the years I have agreed many times to meeting more of these men and women who have shown unusual courage at relatively young ages. Now I am getting to know folk who describe themselves as "the post-Tiananmen generation." To a person, they have learned from the generation before them, and from what I can see they are even more committed to China, its future, and for love's sake, their responsibility.

Their passion for China has stirred me, and I have listened to their longings. So when I was asked yet another time to go further up and further into my involvement with the Tiananmen leaders, I said yes again. This time it was the Beijing Film Academy that invited me, the main film school in China, and they wanted me to speak to their graduate students and professors.[2]

I had to sign various documents before going, promising that I would say nothing "counter-revolutionary." But they also asked if I would bring the film *Amazing Grace*, the story of William Wilberforce and his friends who gave their lives for the abolition of slavery. It had not yet been screened in China, and these lovers of film wanted to see it. Because of my long collegiality with Walden Media, the company was glad to give me many copies to bring along.

As I pondered what to say, I chose to step more fully into the evenings I had had with the Tiananmen leaders ten years prior. In a word, they *loved* China, and yearned to be part of its future. And now, more than ten years later, I was being given the opportunity to speak into the hopes and dreams of the some of the best young storytellers in China, and because of the astounding popularity of Chinese cinema, their visions would shape the society.

We first watched *Amazing Grace*, and as I sat there among the hundreds of students and professors, I was chilled. The film tells the tale of people who, for the love of England and the world, committed themselves to changing the laws of their land—for God's sake. They were men and women who saw themselves implicated in history, responsible for history, and gave the years of their lives to see their culture transformed. The longer I watched, the more sure I was that it was a profoundly counter-revolutionary story. My only comfort, as I pondered my future there, was that they had asked me to bring the film.

I called my lecture "Good Stories, Good Societies." Having been attentive to Chinese film for many years, I knew many of their best directors and films—each were in fact graduates of the Academy. I spent the first part of the lecture explaining why these stories and storytellers were worthy of the students' attention, as well as that of people the world over.

But I also introduced them to the thinking of two gifted artists, the American novelist Walker Percy and the Czech playwright Václav Havel. Percy describes the novelist as "a physician of the soul of society," and in his essay "Another Message in a Bottle," he argues, "Bad books always lie. They lie most of all about the human condition."[3] That insight has become foundational to me, and it is a rare day that I do not draw upon it in conversations. Havel, the playwright-become-prisoner-become-president, in all of his essays and addresses wrestles with the question of human responsibility, especially related to social and cultural conditions. He understood that, after generations of the domination of his country by the Nazis and Communists, unless the Czech people took responsibility for their future, there would be no future. I offered the film students and their professors these words of his: "The secret of man is the secret of his responsibility."[4]

And so I twined together the arguments of Percy and Havel with their own filmmakers, showing how some of their best films reflected insights about the truth of the human condition, especially about the nature of responsibility. I spoke from a manuscript I had prepared as someone standing beside me translated, sentence by sentence. When I finished, I looked out into the auditorium, wondering if anyone had understood.

For a few seconds there was silence. Then a young woman raised her hand and asked a very perceptive question. Someone else did too, and then the room was alive. There were no academic games; instead they each asked honest questions and wanted honest answers. For my part, I will simply say that I loved them for their seriousness about things that matter.

This past year, I was asked again if I would go to China, this time to Shanghai and by a group that has been long committed to asking and answering questions of great consequence. So I spent a week in the most populous city on earth, a city with four times as many skyscrapers as New York City. I had no idea what to expect from such a place, but for a week I lectured, speaking this time to people not only from China, but from all over Asia: Mongolia, Korea, Japan, the Philippines, Hong Kong, Singapore, India and others. They too wanted to talk about culture and their responsibility for the unfolding of the histories of their respective countries. They wanted good reasons to care and had chosen the language of story, a meta-narrative that would make sense of everything: God, human nature and history.

It was not unlike that evening in Washington fifteen years ago. I was once more with people who cared about their cultures and wanted good reasons to do so, reasons that could be sustained over time.

Why is it that we care? Why is it that we see ourselves implicated in the world, in the way the world is and isn't—and in the way it ought to be? And why does it seem that some do not care? I have thought about those questions for most of my life, and they continue to run through my heart.

As I have reflected on why I care about China, I know that the reasons are complex. Some of it has to do with the reality of China's increasing position in the globalizing political economy of the twenty-first century. If we are paying attention to what is going on, we have to be interested in China. Some has to do with the long history of my life and the strange "China moments" that have threaded their way through the years. As a boy, I was fascinated by Chinatown in San Francisco, often visiting there from our home in Davis, California. As a young adult, I lived in a commune in the Bay Area and spent many evenings in that same neighborhood, deepening my love for its people and its food. Twenty years later, my father was invited twice by the Bureau of Specialists in Beijing to come to China and share his expertise on the growing of healthy cotton. He came back full of stories and love for the Chinese people.

But I also know that a lot of it has to do with hearing the hearts of men and women who love their culture and who want more than anything else to be part of its future. They see themselves as responsible for China, for love's sake. And China needs them. But life for most of us does not carry the weight of Tiananmen. The reality is that our lives are very ordinary. In their own ways, of course, my Chinese friends see their lives like this too. How could they not?

Apart from being horribly plagued by hubris, we do not see ourselves as history might. We live among ordinary people doing ordinary things in ordinary places. We are families and we are neighbors, we worship and we work, we laugh and we cry, we hope and we love—the stuff of life for everyone everywhere. But it is also true that whether our vocations are as butchers, bakers or candlestick makers—or people drawn into the worlds of business or law, agriculture or education, architecture or construction, journalism or international development, health care or the arts—in our own different ways we are responsible, for love's sake, for the way the world is and ought to be. We are called to be common grace for the common good.

That is the vision of the Washington Institute, which is my work. Our credo is that vocation is integral, not incidental, to the *missio Dei,* and we work that out in many different ways in our teaching and writing, courses and curriculum. This book is an effort within that larger work, inviting you in its own way to "come and see" that this vision of vocation is being lived into by men and women, younger and older, who are committed to a faith that shapes vocation that shapes culture.[5]

"Seek the well-being of the city" was Jeremiah's prophetic word to the exiles in Babylon, for "when it flourishes, you will flourish" (Jeremiah 29:7 paraphrase). To learn to see—to see ourselves implicated in history, to see that we share a common vocation to care not only for our own flourishing, but for the flourishing of the world—is the vision that has brought this book into being.

1

To Know the World and Still Love It?

*T*here are days we remember to remember for the rest of our lives. We see something of unusual beauty or heartbreaking sorrow. We hear news of wonder and glory or of unbearable sadness. Or perhaps we heard or read something that we know is very important, and because of solidarity with history and the human condition, we know that we cannot walk away from it.

The way that Clydette Powell lives her life makes all of us stop. Several years ago she was asked by USAID and the White House to travel to Africa and spend three months assessing the impact of famine and drought on disease. A physician by training, she had taught at Harvard Medical School before deciding to live for many years in Cambodia, offering her medical skills through the work of World Vision. She eventually returned to the States, taking up the position of physician at USAID, responsible for all US programs for tuberculosis throughout the world. As she explained, "Why this matters now is that most who die of AIDS, die of tuberculosis." So in the early days of Bono's advocacy for AIDS in Africa and of the Bush administration's decision to give $15 billion toward that need, Clydette's judgments were crucial in the calculus of America's response.

It was Christmastime when she returned. As she was a dear friend, we invited her to join us for lunch one day. Our tree was still lit, the fireplace aglow, and big, fluffy snowflakes were falling outside the bay window in our living room—the one our children called the "Peter Pan window." After we sat and chatted for a while, she began to tell us of the horrors she had seen.

"It was outrageous!" she said again and again and again. I remember her words because the contrast was so stark. Christmas glory—and the greatest grief. How do you hold both in your heart? As I listened to Clydette, I wondered how she could know what she now knew and still choose to love her work and the world?

Washington, D.C., is my city. For years I have lived and moved and had my being in what has been the capital city not only of the United States but of the world. One hundred years ago it was not, and one hundred years from now it is unlikely that it still will be. As Rome was, as Constantinople was, as London was, Washington is. For now it is the city where Bono must come to plead for Africa— not Dublin, not London, not Paris, not Beijing, not New York, not Los Angeles. Washington is where decisions are made about the way the world will respond to the AIDS crisis, and it is to the White House and the World Bank that Bono has to make his case.

But if power is the coin of the realm, then cynicism is the atmosphere breathed. People with all sorts of hopes and dreams come to my city, putting their shoulders to history, working to bring their visions of the way the world ought to be into reality. "Potomac fever" is in the air—but with the potential for powerful work to be done, there is also the potential for cynicism to be born.

More often than not, people want to do the right thing. They want their lives to matter, their visions to shape the way the world works for the common good, at least as they understand the good. In a thousand different ways they want their ideas to have legs. That is what makes Washington, Washington.

Several years ago I was sitting in the Senate Dining Room in the Capitol Building talking with the novelist Tom Wolfe, and a few of us were asking questions about his life and work. One longtime journalist in the city asked, "What is the difference between Washington and New York?" Without a blink, Wolfe, a New Yorker, responded, "Washington is the city of ideas. People come here because of ideas, to debate ideas, to see ideas become reality." That seemed remarkably perceptive.

But because that is true, it is likely that those who come to the "city of ideas" will join the generations before them that realized the sober truth that the work of Washington is a very messy business too. As Otto von Bismarck, the nineteenth-century Prussian statesman, noted several generations ago, "If you want to respect law or sausage, then don't watch either being made."[1]

Ideas about who we are and how we live together is the stuff of this city. Laws are imagined, laws are debated, laws are legislated. And it is like making sausage—very messy, very ugly and very smelly. For good-hearted people it is very difficult to know this city and to still love it. In fact I would argue that it is the most difficult task anyone who lives here faces.

Which is why, of course, hearing Clydette's account of her months in Africa weighed upon me so heavily. Now that she had seen so much, could she, would she, still give herself to the vocation of loving and serving God and his world "with gladness and singleness of heart," as the Book of Common Prayer calls us to?

A GOOD QUESTION—NO CHEAP ANSWER

A few days later I was at a college in the Midwest, speaking at a Veritas Forum. My conversation with Clydette still heavy on my mind, I chose to speak about the task of learning in a world that is marked by very difficult realities. I began with Clydette's story, our dinner with her and her repeated words, "It was outrageous!" I asked the students to consider the connection between education and vocation, in particular wanting them to ponder if what they were learning about the world had the intellectual substance that years of living in the world would require of them. Were their ideas strong enough, real enough, true enough, for the complex challenges of the world?

I showed some of the movie *Magnolia*, at the time one of the most fascinating films among university students. Brilliantly imagined, the story is about the nature of the universe, whether it is one of chance and coincidence, or of choices and consequences. But written into its heart is the question, *Can you know the world and still love it?* Or, very poignantly, *Can you know me and still love me?*

And to press the point, I asked, "Will you be able to know the world, as my friend Clydette knows it, and still choose to love it?" Were they learning in such a way that their disciplines would form the foundation for a life of engagement, of stepping into the mess of the world, understanding it and choosing to serve it?

After the lecture, I noticed some young men who were a bit older than the typical undergraduate. They were a group of musicians who called themselves Jars of Clay. I knew of them, but did not know them, and they had their own questions to ask. So we talked and a conversation began that continues to this day. Over the months, they asked about books and essays to read and I was increasingly impressed with their moral seriousness. One day we talked about Africa and their desire to put their creative energy behind an effort to address its complex need for clean blood and water.

And then months later we talked again. They were on their tour bus and were making their way through concerts along the West Coast. They told me that they just played guitars and keyboards, and while they had an honest concern for Africa, they did not know what to do about it, given their gifts and time. Did I have any ideas? I told them that a week earlier I had been in Phoenix, Arizona, speaking at a conference called "The Faces of Justice," and had met a young woman named Jena Lee from Whitworth College who had impressed me with her articulate passion for Africa. Since they were going up the West Coast to Washington on their tour, I suggested they meet my young friend, which they did.

It is a long story, but when Jena graduated that spring, she moved to Nashville to work with the Jars of Clay guys to begin Blood:Water Mission. Those early months were hard ones for everyone—especially Jena. There were many tears and heart-searching questions about the very idea. *Could we? Is it really possible? This is so much harder than I wanted it to be!* And it was. But she held on, and slowly the vision was born.

Years later there are more than a thousand different projects in Africa that have grown out of Blood:Water Mission's work. Jena has done a remarkable job, taking the band's life and hopes, connecting them to hers, and birthing an organization that is healthy and responsible. The board has grown, and one of its prized members has been Clydette, who is still at USAID doing her work on the global threat of tuberculosis. She has brought all that and more to bear for the sake of the vision and work of Blood:Water Mission, with gladness and singleness of heart marking her vocation.

To know the world and still love it? There is not a more difficult task that human beings face. If it is one thing to hope for Africa, to be willing to step into its dreams and needs, it is something else altogether to have the staying power to keep at it over time. If it is admirable to respond to the needs of a village in western Kenya, afflicted by deaths from AIDS and absolutely no access to clean water—and in the physiology of health and disease, they are integrally related—then it is something else altogether to continue to care for the people and their needs when it moves from vision to reality. The complexity of responsible love in the name of justice and mercy leaves us with no cheap answers to any of the important questions.

TO TEACH WHAT IT MEANS TO KNOW

How do we see what is awful and still engage, still enter in? How can we have our eyes open to reality and understand that we are more implicated, for love's sake, now that we see? As Clydette and Jena have been my teachers, so has Simone Weil. In the 1940s, on the last night of her life, Weil wrote, "The most important task of teaching is to teach what it means to know."

They are weighty words. To say something is "the most important" is to commit oneself. We judge and evaluate, and then we step in, arguing that when all is said and done we believe that *this* matters more than anything else. In politics and love, in economics and education, in the whole of life, we live by our judgments.

To teach what it means to know? Found in the journal at her bedside, these were the final words of Simone Weil, the French philosopher who died in the 1940s. While her social position would have allowed otherwise, her own passions and commitments led her to the decision that while others suffered during the war years, she would eat only that which was available to the ordinary people of France. And simply said, she starved herself to death.

Not a suicide—that would make it something other than it was. It was more that she was not a healthy person; her friends saw her as frail. And while in a different day under different conditions she might have made other choices, with an unusual starkness grounded in love she decided to live very simply, as simply as those who suffered. In the quietness of her own room, still very much alive to the world and all that it required of her, she became increasingly weak until one night, after writing in her journal, she went to sleep and never woke up.

Where did this seriousness of heart come from? Why did she see the world as she did? Why did the weightiness of the world mean so much to her? And why would *knowing* become that which mattered most?

Weil was born to a prominent Jewish family in the early years of the twentieth century. By age ten she had decided that she was a communist. Whatever we now think a century later about the Marxist legacy, at the time it meant that she was surprisingly thoughtful and passionate, especially about the needs of those who suffered and groaned. It did not seem right to her that some should have so much, and some should have very little.

As she grew older, eventually studying at the Sorbonne, her beliefs in the communist vision deepened. She read with passion, wrote with eloquence, and finished as the best student in her class, outpacing even the brilliance of Simone de Beauvoir, who later came to prominence herself as both a philosopher and the lover of Jean Paul Sartre. Weil knew, however, that as committed as she was she had yet to even meet a flesh-and-blood communist. So when Leon Trostky came through Paris that summer, it seemed to the young Weil that all her dreams would be satisfied.

But the night he spoke became a line-in-the-sand moment for her. The longer she listened the more sure she was that, while he was a visionary for her cause ("Trotsky, after all!"), he loved his

ideas more than he loved people. He seemed to be enamored with
"humanity," but was indifferent to the lives of ordinary men and
women, the proletariat of Weil's own passions. The following day
she left Paris and her communism.

Weil spent the next years getting to know the farmers and factory
workers of France, the ones whose hopes and dreams her communism was to have defended. She persistently stuck by her commitments, but over time she wanted something more—a more
sustainable reason to love the dispossessed. If the ideas of Marx and
Lenin and Trotsky failed her and her country, was there an answer
to be found anywhere?

She discovered it finally in the God who cries, the God who has tears.

A strange answer? Perhaps, but for her it finally satisfied the
deepest longings of her heart—she wanted a good reason to love
what she knew. Her passion was imbued with new meaning and she
began to write, putting together a body of work that will stand for
generations to come.

Among many essays that she wrote, there is one that I have loved
most, called "On the Right Use of School Studies with a View to the
Love of God." The title seems unusual to us, I admit, but its insights
are profound, speaking to all of us, whether we see ourselves as
students or as lifelong learners, as the vocation of student starts at
the beginning of life and continues on to the end of life—at least if
we are people with ears that hear and eyes that see. Weil argues that
it is in learning to *pay attention* that we begin to understand the
meaning of life and of learning. What does she mean?

To pay attention is to see what matters and what does not matter.
It is to discern rightly, to choose well. Yes, it is to *know* as we ought
to know, to know in a way that leads us to love. She calls this kind
of study *sacramental*, as it is a kind of learning that is born of a love
of God for the world—and in it a calling to love as God loves because we know as God knows.

Her vision is formed by the story of the Good Samaritan, because in it she sees the primary issue as one of having learned, or not learned, to *pay attention* to things that matter. The novelist Walker Percy might have called it "The Story of the Man Who Got All A's and Who Still Flunked Life," as its meaning is cross-cultural and cross-generational, an affliction of everyone's soul. The story of the Good Samaritan is told within a conversation between Jesus and an expert in the Judaic law. This man begins by asking questions that are not fully honest, as he himself knew the answers to his own questions. In response to Jesus' assertion to "love your neighbor as yourself," the expert asks, "So, who is my neighbor?" And Jesus says, finally, "While I am not interested in this kind of conversation, at all—because you don't seem morally serious—I will give you a story."

So he tells of a man on his way to Jericho, who while walking down through the hills east of Jerusalem is beaten and robbed. Two religious leaders, men much like the expert in the law, walk by and do not see a neighbor. They see a man, but do not see a neighbor—someone their law requires them to care for—and they pass by, having justified their indifference religiously, historically and sociologically. They had not learned to pay attention.

In contrast, the Samaritan does see a neighbor and stops to care for him because he has learned to pay attention, to understand what he sees and why it matters. Weil also calls this kind of seeing *sacramental*, because it is a kind of learning that connects heaven to earth. Sacraments always do that—they give us the grace to understand that the universe is coherent, that things seen and unseen are equally real, equally true. And they allow us to understand that the most ordinary elements of life can be made holy—even our learning, even our labor, even our love.

When we see all of life as sacramental, as the graceful twining together of heaven and earth, then we begin to understand the meaning of vocation, which in their very different ways are what the stories of Clydette, Jena and Simone Weil are each about. We can begin to see that all of life, the complexity of our relationships and responsibilities—of family and friendships, of neighbors near and far, of work and citizenship, from the most personal to the most public—indeed, everything is woven together into the callings that are ours, the callings that make us *us*.

THE "COME AND SEE" PEDAGOGY

This is a book about the most difficult task, the most important task. There is nothing we are asked to do that requires more of us than to know and to love at the same time. Mostly we choose otherwise. Mostly we choose to step away, now knowing as we do. Whether it is in the most familiar of relationships, as in marriage, or in the most far-reaching of responsibilities, as in the global AIDS crisis, when we begin to really know what someone is like or what something or someplace is like, the calculus of our hearts more often than not leads us to conclude that it will no longer be possible to love. How can we, after all? Now we know!

But this book is also about the people I know, my community of friends, some in Washington and others in many places beyond the Beltway. One of my deepest commitments is to the "come and see pedagogy" of the Gospels. When the rabbi Jesus was asked about his life, he responded, "Come and see." We learn the truest truths, the most important things, only when we look over the shoulder and through the heart, only when we can see that ideas have legs and that worldviews can become ways of life.

So when I travel around the country and beyond, I talk about people I know who in their very different ways are connecting what they believe with the way that they live in and through their vocations. In fact, they are showing that it is possible to honestly know and to responsibly love as they take up the callings and careers that are theirs. And so time and again, I will say to those who have asked me to speak, "Come and see." Yes, come and see that what I am saying is possible. People actually do live like this—and you can too.

It is possible to live with your eyes open to the realpolitik of this life and to still love what you know. We do not have to play games with ourselves or with history, pretending that the world is a nicer place than it ever can be, that somehow really awful things do not happen, that horribly sad moments are not ours to live with and through.

We do not have to decide that the only livable responses are the most perennial responses, the ones that human beings have made since the beginning of time, those of cynicism and stoicism.[2] Both of course are ways of protecting our hearts from being hurt again, ways of "knowing" that do not ask us to love what we know. Rather they are ways of knowing that allow us to step away from history and from our responsibility for the way that history unfolds. They give us the ability to say no to the tragedies and heartaches of life, and to protect ourselves from being hurt by becoming too close to what will inevitably bring pain.

We can choose to know what is going on in the world and still love the world. But we need good reasons to do so. We are no different than Simone Weil. As we know, the romanticism that was at the heart of Marx's utopian vision eventually imploded. She understood it earlier than most as she saw it painfully incarnate in Trotsky.

She was also right about the God who has tears.

THE COMPLEXITY OF OUR TEARS

One day I was teaching on Capitol Hill and at the end of the afternoon one of my colleagues asked me if I knew a particular woman. I said that I did and he told me that she had been found murdered in her apartment that morning, just a few blocks from where I was standing. I fell back against the wall, screaming inside, *NO!*

Over the next few days, I found myself rethinking everything that mattered most to me. I still loved my wife, but I thought about her differently—that she was alive and very tender to me. I still loved my children, but I thought about them differently—I wanted to protect them from a murderous world, and was sure that in the end I couldn't. I still loved my work, but I thought about it differently—would I be able to teach my students to honestly step into the sordidness of the city and world, knowing that they too might suffer?

What I wasn't sure about was God. Those were dark days for me, as it seemed that I had now seen enough to know that what I had believed about faith and hope and love was not sustainable. This was one too many stories of horrible sorrow. How could it all still be true in the face of a friend being stabbed to death? And I began to wonder, *Is there something that is more true than what I have believed? Is there an account of the universe that makes more sense of griefs like this?*

We gathered together to mourn our friend's death, and we cried and cried. While the days are a blur in some ways, I still remember wondering about God and the world, perplexed as to what could be honestly believed.

In those same weeks, *Harper's Magazine* featured an evening-long conversation between two professors, Neil Postman and Camille Paglia, about the meaning of television for persons and for politics. Yes, the stakes were raised by the technology of TV: was it a social good, or not? At that time, Postman was the most honored and widely read observer of technology and its meaning for who we are and how we live; Paglia was a celebrated feminist philosopher with sometimes surprising views of the way the world is and ought to be. He was critical of television, and she was not.

The magazine gave them a glorious meal together, a multicourse dinner—and recorded every word of their conversation. So from appetizers to salads and soups, on to the main dishes and desserts, *Harper's* allowed us to listen in as these two remarkably bright people debated the virtues of a television-shaped society.

Toward the end of the meal, Postman made an observation that summed up his criticism: "How is it possible to watch the evening news, and in five minutes hear about a plane crash in India, an earthquake in Chile, a rape in Central Park, that the Mets beat the Cardinals, and finally an ad for hemorrhoids medicine—and somehow take it all in?" He argued that as human beings we cannot do so, and we choose to step back, unable to respond to the torrent of information, poignant and horrific, playful and commercial as it is. Paglia responded, "But Neil, that's the way the world is. Buddha smiles at it all."[3]

When I read her words, I recoiled, knowing that was not an adequate response to my friend's murder. How could it ever be? There was a profound moral and metaphysical equivalency in her judgment, and it seemed completely out of touch with the painfulness and evil of cold-blooded murder. But I realized she was not alone in her conclusion. Reflecting on what I knew of the world and the worldviews of it, I knew that one of the deepest streams in the human heart is stoicism, and that its vision of life under the sun is manifest in both the East and the West, in pantheism as well as materialism.

I also found myself thinking again about God and what in fact his tears mean. About fifteen years earlier I had read an essay by Benjamin Warfield, a professor at Princeton Theological Seminary at the turn of the twentieth century. In the first paragraphs of "The Emotional Life of Our Lord," he argues that the Gospels were written within a Stoic culture, so that the incarnation must be seen as an alternative account of that universe. In particular, he maintains that the incarnation is a counter-argument to stoicism.

Paglia's "Buddha smiles at it all" seemed a million miles from Warfield's reading of the Gospels, especially his lengthy account of

John 11 and the response of Jesus to the death of Lazarus. That biblical story was significant to me even then, but the murder of my friend pushed me to the wall and forced me to ask, *Does this still make sense of what I see and hear? Does it still make sense of the world as I know it?*

Warfield lingers, theologically speaking, over the time when Jesus enters into Bethany, hearing the wails of the village and especially of his friends Martha and Mary. John does record, "Jesus wept," but Warfield digs deeper and opens windows into the heart of God, incarnate in Jesus, who twice is said to have "groaned severely in his spirit." He does what a good reader of the text will always do and asks about the meaning of John's words. What he found surprised me. The very words that are used are the same ones that Greek poets used to describe a warhorse ready to enter battle, a stallion rearing on his hind legs, nostrils flaring, angry at what he sees and ready to enter the conflict as a warrior himself, even as he carries a warrior in armor on his back.

That Jesus responded like this matters immensely. There are moments when we can do nothing else than cry out against the wrongs of the world. *It is just not the way it is supposed to be! Outrageous, it is outrageous!* Tears matter, and sometimes they are very complex.

COME AND SEE

We all cry—but what is important here is why we cry and when we cry and what our crying means for who we are and how we live.

As a father of young children, I saw lots of tears. Each one— Eden, Elliott, David, Jessica and Jonathan—moved from the innocent tears of their early weeks to the stubborn and selfish tears of their early years. And along the way, with each one, I tried to explain that tears were good gifts to us, so that we needed to take care of them, "saving them for when we really need to cry someday— so don't use them all up right now, because someday you will need to cry." Even for the littlest ones among us, tears are complex.

And they only become more so. Most who know anything at all about the Oxbridge professor C. S. Lewis know that he wrote two books on pain and sorrow. One is more an apologetic on the nature of suffering, *The Problem of Pain,* and another he wrote after watching his wife, Joy, die of cancer, *A Grief Observed.* They are two different readings on the same human heart, trying to understand what we do with the wounds of the world.

A caricature of Lewis is portrayed in the film *Shadowlands*: an academic who had lived his whole life in an ivory tower, limiting his knowledge of sorrow to the theoretical. But the truth is that Lewis had known unbearable pain from his boyhood on: from his mother's death when he was ten, his horribly lonely adolescent years of schooling in Dickensian places of pedagogical horror, to his wounding in World War I and more. Because these experiences were true of Lewis, I have been able to learn from him, knowing that he knows.

Most of life is autobiographical for all of us—and so it was for Lewis. Growing out of his years of sorrow, especially the ones of watching his mother become sick and die, *The Magician's Nephew* tells the tale of a boy named Digory who enters into the world of Narnia on the day of its creation. Digory has mixed motivations, which is the way it is for all of us. On the one hand, it is for his friend Polly's sake that he takes up the adventure that leads him into Narnia, sure that she is in distress and wanting to help. But on the other it is because of his mother's sickness and his own great grief that he is willing to do anything for anyone that might make her better.

Aslan, the lion who is king of the new world of Narnia, draws Digory into a conversation. In his heart, Digory begins to imagine that he can make a deal with Aslan: *I will do this for him if he does this for me.* But the closer he gets to the great lion, the more sure he is that no deals can be struck. It is then that he looks up at the lion and sees tears streaming down his tawny face. Lewis writes that Digory was then "sure that the lion cared more about my mother than I did myself." And knowing that to be true, he opened his heart to the calling that became his, as Aslan had work for him to do in addressing the heartaches of that very new world.

"A children's story which is enjoyed only by children is a bad children's story. The good ones last," Lewis once wrote.[4] Over the years, in the moments when life seems bleakest, when I can only sigh or groan, I have come back again and again to *The Magician's Nephew*. Not unlike the insights of Weil and Warfield, Lewis gives us an image that is profoundly rich and wonderfully tender. We need both.

The tears of God are complex. They must be tears of sympathy, even empathy, as Aslan weeps for Digory's mother and as Jesus weeps with his friends at the death of their brother. But sometimes they are also tears of anger at the unnaturalness of death, at the distortion of death, at the skewing of human hopes, as Jesus "groaned severely in his spirit" at the death of Lazarus.

As the days passed after my friend's murder, I entered again into the tears of God. It mattered, supremely, that Jesus wept, tearful about our sorrows, weeping with those who wept, *and* that he groaned severely, being angry at the distortion of life that death is. Years have come and gone since those weeks of great sadness and there have been other days of tragedy, as there will be in the days to come. But I am sure now that I need John 11 to be in the Bible. I need for God to have tears, even, and especially, complex tears, because some days I do too.

So, reader, come and see. In these next pages, you will meet my friends from near and far, men and women who incarnate the reality that we can know and still love the world, even in its wounds—perhaps especially in its wounds—whether they be in family or friendship, psychological or sociological, in economic life or political life, in the arts or in education, in small towns or on complex continents. As the poet Bob Dylan once sang, "Everything is broken." Yes, *everything*, and so we must not be romantics. We cannot afford to be, just as we cannot be stoics or cynics either.

But the story of sorrow is not the whole story of life either. There is also wonder and glory, joy and meaning, in the vocations that are ours. There is good work to be done by every son of Adam and every daughter of Eve all over the face of the earth. There are flowers to be grown, songs to be sung, bread to be baked, justice to be done, mercy to be shown, beauty to be created, good stories to be told, houses to be built, technologies to be developed, fields to farm, and children to educate.

All day, every day, there are both wounds and wonders at the very heart of life, if we have eyes to see. And seeing—what Weil called learning to know, to pay attention—is where vocations begin.

2

If You Have Eyes, Then See

When there's all kinds of chaos
And everyone is walking lame
You don't even blink now do you

BONO, "WHEN I LOOK AT THE WORLD"

*N*ot so many years ago *The Last Butterfly* came to an arthouse theater in the Georgetown neighborhood of Washington, D.C. Surprisingly beautiful and unusually engaging, the film was serious about serious ideas and issues that have consequences for who we are and how we live.

It is a story of vocation lost and vocation found. Worn down by personal failures and political pressures, a man loses his way in the world. But as he walks into the refiner's fire of realpolitik, forced to decide what he believes about what is real and true and right, he finds himself and his vocation once again. *The Last Butterfly* is about moral imagination, about learning to see with the heart in the context of one's calling, right in the middle of the push and shove of life, full as it is of complex responsibilities.

Set in 1940s Europe, the gifted Czech director Karel Kachyna's story begins in Nazi-dominated Paris.[1] Antoine Moreau is the most famous mime in Europe, the featured artist on stages in every capital city of the continent. But as the war progresses, his artistic vision gets lost in the swirl of too much alcohol and the political propaganda of Vichy France. Rather than a celebrated mime, he becomes a clown. But he does not completely forget: he dreams of what might be. And then one night, with a Parisian theater full of the Gestapo, he decides to again connect calling and career, giving the speech of his life—in silence.

He is heard, too loudly, and is "invited"—with arm twisted behind his back—to give a performance for Jewish children in Theresienstadt, the Czech city maintained by the Nazis as a showplace to the world, maliciously maintaining that they were in fact taking good care of the Jews. With the promise of a return to Paris once he performed, he plans his show to entertain the children.

Moreau decides on the fairy tale "Hansel and Gretel" and finds wide interest among the children of Theresienstadt, who beg to join him in the play. To his surprise, he also finds musicians who want to help with the production as well. Several are individuals he has known from his travels throughout Europe—the maestro of an important orchestra in one city, the first violinist of another—as well as some of the best musicians in Europe who have gathered in this "city of the Jews."

What he does not understand is that the uncommon interest in his work is because it is literally a matter of life and death for the Jews, children and adults alike. Theresienstadt, rather than being a showplace, is in reality "an outpost of hell," as the Jews saw it. It is the last stop on the train line to Auschwitz. Week after week, cars full of Jews leave Theresienstadt for the death camp.

The gifted mime is slow to see. But painful experience by painful experience, he begins to understand where he is and

therefore what his responsibility is. How hard that is for human
beings. Our propensity to deceive ourselves about our place and
purpose makes it so very difficult to see the truth of our lives, to
understand the meaning of our moment in history and our responsibility to it.

So Moreau transforms the story from the traditional tale of
children lost in the woods with a witch to one in which the cosmic
conflict between good and evil is played out on stage. Rather than
the children winning in the end and having a gingerbread feast, the
witch pushes them into a fiery furnace, silently cackling all along
the way.

If you have eyes, then see.

The grand day of the performance finally comes. The posters are
in the streets. Flowers have been put in window boxes. Bread is
given out to children in the park. The show is on, and the play
begins. Seated in the front row and beaming at their ability to con-
found the International Red Cross which is there to assess whether
the Jews are in fact being well cared for, the Nazi officials begin to
squirm in their seats as they hear and see that the mime has spoken
forcefully and powerfully against them. The silence of his story has
spoken volumes.

Works of art that last do so, in large measure, because they ask
and answer the perennial questions which press upon human
beings in every century and in every culture. The importance of
The Last Butterfly is that it asks the viewer this probing question:
In the context of one's calling, how does one learn to see with the
eyes of the heart, to see oneself as responsible for the way the
world is and isn't?

THE OBEDIENCE OF CORPSES

"Corporate evil does not begin with the gas ovens. It begins, more
often than not, processed in triplicate."[2] So observed Hannah

Arendt as she reflected on the horrors of the Holocaust, understanding our ability as human beings to excuse ourselves from accountability, fragmenting the moral universe as we do—*It was him, you see. He did it. I only signed my name to a small paper. We all did. What difference did that make anyway?*

Arendt was born a German Jew. As a student of the history of ideas, she was intensely interested in their meaning for human life, so she focused on the existentialist writers of the mid-twentieth century. She also immersed herself in the *Confessions* of Augustine of Hippo, writing a dissertation titled *Love and Saint Augustine,* in which she asked this very searching question: What is the relevance of the neighbor, especially of love for one's neighbor?[3] This became the question of her life as she kept finding reasons to ask it again and again.

After the publication of *The Origins of Totalitarianism* in 1951, Arendt's effort at making moral sense of Hitler and Nazism, one reviewer called her "the most original and profound—therefore the most valuable—political theoretician of our times."[4] A decade later, she offered the world *Eichmann in Jerusalem: A Report On the Banality of Evil,* a compilation of her essays for *The New Yorker* on the trial of Adolph Eichmann, the Nazi official given primary responsibility by Hitler to answer "the Jewish question."[5] The book is a fascinating account of a man's life, from childhood through his last hour on earth. Fifteen years after the war, he was captured in Argentina and he was tried in 1962 in Jerusalem for his crimes against the Jewish people. With an unusual eye, acting as both journalist and moral philosopher, she interpreted what she heard as she sat in the courtroom, trying to make sense to herself and the world the nature of Eichmann's responsibility.

Banality. It was the *ordinariness* of Eichmann's life that so struck Arendt. He did not get up in the morning announcing his ambition

to inflict horror and terror; rather, he was simply obeying orders.
He was just doing his job. In a captivating though sobering chapter,
"The Duties of Law-Abiding Citizens," she described Eichmann as
reading his world through this lens:

> This was the way things were, this was the new law of the land,
> based on the Führer's order; whatever he did he did, as far as
> he could see, as a law-abiding citizen. He did his *duty*, as he
> told the police and the court over and over again; he not only
> obeyed *orders*, he also obeyed the *law*.[6]

The distinction mattered to Eichmann. In the pharisaism of his
heart, he understood his employment as a public vocation with
professional responsibilities, so that it was important to not only do
one's duty but to obey the law—even if the law was one and the
same with the fatally flawed Führer himself. Arendt painstakingly
set forth the historical details of the Nazi vision in general, and
Eichmann's role in particular, always returning to the question,
Why didn't he see these people as neighbors? What perversion of law
and order made it possible to go to work day by day, year after year,
making choices with horrific consequences, and to see it all as
"my duty"?[7]

To Arendt's dismay, the prosecutor, counsel for the defense and
judges all missed the *meaning* of Eichmann: "Alas, nobody believed
him." Their conclusion instead was that he deliberately misrepre-
sented himself, skewing what he knew and what he did—in the
name of "I was just doing my duty." She thought that they were "too
good" themselves,

> perhaps too conscious of the very foundation of their pro-
> fession to admit that an average, "normal" person, neither
> feeble-minded nor indoctrinated nor cynical, could be per-
> fectly incapable of telling right from wrong. They preferred to

conclude from occasional lies that he was a liar—and missed the greatest moral and even legal challenge of the whole case.[8]

Also perplexed by Eichmann and the court, she tried to find language sufficient to communicate the moral meaning of his actions, and offered the word *thoughtlessness*—he did not think things through, he was not thoughtful about what he did and what it meant. In the narrowness of his vision of neighbor, of citizen, of employee, he failed to follow through on the moral implications of his beliefs and behavior. In the postscript to her story, she writes,

> *He merely,* to put the matter colloquially, *never realized what he was doing.* . . . It was sheer thoughtlessness—something by no means identical with stupidity—that predisposed him to become one of the greatest criminals of that period.[9]

In his moral obtuseness, Eichmann protested, "With the killing of Jews I had nothing to do. I never killed a Jew, or a non-Jew, for that matter—I never killed any human being. I never gave an order to kill a Jew or a non-Jew; I just did not do it."[10] Arendt observes,

> The fact is that Eichmann did not see much. . . . He never actually attended a mass execution by shooting, he never actually watched the gassing process. . . . He saw just enough to be fully informed of how the destruction machinery worked: that there were two different methods of killing, shooting and gassing; that the shooting was done by the Einsatzgruppen and the gassing at the camps, either in chambers or in mobile vans; and in the camps elaborate precautions were taken to fool the victims right up to the end.[11]

And yet, he did see *enough to be fully informed* and therefore he was responsible.

On morally and legally conflicted grounds, for Arendt at least, the court found Eichmann guilty. Not as a man so numbed to his humanity that he acted inhumanely, but as a liar—someone who knowingly distorted his responsibility. Eichmann was profoundly disappointed at the verdict—shocked, really—when he was found guilty of crimes against humanity. He had been so impressed with the sincerity of the judges, so sure that their honest interest in him and his motivations would lead them to understand that he was only doing his job and simply following the law. In a chilling self-assessment, he stressed that he had offered his nation blind obedience, *Kadavergehorsam*—the "obedience of corpses."[12]

Eichmann's failure to see truthfully enabled him, by just doing his job, to oversee Theresienstadt, the "city of the Jews" in *The Last Butterfly*. The film is what we call historical fiction, but Eichmann's role was far from fictional. Blind to the meaning of who he was and what it meant, he made sure that the trains left on time for Auschwitz, going to bed at night certain that "with the killing of Jews I had nothing to do."

THE MURDEROUS, MECHANIZED TWENTIETH CENTURY

The stories of Nazis and Jews continue to ripple through contemporary consciousness. They are worth telling and telling again as their moral starkness continues to show where the philosophical and political lines in the sand are. We see our own choices more truthfully, our own beliefs more plainly, when they stand next to the hallmark of horror which was the Holocaust.

And yet to most of us, its dreadfulness seems a long way from where we live and move and have our being. In the ordinariness of our lives, full of study and play, work and worship, full of relationships with family and friends, what have we to do with *Kadavergehorsam*? With rare exceptions, the choices we make and the consequences which follow from them pale before the heartlessness of "the obedience of corpses." We are butchers and bakers and candle-stick makers—not Nazi commandants and bureaucrats. Yes, yes and yes again.

But the harsh truth is that the twentieth century produced other holocausts, some more terrifying than that of Nazis, and to own that history is part of our human responsibility even in the midst of our ordinary lives in ordinary places. Larger and smaller, they span the century, giving our collective memory names which send shivers through our souls: Stalin, Pol Pot, Idi Amin, Saddam Hussein, Somalia, Bosnia, Rwanda, the Sudan, each a name that remind us of humanity at its worst. The distinguished and brilliant writer Walker Percy, in looking back across the last one hundred years, sadly pro-claimed it "that murderous, mechanized 20th century."

Take Rwanda. Before it became synonymous with sorrow, it was a relatively small African country unknown to the global com-munity until the world watched as it imploded in the mid-1990s. Most of us saw it as someone else's problem. Rwandans were not our neighbors. For political, sociological, historical and economic reasons, they were something even less than neighbors.

But then, slowly, the stories began to leak out of mass murders, hundreds of thousands of human beings hacked to death, killed in the most hideous ways. When it was all over, with the grieving, groaning Rwandan people left to the count their dead, the United Nations decided to investigate, assembling a team of attorneys from all over the world.

The United States chose Gary Haugen to represent its interests. A Californian who early on was captivated by the biographies of Abraham Lincoln and Martin Luther King Jr., Gary began studies at Harvard University in the early 1980s. In those same years the university celebrated its 350th anniversary. Gary was fascinated by the university's seal, with the motto *Veritas, Christo et ecclesia,* which is still pictured in the stained-glass windows on campus. The words intrigued him—*Truth* as the central flag, *Christ and the church* as banners unfurled alongside—as they called for an understanding of truth imbued with philosophical and theological meaning that was far from what Harvard had become by the late twentieth century.

Undergraduate though he was, Gary stepped into the anniversary celebration with an effort called *Veritas Reconsidered*, a magazine-length collection of stories of professors and alumni whose Harvard experience included engaging truth within the Christian story. The publication went all over campus, and then it went all over the world.

Upon graduating, Gary went to South Africa to work with Michael Cassidy of Africa Enterprise, which for a generation had been a leading voice for reconciliation among the deeply divided peoples living under apartheid. That apprenticeship profoundly influenced Gary, giving him eyes to see that social and political responsibility could be integrally connected to his beliefs about God and history, Christ and the church.

Several years later, law degree in hand, Gary came to Washington, D.C., and took a position with the Justice Department. There his primary caseload focused on police brutality within the United States—a tough assignment for anyone. It was from that setting that Gary was called in 1994 to represent the United States on the United Nations commission to investigate the genocide in Rwanda.

Because of a leadership collapse, Gary was made the chief investigator of the commission. That meant he was given the responsibility to spend months of his life walking the killing fields of Rwanda, seeing and smelling the unimaginable, trying to make sense *for* the world of what had happened *when* the world had decided to sit in silence.

Good societies anywhere require people with a similar sense of calling, folk who see into the messes and horrors and complexities of human history and decide to enter in for justice's sake, for mercy's sake.

And yet it is with some irony that Gary had his undergraduate formation at Harvard in the last quarter of the twentieth century. In the same period of Gary's schooling, a graduate student orator at a Harvard commencement observed,

> They tell us it is heresy to suggest the superiority of some value, fantasy to believe in moral argument, slavery to submit to a judgment sounder than your own. The freedom of our day is the freedom to devote ourselves to any values we please, on the mere condition that we do not believe them to be true.[13]

The moral vacuity of that kind of education leaves citizens and their societies exposed to the malice and thoughtlessness of tyrants of whatever time, of whatever place—whether of Theresienstadt in the mid-twentieth century or Rwanda of the late twentieth century. Or choose your own.

If it is heresy, fantasy and slavery to believe something to be true for everyone everywhere, then on what basis would someone say *no*? Educated to discern justice, for several years an employee in the Department of Justice, in his own way in his own time an incarnation of justice, in and through it all, Gary believed that some things are true and right and that some things simply, profoundly are not.

An unusual courage and compassion marked Gary's decision to enter the morass of Rwanda, but the decision he made upon his return was equally unusual. Pondering all that he had seen and smelled, he found himself unable to walk away from its moral meaning. He wondered what those weeks could and should and would mean for him, for his vocation. He could easily have said, "I did my part. Well done. Now, I'm going to go off and have a good life. I have an excellent education and it's time to enjoy its privileges, to do something easier, something less soul-stretching."

Instead, Gary kept hearing in his heart sorrowful stories from
every corner of the earth. One in particular caught him. I remember
him telling me about missionaries in the Philippines who had
found themselves in tension with the local police. How did this
happen? Part of their ministry involved offering Bible studies for
children. Boys and girls alike attended, and then soon after their
twelfth birthday the girls began to disappear, too regularly to be by
accident. They no longer came and were nowhere to be found.
Eventually they were discovered, held in forced prostitution.

A problem the world over, yes, but here it had an unusual bite.
The police owned the brothels—and if the missionaries protested,
they would lose their papers and be forced out. It was a grievous
situation, full of sorrow and injustice. Someone had to say *no*—
plainly, clearly, with legal and political force.

Over time Gary decided to leave the Department of Justice to find
a way to address injustices small and large wherever they might be
found. If in the Philippines it was child prostitution, in India it was
child slavery. And so three years after the Rwandan genocide, the
International Justice Mission was formed. Now, fifteen years later,
IJM has developed networks of attorneys, investigators and trauma
social workers in nations on every continent.

Two stories, one century: Eichmann and Haugen. Highly skilled,
politically astute, two men set amidst the strains of history with its
tensions and terrors—and yet two very different responses. Where
one did not see a neighbor in need, the other understood that
moral, political and social injustice is in fact always one more
window into a neighbor's need. The question that searches the
deepest places is this: Why did Gary feel responsible? Why did he
see himself as implicated? In stark contrast to Eichmann, who
protested all the way to the gallows that he was not responsible for
the deaths of Jews—"I was only doing my job!"—Gary had eyes
to see that he was in fact responsible to do something, because

someone had to say no. And he found a way in the context of his calling to do just that.

WHAT AM I GOING TO DO?

Some years ago I was asked by the Institute for Advanced Studies in Culture to give a "town-and-gown" lecture at the Bayly Art Museum at the University of Virginia, speaking to an audience from both the university and the community. I remember it was a beautiful afternoon, springtime in the Shenandoah Valley, driving from Washington to Charlottesville.

The substance of what I said contrasted the music of Smashing Pumpkins with the literary vision of Walker Percy, reflecting on St. Augustine too. That year the Pumpkins were the biggest musical act in the world—everyone knew their *Mellon Collie and the Infinite Sadness* album. I told a story about taking my sons to their concert, listening to Billy Corgan scream out, "God is empty just like me!" and about the conversation with my sons after the concert about adolescent suburban angst. But then I spent most of the lecture talking about Percy, the man and the writer, arguing that he had his own reasons for melancholy and sadness. I explained that he had chosen a simple life in a small town in Louisiana, loving his wife and daughters, being a good neighbor in his community, and working at his craft of writing, a vocation he described as "a physician of the soul of society."

There were several good questions, one from a fourth-year, as the University of Virginia calls its seniors. He asked about family sadness and the ways that can affect what we see and how we live. I responded, setting forth the contours of an answer, but then said, "Come take a walk in our woods, and we'll have a longer conversation." A week later he wrote, asking about that possibility, saying that he was "about to leave Mr. Jefferson's bubble," and he needed to think things through if he was going to choose well in the future. We did walk in the woods, and talked—and off and on are still talking.

He is now a husband and father, a very good teacher who has become a headmaster of a school, and someone who has had his own sadnesses to bear in his young life, none that were conceivably on the horizon when he asked me the question that night. Knowing some of the wounds of the world in ways that no one would choose, he has chosen to love the world, incarnate in the realities of his life, in the relationships and responsibilities that are his.

He is not unlike Percy in that way.

Over the years I have read and reread Percy's work, dwelling in his vision of learning and life. He is, after all, the one who wrote that "it is possible to get all A's and still flunk life." An observation about the human condition from his novel *The Second Coming*, the second of two novels about Will Barrett, his words are a warning about the temptation that lurks around the corner of everyone's heart—to believe that competence can be separated from character, that excellence can be defined in merely academic terms without a corresponding concern for the kind of people we are. Do we have eyes to see what is really important? What really matters?

He is also the one who offered the timeless wisdom about books and the truth of the human condition that I have taken all over the world. From conversations with artists of all sorts in the New Yorks, Nashvilles and LAs of this life, to lectures in countless universities, I have drawn on Percy's insight, time and again. It is one of the truest truths of the universe.

His wisdom was hard won. Born into a country-club lifestyle in Birmingham, Alabama, generations of Percys were colonels and senators, owners of land and newspapers, the gentry of the Old South. But at age ten, his father committed suicide—as had his grandfather in the previous generation. No scandals loomed, no notoriety was about to be exposed; rather, it was a uniquely Percy legacy. Neither his father nor his grandfather could figure out how to live with their melancholy and sadness.

Walker was the oldest of three brothers. His mother first took them to live in her family home in Athens, Georgia, and a year later to the Percy family home in Greenville, Mississippi, where the boys grew up. Five years after his father's death, Walker's mother died in a strange accident. She drove off a levee outside of town and drowned. No one ever knew what happened, and for Walker the not knowing only added to the plagues of his young life. Did she want to die? Did she too not care about me? What really happened? Am I fated to kill myself someday?

Walker's Uncle Will raised the boys, offering them a safe home and an intriguing window into Southern culture. A lawyer and farmer, he was also a writer, and he entertained other writers like William Faulkner in the years that the Percy boys were in his home. Walker made a very conscious decision in those years to begin thinking in certain definite ways; he was forming a way of seeing the world, a task common to every adolescent. What did he believe, and why? If people could not be trusted, what could be? In the 1930s, that one thing was science and the promise of indubitable certainty. A person could trust science because its questions and answers were sure. So with surprising determination, he began planning for a career in science; he would become a physician, but not a family doctor as that involved too much interaction with people. He wanted to become a pathologist, a scientist-physician.

First he went to the University of North Carolina as a pre-med student, then to Columbia University's medical school. While he flourished in the city and in his studies, before his work was done he contracted tuberculosis. First it was, "Take a year off to get better, and then come back." But a year later, the TB remained and he was told that he would have to leave medicine, even the work of a scientist-physician. For the third time, he suffered a profound loss—first his parents, then his carefully chosen career. All lost.

The next years could be perhaps best described as "lost in the cosmos," to use the title of his collection of essays. He wandered, and wondered, not knowing what to do. Reading the existentialist philosophers of the mid-twentieth century, he began to see his own struggles within the larger story of alienation, interestingly a term used by both the Marxists and the existentialists to make sense of life in the modern world. Along the way, principally in conversations with good friends, he was drawn to mere Christianity, to the gospel of the kingdom which was strange good news for someone like him who longed for something to believe about life and the world that could make sense of his life in the world.

Percy began to write, mostly philosophical essays on the meaning of language. No one wanted to read his work. But he kept at it, and at age forty-five submitted the manuscript for *The Moviegoer* to a New York publisher. Before the year was out, he had won the National Book Award for fiction. His subsequent novels each in their own way explored the same themes of identity and modernity, hopes and fears, longing and loss. Often apocalyptically named—*The Last Gentleman, The Second Coming, Love in the Ruins, The Thanatos Syndrome*—his characters were always wrestling with alienation from God and the world, so much so that the New York reviewers decided that Percy was "the American Camus." While honoring Camus's work and understanding his despair better than most, Percy resisted this identification with the famous philosopher-novelist, saying, "But I always want some hint of hope in my writing."

What the literati saw in Percy's work was his unflinching willingness to look at sorrow and anguish and not blink. Eyes that see, yes—but what do we see? He was not a romantic—that was not a possibility. Rather he was a realist to the core. What the reviewers missed was his deeply rooted commitment to seeing human beings as "pilgrims in the ruins," that we are glories and shames at the same time. He was not fooled by the optimism of the optimistic humanists, but at the same time he did not make a final peace with the pessimistic humanists either. His anthropological vision was more nuanced, more grounded in the truth about the human condition, and it gave him a place from which to see and hear the world that brought him a loyal reading and literary acclaim.

"But I always want some hint of hope in my writing." What did he mean? And why did it matter? Honest readers of Percy's work acknowledge that he was painstakingly honest about the sorrows that are ours as human beings, and his hints of hope were never more than that. Some of his stories are very hard to read, so full of anguish as they are—*Lancelot* stands out as an example. Every one of his novels is about someone who has lost his way and is struggling to find a way out. In one essay, he maintains that this is also true of the people we meet in the Gospels. But never do we meet someone for whom the end of the story is one happy day after another, as if the struggle to find a way out can be finally done in this life. We are always pilgrims in the ruins.

There is one great question in his work: "Knowing what you know about yourself and the world, what are you going to do?" Of course the question is story-shaped, and so it comes to us in the characters of Binx Bolling, Will Barrett and Tom More, the people whose tales are told on the page of his novels. In their own voices, the question is simply, *What am I going to do?*

Will Barrett's story is told in *The Last Gentleman* and *The Second Coming*. In the first novel, Will follows his father and grandfather to Princeton University where he takes his coursework seriously. But after two years of reading and reflecting upon life and the world, he decides to drop out. He doesn't know what to do with all he has come to know. In the second book, several decades later, Will is now retired from Wall Street and planning to play golf in the mountains of North Carolina for the rest of his life—and that becomes the problem of his life. *What, really, am I going to do?*

Tom More is the man for all seasons in *Love in the Ruins* and *The Thanatos Syndrome*. The fictional descendant of Thomas More, the sixteenth-century English social philosopher, statesman and friend of Henry VIII, Tom slowly but decisively begins to answer the question first raised by Percy in his earliest novels, *Knowing what I know, what will I do?* Taking the pulse of our society, full as it is with ills of all shapes and sizes, with groaning and sighing across the spectrum of human experience—psychologically, sociologically, politically, economically, aesthetically—he invents "the qualitative-quantitative ontological lapsometer," in one fell swoop capturing the debates of the Enlightenment and its empty promises. And of course he answers the obvious question, explaining that the lapsometer measures lapses, a stethoscope of the spirit, "the first caliper of the soul."

More himself suffers from lapses, so much so that between the first and second novels he is sentenced to prison for prescribing pills to the women in a local bridge club who wanted help with their diets. *The Thanatos Syndrome* begins with More returning to private practice and wondering why people are nicer than ever before. He sees as a psychiatrist sees, listening to the longings and anxieties, and does not understand.

The story is wonderfully told, playful even as it is profound—*thanatos* being the Greek word for "death." What More slowly discovers is that some enlightened citizens are drugging the population, putting chemicals in the local water supply so that life will be happier for all. Not surprisingly, good story that it is, the rest of the novel is bound up with the great question, *Knowing what you know, what will you do?* Seeing people as they are, seeing the world as it is, More knows that he is implicated and decides to step into history with the commitments implicit in his own calling—and that is the drama that draws us into the story.

Simply said, he is a pilgrim in the ruins, and Percy would not have it any other way. These are only stories, of course—yes, only stories. Attentive as he was to life, and to his life, Percy was writing about the challenge of being alive in the modern world. So much to see, so much to hear, so much to know—what will we do?

BANALITY GOES BOTH WAYS

I recently had lunch with a former British boarding school chaplain. He remembers being with the boys in his school the morning thirty years ago that the very first pictures of widespread starvation in Africa were shown on the BBC. "We were dumbstruck. Having the children's faces in our faces made a tremendous impression. I will never forget the feelings I had that day." He has seen and heard a lot since then, given who he is and what he does. "But then, after awhile, what do you do?" he asked.

That is the most difficult dilemma for thoughtful, serious human beings: *What will you do with what you know?*

Whether our reading of the world began pre- or post-early 1980s, the images which caused the British chaplain and his students to be dumbstruck may or may not have been part of our experience. But each one of us knows the feeling. We know in our deepest places how hard it is to keep our eyes open to the complexity of the broken world around us, to keep feeling the pains of a world that is not the way it is supposed to be and, knowing the difficulty, choosing to engage it rather than being numbed by it.

Eichmann represents one side of this story. Not able, or perhaps not willing, to see that it was the small choices of his daily life that implicated and condemned him, he had eyes that did not see. *Banality* was Arendt's word, trying to capture the surprising ordinariness of the man. But history is mostly that, very ordinary people in very ordinary places. One of the graces of Percy's fiction is that it artfully insists on the commonplace character of responsibility.

Most of us cannot and do not live extraordinary lives. Instead we live in families and in neighborhoods, working and worshiping week by week in rhythms that make the sum of our lives, season after season, year after year. Life cannot be other than that.

I am a teacher, and for years I have taken students of all sorts to the Holocaust Memorial on the Capitol Mall in Washington. We walk through its story of "the banality of evil" in the lives of countless men and women all over Europe who did not see themselves as implicated in the world around them. In Weil's terms, they did not see their neighbors as neighbors. They did not pay attention to what was going on next door and on their street. They did not pay attention to what Nazism meant for Europe and the world. *Thoughtless* is the simple, tragic summary of Arendt's judgment.

But banality goes both ways. If most of Europe was Eichmann-like, offering "the obedience of corpses" in thousands of terribly ordinary ways, there were exceptions. In every nation there are people who choose otherwise, who have eyes to see that something is wrong and that they can do something about it. Germany had its students, France its farmers, Denmark its fishermen and Holland its shopkeepers. Taken together they are some of the best stories in the whole of history, reminding all of us what it means to be a neighbor, what it means to have eyes that see.

The undergraduate student group known as the White Rose at the University of Munich gave their lives as a testament to the truth about the Fatherland amidst the Holocaust horror. They were very ordinary young men and a very ordinary young woman together insisting, as only students can, that their nation was wrong. The villagers of Le Chambon in the hills of France hid thousands of Jews in their basements and barns. In one of history's strange co-incidences, Albert Camus wrote *The Plague* in Le Chambon at this very time as he wrestled with God, suffering and death, vocation and responsibility, all while surrounded by this conspiracy of simple goodness.[14] The whole nation of Denmark also refused to go along with the genocide, choosing *en masse* to secretly send every Jew to Sweden by boat. It is evident that this was not only an individual responsibility; the Danish people as a people said *no*. In thousands of important and different ways, each is a story formed by the asking and answering of the question, *Knowing what I know, what will I do?*

The nation of the Netherlands is its own poignant window into this question. Over the years of my visits to the Holocaust Memorial, what stands out is that one of the smallest nations in Europe had the most people who said, "It will not be like that here." Their names are listed, one after another; every person who took part in the resistance is remembered, each one a righteous Gentile. What is remarkable is the banality of goodness in the stories of these people. None lived as great people of history, though each one was in fact a great person; but the greatness was seen in the ordinariness of their lives. Shopkeepers and farmers mostly, men and women living simple lives as neighbors to neighbors, Jew and Gentile alike. What marked them was that they had eyes to see into the complexity of history, understanding that they were responsible, for love's sake, for the way the world turned out.

Always and everywhere, this is our challenge as human beings. Can we know and love the world at the very same time? Knowing its glories and shames, can we still choose to love what we know? Is there any task more difficult than that? Think it through. From roommates to parents to siblings to friends, from neighborhoods to cities, from countries to cultures to continents—once you begin to really know what a person or a place is like, can you still love them, can you still love it?

At the dawn of the twenty-first century that question is a hard one to answer. Perhaps the honest human in every century and every culture would say the same. But this is our moment, and in it we face a world shaped by pressures that *feel* unique—whether they are or not. On the one hand, answering the question seems especially difficult given the challenge of the sociological stoicism of the information age, what some have perceptively called "the info-glut" culture; and on the other, we live with the worst face of modernism-become-postmodernism, what might be called "the culture of 'whatever.'"

These are not abstractions. In their own ways the sociological and philosophical faces of our world conspire to haunt us. Attending to the info-glut character of contemporary culture carries with it the ironic edge that the more we know, the less we care; the more information we have, the less engaged by it we are. Responding to the critique of postmodernism—a word that Percy was using as early as the 1960s to explain the soul-strained character of contemporary life—makes most of us wonder whether anything is ever really true for everyone all the time. We do not need to read the philosophers to understand this. As the twentieth has become the twenty-first century, the air we breathe is full of the ether of "whatever." In the next chapter we will explore the meaning of both, weighing their influence upon our ability to be fully and responsibly human.

Knowing what I know about the way the world is, what am I going to do? A mime in Europe had to answer, as did the Nazi bureaucrats, as did the Justice Department lawyer, as do all of us. Percy's question echoes through the heart of every human being, and it is especially poignant for those coming out of the starting blocks of early adulthood with a life of knowing and doing on the horizon. The question requires an answer if we are going be human.

3

The Landscape of Our Lives

Orwell feared we would become a captive culture.
Huxley feared that we would become a trivial culture. . . .
Orwell feared that what we hate will ruin us.
Huxley feared that what we love will ruin us.

NEIL POSTMAN, *AMUSING OURSELVES TO DEATH*

*W*e are the "froth riding on a wave . . ." was Allen Ginsberg's metaphor of choice, trying to make sense of the dynamic relationship of the arts to life at large.

As cultures have coursed their way through the centuries, time and time again artists feel things first, artfully sensing what a culture is, what matters most and where the culture is going. In *Irrational Man,* his classic study of existentialism, William Barrett writes,

> Every age projects its own image of man into its art. The whole history of art confirms this proposition, indeed this history is itself but a succession of images of man. A Greek figure is not just a shape in stone but the image of man in the light of which the Greeks lived. If you compare, feature by feature, the bust of a Roman patrician with the head of a me-

dieval saint—as André Malraux has done with a spectacularly
sharp eye in his *Voices of Silence*—you cannot account in
some formal terms for the difference between them: the two
heads stare at each other and cancel each other out; they give
us two different images of the destiny and possibilities of
being a man. . . . Whenever a civilization has lived in terms
of a certain image of man, we can see this image in its art.[1]

Donald Drew, the wise and much-loved teacher of literature to
English boarding school students and who later spent several years
as the Master of the Farel House in the Swiss community of L'Abri,
argued similarly in his *Images of Man: A Critique of the Contemporary Cinema*. Taking off from Descartes's "I think, therefore I am,"
Drew maintained that films are cinematic images of the human
condition, windows into diverse understandings of what it is that
makes us human. I play, therefore I am. I work, therefore I am. I
kill, therefore I am. I copulate, therefore I am.

With unusual insight he suggested that movies, like every art
form, both reflect and promote certain visions of the way life is and
ought to be. They can never be neutral. Someone is always com-
municating something—and not always because its creator is intentionally making a statement, but more so because the dynamic
of reflect and promote is implicit in the act of creation itself.

And so if one wants to understand Greek culture in the fourth
century B.C., the surest way is to study its sculpture, as it is there
that the hopes and dreams are most plainly seen. If one wants to
understand Italy in the twelfth century A.D., then it is in its paintings
and its poetry where the attitudes and thought patterns are manifest. Generation after generation, it is the art of Michelangelo, of
Rembrandt, of Durer that tells a story of human life under the sun,
as do the novels of Jane Austen and Victor Hugo. The plays of
Samuel Beckett and T. S. Eliot, the paintings of Pablo Picasso and

Georgia O'Keeffe, the stories of Albert Camus and Flannery O'Connor, the music of Duke Ellington and Elvis Presley, each in different ways are an account of what it felt like to be alive in the middle years of the twentieth century. And names like J. D. Salinger, Jackson Pollock, Chinua Achebe, Woody Allen, Ingmar Bergman, John Lennon, Annie Leibovitz, Mick Jagger and Alice Walker are synonyms for the last years of the century, each offering an account of what it means to be human; just as the early twenty-first century is known through the work of Isabel Allende, Cormac McCarthy, Douglas Coupland, the Coen brothers, Paul Thomas Anderson, Eminem, Lady Gaga and U2.

To understand this cusp of a new century—marked as it is both by the sociological reality of the information age and the philosophical movement we call postmodernism—we have to pay attention to the novelists, filmmakers and musicians who are culturally upstream, as it is in their stories, movies and songs where we will feel the yearnings of what human life is and ought to be. Whether staged or celluloid, in print or on computer disks, they are fingers to the wind. Why? Artists get there first.

Too Much Is Not Enough . . . I Feel Numb

Take U2, for example. It is hard to imagine students of history in some future era making sense of the dawn of this millennium without studying their music. No group of musicians ever has been so culturally engaging on a global scale as has this band of boys from Dublin. Song after song, album upon album, for more than thirty years their passions for God and the meaning of human history have been played out upon stages the world over. Pop icons, yes. But prophets as well, as they have set out for themselves and their audience a vision of human life under the sun that has been as enormously entertaining as it has been politically and socially attentive.

While there are scores of songs that offer artful windows into the human heart, in their album *Zooropa,* the song "Numb" captures better than almost anything else what it feels like to be alive in the information age. In almost countless settings I have shown the MTV version of it to people young and old, students and faculty, in universities and beyond. My hope has been that it might allow some to hear and to understand the meaning of this moment.

Drip . . . drip . . . drip. The first image is of a faucet leaking. And then the member of the band who calls himself "The Edge," with eyes straight ahead, begins what sounds like a levitical litany, "Don't suggest. Don't try to make sense." Don't, don't and don't again and again and again—sketching the contours of human life, but each time, "Don't." All the while various people come to him as he sits, staring. Little girls want to play, big girls begin to lick his ears, someone else offers ice cream, another wraps a rope around his neck, someone else blows smoke in his face, and on and on. Pleasures and pains of all sorts, and he just sits and stares straight ahead, rarely even blinking. About half way through, the rest of the band begin to sing into his ears, "I feel numb . . . I feel numb . . . I feel numb. Too much is not enough . . . I feel numb."

It is an unsettling song. I remember showing it once during a lecture in an auditorium full of literally thousands of people and had two very different responses. A group of students were shocked, and wondered why I wasn't; or perhaps more, why I had shown something so crude, so in-your-face? But then over lunch, a man in his late seventies said to me, "Now I understand. That was the most perceptive reading of the culture that I have seen in years. That is the world we live in, isn't it?"

What is it about? In MTV music, images always mean something—even if they intend to show that nothing has meaning. But U2 can be counted on to be very purposeful, very intentional, very meaningful. In "Numb" the faucet is an image of the droning, incessant, twenty-four-hours-a-day character of the information age. It is "on" all the time. Edge is seated on a stage, looking at something. What? He seems to be looking at the camera, looking at us. Maybe. But there is a flickering translucence that constantly crosses his face, and somehow it feels familiar. Distraction by distraction, people come and go, some with kisses and some with smoke. He will not be bothered. Eyes glued ahead, he bears up against anyone and everything, continuing his drone, "Don't . . . don't . . . don't." He will not be unplugged.

For those with eyes to see and ears to hear, the song is a finger on the pulse of the ABC/BBC/CBS/NBC/CNN/FOX/MSNBC on-all-the-time culture. And U2 gets at it brilliantly, profoundly. Artists do get there first. *I feel numb.*

Try this one. Several years ago I was on a way-too-crowded plane flying to Martha's Vineyard to speak to a group of college students at the FOCUS Study Center and saw on the lap of the person next to me a book, *The Diagnosis.*[2] Intrigued, I kept looking, while still trying to be polite. On the back cover I saw these words, attributed to the *Chicago Tribune*: "A searing vision of our helter-skelter and spiritually debilitating technocracy." I wrote down the title, and when I got to the Vineyard I went to find a bookstore. What I found was the novel form of U2's song.

Written by a former MIT professor, Alan Lightman, *The Diagnosis* is the tale of a businessman who day after day takes the train from suburban Lexington to downtown Boston, where he works for a company whose motto is *the maximum information in the minimum time.* The story begins on the train, one more day watching people open up their laptops, talking into their cell phones—plugged into the information age before they even get to work. But this day is different. He notices; he cannot stop noticing. Beginning to feel strangely uncomfortable, he starts to feel a little warm. So he loosens his tie, and takes off his coat—and then his shoes, and his shirt, and finally his pants.

By the time he is downtown, he has forgotten his name, where he works and where he lives. He is lost in the cosmos of Boston. Knowing that something is wrong, he eventually finds his way into a hospital's emergency ward where he is finally brought into an examining room for a diagnosis. With highly skilled physicians and a brand new machine, he is hooked up and test results are on their way. But when the doctors leave the room, so does he. And he wanders the streets with no name and no idea where and how to find his way home.

After hours of futility, he walks by a big building and the doorman greets him, with the kindness and familiarity of someone he knows. The good news is that he gets home that night. The bad news is that when he wakes up the next day, his fingers are numb—which is a problem for someone who works for a firm that lives by its ability to process "the maximum information in the minimum time." He finds that he cannot use the keyboard as quickly as he must to keep up with the flow across his screen. Others begin to notice too. As the days pass the numbness grows, moving through his hands to his feet, limb by limb, slowly immobilizing him.

And so more tests are done. Massachusetts General Hospital offers its diagnostic tools, results are sent to the Mayo Clinic and Duke University's Medical School. Each reply with the same, sober response: there is nothing wrong.

A new round of tests is called for, this time with psychiatrists and psychologists; if it is not his body, is it his brain? Hours are spent in conversation, but each skilled professional offers the same diagnosis: there is nothing wrong.

But of course there is.

There is no happy healing at the story's end. Inch by inch the man becomes numb, from head to foot—no longer able to move or to talk or to be the human conduit for the maximum information in the minimum time. *I feel numb.*

The artists get there first.

But others are feeling it too. A cover story in *Harper's* called "The Numbing of the American Mind: Culture as Anesthetic" began with these words of Nietzsche:

> The massive influx of impressions is so great; surprising, barbaric, and violent things press so overpoweringly—"balled up into hideous clumps"—in the youthful soul; that it can save itself only by taking recourse in premeditated stupidity.[3]

Unusually insightful about the phenomena of the flood of information and its psychological and political implications, Thomas de Zengotita observed, "Nietzsche was not thinking IQ or ignorance when he used the word 'stupidity.' He meant stupidity as in clogged, anesthetized. Numb."[4] Moving through an accounting of the Information Revolution with its Web, satellite cable TV, mobile phone, DVD and Ethernet, he explores the difficulty of distinguishing reality from fabrication, arguing that we are totally immersed with "stuff" and "choices" in ways "unprecedented in human history." In what is the most pointed analysis in his essay, de Zengotita writes,

> When you find out about the moving cursor, or hear statistics about AIDS in Africa, or see your 947th picture of a weeping fireman, you can't help but become fundamentally indifferent because you are exposed to things like this all the time, just as you are to the rest of your options. Over breakfast. In the waiting room. Driving to work. At the checkout counter. All the time. I know you know this already. I'm just reminding you.
>
> Which is not to say that you aren't moved. On the contrary, you are moved, often deeply, very frequently—never more so, perhaps, than when you saw the footage of the towers coming down on 9/11. But you are so used to being moved by footage, by stories, by representations of all kinds—that's the point. It's not your fault that you are so used to being moved, you just are.
>
> So it's not surprising that you have learned to move on so

readily to the next, sometimes moving, moment. It's sink or
surf. Spiritual numbness guarantees that your relations with
the moving will pass. And the stuffed screen accommodates
you with moving surfaces that assume you are numb enough
to accommodate them. And so on, back and forth. The dia-
lectic of postmodern life.[5]

I feel numb.

AN INFO-GLUT CULTURE

But do a song, a novel and an article make a persuasive argument?
A growing chorus of critics brings their voices to bear on the
meaning of the information age, wondering what it means, and will
mean, for all of us. Of the best, none are Luddites, expecting or
hoping that we will somehow find our way back to a less complex
world; rather they have invested years and careers to this age's stewardship and analysis.

The most intriguing is James Billington, the Librarian of Congress, whose task it is to oversee the largest library in the world.
Built from six thousand volumes donated by Thomas Jefferson, the
Library of Congress now receives thousands of books each week.
With the advent of electronic communication, the challenge of
making its resources accessible to the nation is enormous. But
Billington believes that the more searching question is one outside
of the library. As complex as it is to develop administrative avenues
to handle the flow of information coming its way month after
month, he argues that it is even more difficult for the nation to
know what to do with it all. Describing the contemporary world
as "an info-glut culture," he has asked with probing seriousness,
"But have we become any wiser?" The words echo across the landscape of our time.

One of the earliest to weigh in was Theodore Roszak, an attentive seer of the twentieth century. Intrigued by the interaction of ideas and culture, his work through the 1970s and 1980s addressed the social and philosophical influence of the Enlightenment upon life and learning.[6] His book *The Cult of Information* focused his criticism on the knife's-edge character of the computer: as innocent as it seems, it can hurt us because it changes the way we know what we know. It was not a cheap critique. What he saw was "a glut of unrefined, undigested information flowing from every medium around us," "a statistical blizzard that numbs the attention," "tons of obfuscating data glut."[7]

"The more information accessed, the less significance possible" is the way that Michael Heim understands the dilemma in *The Metaphysics of Virtual Reality,* raising the stakes for all of us. Yes, but knowing that to be largely true, what do we do with it? There are no easy answers, at least for those who take the question seriously. With a wide-ranging critique, Todd Gitlin calls it *Media Unlimited: How the Torrent of Images and Sounds Overwhelms Our Lives,* observing,

> In recent decades, the media torrent is where speed-up is most unmistakable. The images steadily thicken, the soundscape grows noisier, montage more frenetic. This process transcends the conventional polarities of politics. It is a curiosity of our present civilization that many of those who call themselves conservatives embrace the revolutionary daemon of capitalism, the most reckless, hard-driving force in the history of the world, and celebrate Joseph Schumpeter's 'gales of creative destruction' that blow through production, marketing, taste, and everyday life. But among radicals, too, who will organize Students for a Slow Society? Not the rocking and rolling, post-MTV, music-downloading, raging-against-the-machine cultural left. Who is against upgrades, jump cuts, more channels, better speakers, the Sensurround pleasure dome of everyday life?

The real answer to the rhetorical question is: hardly anyone.[8]

Looking into his life and out to the wider world, Kenneth Gergen writes about *The Saturated Self: Dilemmas of Identity in Contemporary Life,* arguing that "social saturation brings with it a general loss in our assumption of true and knowable selves."[9] To flesh out his thesis, he offers a window into his life.

> I had just returned to Swarthmore from a two-day conference in Washington, which had brought together fifty scholars from around the country. An urgent fax from Spain lay on the desk, asking about a paper I was months late in contributing to a conference in Barcelona. Before I could think about answering, the office hours I had postponed began. One of my favorite students arrived and began to quiz me about the ethnic biases in my course syllabus. My secretary came in holding a sheaf of telephone messages, and some accumulated mail, including an IRS notice of a tax audit and a cancellation notice from the telephone company. My conversations with my students were later interrupted by phone calls from a London publisher, a colleague in Connecticut on her way to Oslo for the weekend, and an old California friend wondering if we might meet during his summer travels to Holland. By the morning's end I was drained. The hours had been wholly consumed by the process of relating—face to face, electronically, and by letter. The relations were scattered across Europe and America, and scattered points in my personal past. And so keen was the competition for "relational" time that virtually none of the interchanges seemed effective in the ways I wished.

And he goes on, noting that even ten years earlier none of these observations could have been made. Two decades later, each is even more true. In a sober summary, he states, "The fully saturated self becomes no self at all."[10] Yes, I feel numb . . . I no longer feel what I need to feel to be human.

One of the best known voices bringing a critical eye to bear upon the information age is Neil Postman, who for twenty-five years wrote as widely and perceptively as anyone on the challenge of learning to learn and live in a technological society. Of all that he wrote, *Amusing Ourselves to Death* won him the widest audience. With an uncanny eye and ear, he picked up on the tremendous challenge of holding onto one's humanity in an information-saturated culture.

Taking off from two seeing-into-the-future works, George Orwell's *1984* and Aldous Huxley's *Brave New World*, he made a convincing argument that the latter won, hands down. The totalitarian face of Big Brother did not take over at century's end; rather we had entered headlong into a Huxleyan-imagined "amusing ourselves to death" time in history.

> What Huxley teaches is that in the age of advanced technology, spiritual devastation is more likely to come from an enemy with a smiling face than from one whose countenance exudes suspicion and hate. In the Huxleyan prophesy, Big Brother does not watch us, by his choice. We watch him, by ours. There is no need for wardens or gates or Ministries of Truth. When a population becomes distracted by trivia, when cultural life is redefined as a perpetual round of entertainments, when serious public conversation becomes a form of baby-talk, when, in short, a people become an audience and their public business a vaudeville act, then a nation finds itself at risk; culture-death is a clear possibility.[11]

Summing it up, "Orwell feared we would become a captive culture. Huxley feared that we would become a trivial culture. . . . Orwell feared that what we hate will ruin us. Huxley feared that what we love will ruin us."[12]

A generation later, in this long conversation that has become an internal cultural critique, Nicholas Carr has written as well as anyone; first an essay in *The Atlantic,* "Is Google Making Us Stupid?"[13] and then later the book *The Shallows: What the Internet Is Doing to Our Brains.*[14] Not a Luddite for a moment, Carr sees the gifts of modern technologies, understanding that we can now do work in ways that are unprecedented in human experience. But he also sees a harder edge, one that has less to do with the content of media as with modern media itself—what one of the earliest critics, Marshall McLuhan, saw as "the medium is the message," or *massage,* as the case might be. While there are dangers to what comes across internet screens, and the dangers are not small, Carr instead draws on brain physiologists to argue that our very brains are being re-wired so that we are seeing life differently, and we are reading the world differently. Scanning our way down the computer screen, hyperlinking as we do, we are decreasingly able to read more care-fully, with the kind of discernment that critical reading requires. It is a million miles from the time-honored *lectio divina* that the best reading has always been, where words are taken into the deepest places of the heart, because of course we want our reading to transform us, to teach us about the world and our place in it. In a word, Carr calls our contemporary practice "the shallows."

Of all that has been written on this phenomenon, Colin Gunton's Bampton Lectures at Cambridge University, *The One, the Three and the Many: God, Creation and the Culture of Modernity,* seem the wisest. Brilliant and far-ranging, he argued that disengagement is the essence of modern life. Looking out at the world, we want to understand it, we want to respond to it—and yet we find it so very hard to do so in any morally meaningful way. *Knowing what I know, what am I to do?* For sociological reasons, for philosophical reasons, we see the immensity and the complexity and we step back. We disengage, hoping to hold onto ourselves, to that which matters most to us, trying to protect ourselves from being overcome and overwhelmed.

What sets Gunton off from the other critics is that while his critique is rigorous, his vision of what might be, of what ought to be, is equally so. From beginning to end he argues "that a renewed thinking and expression of how we belong in the world, of the human habitation of reality"[15] is a most critical task. With a rare moral intelligence, over the course of his book he develops a way out of the desire to disengage, arguing for a relational universe rooted in Trinitarian theology, a world where responsiveness and responsibility are written into our humanness. But to say more is to get ahead of ourselves.[16]

An info-glut culture? Yes, in more ways than we know, on more levels than we can understand. *I feel numb.* While the artists get there first, the world at large catches up, and we all wonder, *What am I going to do?*

THE CULTURE OF WHATEVER

As probing as that question is for all, some have decided, with a shrug of the mind and heart, *whatever.* Sometimes playful, often more cynical, the word itself is a window into the complexity of life; we feel overwhelmed in so many different ways all at once. How else to respond than with a heartfelt "whatever"? From casual conversations in families and among friends to core curricular commitments at major universities, "whatever" seems to many the best response to the way the world is—and isn't.

And yet there are ideas and issues that seem beyond "whatever." Some times and in some places, it is, simply said, inadequate. The reality of pain and evil in this life requires a response that is more than the culture of whatever provides. Some choices are awful choices; they do not and cannot exist in a moral universe of their own making. Thoughtful, honest human beings wonder, *Knowing*

what I know, what am I going to do? To do nothing seems less than
human, seems less than right.

For example, several years ago I visited with a woman who directed the Protection Project, an initiative addressing human trafficking—the sadness that in earlier days was called slavery—which
was then under the auspices of Harvard University's Kennedy
School of Government. If centuries ago it was Marco Polo carrying
spices along international trade routes, today it is very sophisticated networks of traders who traffic in human flesh—all over the
world, on every continent and in every culture. The Protection
Project's annual report is an important, though terrifying and sobering, account of the human capacity for malice and greed; its map
of trade routes and hot spots show the problem to be horribly
global. As we talked about the Protection Project and its place in
the city of Washington among human rights organizations of all
sorts and sizes, I asked, "So why do you care about this?"

She told me the story of her heart opening to the cries of women
and girls who were sold into slavery, often a sexual bondage. Years
earlier she had written a paper in law school where one aspect of
the question interested her, and then over time that paper and the
issues it addressed kept bubbling up as others read her work. Eventually the Kennedy School asked if she wanted to pursue the questions in Boston or Washington, and she chose Washington. We
talked at some length about how hard it was to argue for human
rights in an issue-weary city, about how hard it was to keep going,
to keep believing in the idea that brought the "issue" into being.

As we talked in her office, I watched her staff walking by in the
hallway outside her door, and their serious and eager faces impressed me. I think she must have noticed because she eventually
said, "I get the most interesting applications here. Just imagine.
Harvard University . . . Washington, D.C., . . . human rights. It's a
powerful combination, and it draws unusually gifted young women

and men from the best universities in America."

But then she surprised me with these words, "After a few weeks they almost always find their way down the hall, knock on my door and ask to talk. Now, I know what they are going to say. After thanking me for the position and the opportunity, a bit awkwardly they ask, 'But who are we to say that trafficking is wrong in Pakistan? Isn't it a bit parochial for us to think that we know what is best for other people? Why is what is wrong for us wrong for them?' To be honest, I just don't have time for that question anymore. The issues we address are too real, they matter too much. I need more students like the one you sent me, because I need people who believe that there is basic right and wrong in the universe!"

Whatever? No one really wants the world to be like that, at all times and in all places. We prefer to choose the circumstances where right and wrong are up for grabs, where tolerance of everything by everyone is truly the rule of the day, because we know that "whatever" only works some times and some places. But this amoral vision is characteristic of our time, of the movement from modern to postmodern, from twentieth to twenty-first century. Whether we read the philosophers or not, the belief that we have no access to certainty, particularly to moral absolutes, to the world of "basic right and wrong in the universe," is in the cultural air we breathe.

It is important to be clear. This is not the worst of all worlds. There is no golden moment historically. Pre-modern, modern, postmodern: every age is marked by graces and groans. If there were curses in the pre-modern world—little access to medical care and education, inadequate housing and plumbing, no electricity—then there were gifts too; in sum, a world of much less fragmentation. If there were strains built into the modern world—the disruption of our relationship to people and places being one of the most far-reaching, what the poet T. S. Eliot captured in his image of the philosophical, sociological and psychological "wasteland" of twentieth-century society—then there were advantages too, such as life-saving medicines, near-universal education and widespread religious freedoms. The Enlightenment's crowning achievement is what we have known as the modern world; again, tragically and poignantly called "that murderous, mechanized 20th-century" by Percy. Scientific advances? Yes. The experiments of Nazi doctors, no. Electricity? Yes. A neon culture, no. Freedom of speech? Yes. The pornographic world, no.

That same blessing/curse character is true of what we call post-modernism, the movement beyond the Enlightenment, beyond the modern. At its best it is a criticism of the modern world's flaws, the Enlightenment's hubris. For example, it gives us the ability to see the clay-footedness of scientism's claim to be the sole arbiter of reality and truth. All reality cannot be weighed and measured, as if it is most truly known when it is quantified. The scientific method gives us limited access to certain "true" truths, but it cannot speak to most of what matters to human life. And there is not an "objective world" solely discernible to unbiased, unprejudiced opinion, just as there is not a "subjective world" accessible only to those who prefer its patterns and opinions to all others. The "Cartesian split" (in honor of Descartes's pioneering effort at the dawn of the Enlightenment to frame ways of knowing, ways of making sense of what we see and hear) no longer holds sway under the postmodern critique. So the world of indubitable "facts," distinct from the world of privately held "values," assumes a language and universe that is judged passé in postmodernism.

Rather we are promised a place for everyone at the table of ideas. No one is "privileged," not the scientist, not the philosopher, not the white male, not the black female, not the American, not the Indian and, of course, not the Protection Project and its advocacy for human rights, its argument on behalf of those in the chains of twenty-first-century slavery. But that is the rub. In a post-Enlightenment world, there is no voice, no perspective that carries more weight than any other, because no one has access to certainty about anything. There is no Story to make sense of stories, no Truth to make sense of truths, no Metanarrative to make sense of narratives. All claims to the contrary are "totalitarian" and are not to be tolerated. The worst face of postmodernism is that nothing has metaphysical or moral weight; it is the culture of whatever, a nihilism for Everyman.

In his brilliant analysis "Can Humane Literacy Survive Without a Grand Narrative?" David Lyle Jeffrey tells the tale of the postmodern vision, a world where "there is now deemed to be no such thing as a 'wrong answer.'"[17] Reflecting upon Jean-François Lyotard, he writes,

> We are to understand that postmodernism refers above all to a shift away from traditional theories of knowledge and the knower, particularly such theories of knowledge as imply a philosophy of history—or world view—as a means of legitimating that knowledge. Lyotard's simplest definition of postmodernism is "incredulity toward metanarratives."[18]

With unusual insight, Jeffrey examines the landscape of life and learning in a world "without a grand narrative," a world without windows to transcendence and truth, by listening in on some of its most important voices.

Richard Rorty is by some counts the most influential philosopher of our time, and one who represents this vision of human life. In effect, Rorty argues that when humans make sense of the universe and their place in it, making judgments that shape both what we know and how we act, in the end—as Jeffrey paraphrases it—"our saying so makes it so." Jeffrey continues, "When conventional associations make this awkward for us, we simply redefine key terms."[19]

Jeffrey reflects on the relatively small universe that someone like Rorty inhabits:

How convenient—and how resistant to learning, to others, to reality. . . . When Rorty says that the essential postmodern theme is that "what is most important for human life is not what propositions we believe but what vocabulary we use," he quickly observes that philosophers like Nietzsche and William James have been instrumental in developing this thesis by teaching us to give up "the notion of truth as corresponding to reality." Henceforth, instead of saying that the function of language is to "bring forth hidden secrets to light," they said that new ways of speaking could *help us get what we want.*[20]

To get what I want when I want it. To do what I want to do when I want to do it. Baldly stated, that is the way I have described morally malformed people to my children over the years, like a driver along the interstate who bullies everyone else, a politician who with Machiavellian cynicism skillfully uses the system to advance his own ambitions. Very, very bright people do not always make very, very good people. You can get all A's and still flunk life.

One who felt the personal and political pains of this in the Soviet prisons was the great Russian novelist Aleksandr Solzhenitsyn, a prophetic voice crying in the wilderness of contemporary culture. Neither an oracle nor infallible, his judgments are torture-tested, wrought out of his years of suffering the injustice of Soviet imprisonment and his attentiveness to the complex ways in which ideas have legs. In the words of his autobiography, he was a "calf against the oak," a small man fighting against systemic and politically powerful evil.

Inch by inch the world began to hear him, first through samizdat networks in the Soviet Union, and from there his stories of the Stalinist persecutions and the larger problems implicit in the Marxist and Leninist dream made their way into the West. With his emergence as a writer of international reputation and his receipt of the Nobel Prize in Literature, he was given the freedom to leave Russia in 1974. For a few years he was the darling of the intellectual world in the West, that is until he began to warn the West in a series of addresses that began with speeches to trade union leaders in Washington and New York, a speech to the US Congress, and interviews and speeches over the BBC. This culminated in his famous commencement address at Harvard in 1978. The Western world listened in over the shoulders of those gathered in Harvard Yard and did not like what it heard.

While beginning with the words "I am sincerely happy to be here with you on the occasion of the 327th commencement of this old and illustrious university," he continues with a piercing critique of the university's, and the West's, retreat from *veritas*.

> Many of you have already found out and others will find out in the course of their lives that truth eludes us as soon as our concentration begins to flag, all the while leaving the illusion that we are continuing to pursue it. This is the source of much discord. Also, truth seldom is sweet; it is almost invariably bitter. A measure of bitter truth is included in my speech today, but I offer it as a friend, not as an adversary.[21]

In his speech, Solzhenitsyn analyzed the world split apart: politically, economically, socially, historically and morally, all the while continuing to ponder the meaning of truth in relation to human beings and their societies. As he drew to a conclusion, Solzhenitsyn asked, "How did the West decline from its triumphal march to its present debility? Have there been fatal turns and losses of direction in its development?"

And then with an eagle's eye he descends upon the mistake "at the root" of the West in the modern-becoming-postmodern world. His chronicle moves from the Renaissance into the Age of Enlightenment and observes that philosophical commitments about human nature and history "became the basis for political and social doctrine and could be called rationalistic humanism or humanistic autonomy: the proclaimed and practiced autonomy of man from any higher force above him. It could also be called anthropocentricity, with man seen as the center of all."[22] His argument comes to this crescendo:

> Mere freedom per se does not in the least solve all the problems of human life and even adds a number of new ones. And yet in early democracies, as in American democracy at the time of its birth, all individual human rights were granted on the ground that man is God's creature. That is, freedom was given to the individual conditionally, in the assumption of his constant religious responsibility. Such was the heritage of the preceding one thousand years. Two hundred or even fifty years ago, it would have seemed quite impossible, in America, that an individual be granted boundless freedom with no purpose, simply for the satisfaction of his whims. . . . All the celebrated technological achievements of progress, including the conquest of outer space, do not redeem the twentieth century's moral poverty.[23]

In the days that followed, editorials appeared in America's most important newspapers and overwhelmingly—with great intelligence and eloquence—dismissed his criticism and concern as coming from a forlorn Russian who misunderstood the genius of the West, that is, our understanding of freedom.

Human lives and history are at stake here. No wise person, therefore, will step into this analysis with a cheap critique. But Solzhenitsyn's analysis of the notion that "it would have seemed quite impossible, in America, that an individual be granted boundless freedom with no purpose, simply for the satisfaction of his whims" was profoundly prescient. He saw where the line in the sand was, and would continue to be, in the culture of whatever.

What Am I Going to Do?

Few films have captured this dilemma with as much cinematic brilliance as *Run Lola Run*. As postmodern a picture as has ever been done, it begins with a series of questions offered in cartoon-like art, but the questions are the most probing ones we ask: *Who am I? What is the world really like? Is there any meaning to life, and to my life?*

Set in a German city, the film shows a young man on a train who is a runner for drug dealers. His task is to take the money from one person to another in the business of a drugged subculture. Through a completely innocent "chance" circumstance, he loses the bag with the money. He was not inattentive, really—it just happened.

In desperation, he calls his girlfriend, pleading, "Lola, I need help! If I don't have the money in twenty minutes, I'll be killed! I need you to get me money." *Run, Lola, run!* And she does, leaving her apartment, descending the stairs, running through the streets, yearning to save the life of her friend. But when she arrives, he has begun a robbery of a store in an attempt to get the money he needs, and there is a shoot-out. Well, it seemed to me that the movie was over far too soon.

But then, the phone in her bedroom rings again. And the story starts all over. Once more the boyfriend tells Lola that he is in a desperate place, and needs her help. With exactness the scene is played over again. But this time Lola leaves the apartment a bit differently. This time she jumps over the dog rather stumbling over it, and once out on the street, runs around the car rather than into it; moment by moment she makes small but different responses to the circumstances before her. And this time, when she gets to the center of the city where her friend awaits, something different happens.

I found myself beginning to catch on. A different narrative, a different universe, but each a response to the perennial question at the heart of every heart: *Knowing what I know, what am I going to do?* Yes, the boyfriend calls a third time, repeating the scene once more, "Lola, I need help!" She runs down the stairs, reacting bit differently to what she sees and hears as she races across town to help her friend. And a third time they meet, with a third very different conclusion to the story. In each of the stories, people do not make choices for which they can be held accountable, for which they are responsible; rather, what happens happens. It just happens.

Strange? Yes. But with uncanny insight it offers a window into the world of whatever. The poet Steve Turner sums it up with his gift of seeing things as they are, with words that are "bright as a light, sharp as a razor."

> We believe that each man must find the truth
> that is right for him.
> Reality will adapt accordingly.
> The universe will readjust. History will alter.[24]

This is the "creed" carved into the portals of the postmodern world at its worst. It is what is believed, and lives are staked on its plausibility. In the metaphysical and moral universe of *Run Lola Run,* there are no windows to transcendence, no windows to truth, no grand narratives, and so no Story to make sense of the stories. The stories themselves are "chance" encounters with no more meaning than bumping into the universe as one meets it, hoping against hope.

For the foreseeable future, we will never become a completely postmodern culture. At best, we are stretched taut between times. Airplane schedules, with all the technological complexities of air traffic controllers, with the mathematical precision required in allocation of air space, with the interrelatedness of computers across continents and oceans, require modern consciousness, the ongoing commitment to certain things—"facts"—being true for everyone all the time. But the on-the-street ethos, the air we breathe, is plainly that of postmodernism, and its worst face is the culture of whatever.

A RAT IN THE CAGE?

Seeing what I see, hearing what I hear, what am I going to do? A
few years ago, I was invited to spend a weekend with a group of
graduate students from Yale University. A home on Cape Cod was
offered, and we stepped into intense conversations Friday evening
and continued on through the weekend. As we were thinking
through the dynamics of belief and behavior, living between
modern and postmodern consciousness, we pondered the philosophically pregnant lyrics of the music of the Smashing Pumpkins,
as well as similar themes in films and novels. Late on Saturday
night, one of the students came up to me with a serious look and
an equally serious question. He was doing PhD studies in literature,
and he put it this way:

> I believe in God. I believe there is meaning in the universe.
> But sometimes, maybe even often, when I am driving back to
> New Haven from New York, I turn on the Pumpkins, open the
> windows of my car and sing with the loudest voice, "Despite
> all my rage, I'm still just a rat in the cage!" Because that's how
> I feel—it seems to capture just the way I feel. I'm studying
> here and am doing well in my coursework. But in my de-
> partment we are very suspicious of any claims to certainty. We
> have narratives, but no metanarrative. And so nothing really
> to make sense of everything. There are times in the day when
> it seems that I'm just that, a rat in the cage—and I don't know
> what to do about it.

Listening to him, my heart sighed. *Seeing what I see, hearing what I
hear, what am I going to do?* The Pumpkins would not have sold as
they did without there being a ring of truth, a resonance in their
words that touched the deepest chords for thousands and thousands all over the world. Artists do get there first.

From across the Atlantic, writing out of very different cultural

conditions than the Smashing Pumpkins, feeling very different vocational pressures than the Yale student, was Václav Havel. The
public character of his protest against totalitarianism with a Communist face made him a persona non grata in Prague, so in the
1970s he left for the Tatras, the mountains one hundred miles away.

In an interview titled "It Always Makes Sense to Tell the Truth,"
he was asked, "What would you say about your plays? What are
they about?" He responded, "All my plays so far have been about a
single theme: the crisis of human identity. I keep coming back to it
in different ways and in different forms, but always in the end—
whether I want to or not—that theme somehow appears in what I
write." The journalist pressed him, "Could you expand on this idea
of human identity?" Havel replied,

> I believe that with the loss of God, man has lost a kind of
> absolute and universal system of coordinates, to which he
> could always relate anything, chiefly himself. His world and
> his personality gradually began to break up into separate, in-
> coherent fragments corresponding to different, relative coor-
> dinates. And when this happened, man began to lose his inner
> identity, that is, his identity with himself. Along with it, of
> course, he lost a lot of other things, too, including a sense of
> his own continuity, a hierarchy of experiences and values, and
> so on. It's as if we were playing for a number of different teams
> at once, each with different uniforms, and as though—and
> this is the main thing—we didn't know which one we ulti-
> mately belonged to, which of those teams was really ours.[25]

A poet, a playwright, a prisoner, a politician. In and through his
occupations, Havel's vocation had been sustained. He was a seer, his
vision piercing; time and again he understood just where the line
in the sand was drawn. And in that interview, he raised the stakes
for all of us, identifying the reasons for our loss of ability to make

sense of who we are and where we are with the loss God.

Seeing, hearing and feeling the world—what are we to make of it? Is it possible to look into its complexity—sociologically and philosophically, politically and personally—and find a way to live responsibly? To find a way to love the world? Or are we all just rats in the cage with no way out?

I have been in a room with Bono, sitting in a circle with others, and asked him to reflect on the song "Numb," particularly in light of his challenge to care for Africa and the global AIDS crisis it represents. Knowing what he knows of the numbing character of more information, how is it possible to communicate knowledge about the issue without becoming anesthetized to it at the very same time? A hard question for all of us, and a hard question for Bono too.

Numbed, overwhelmed, trapped. I was just doing my job. The more I know, the less interested I am. Free to be me, but I have no Story to provide a lens through which to understand my freedom. Unable to make any true choices, we only react, and what happens happens. What is left to be said but a simple, sad, *whatever*?

From mime artists in Paris, to attorneys walking the killing fields of Rwanda, to young, eager human rights activists in Washington, to graduate students at Yale, how does one learn to see with the eyes of the heart, to see oneself as responsible for the way the world is and isn't? Not a cheap question, and there are no cheap answers.

4

Knowing Is Doing

I can only choose within the world that I can see.

IRIS MURDOCH, *THE SOVEREIGNTY OF GOOD*

A mind without a heart is nothing.

Few stories capture the poignancy of parenting and politics, particularly of the ways in which fathers and their sons together learn to care about the world, as does Chaim Potok's *The Chosen*. The story of two Jewish families in Brooklyn in the 1940s, it begins on a blacktopped baseball field. The Reform sons are playing against the Hasidic sons, distinct communities within a community, each struggling to understand the meaning of their heritage in twentieth-century America.

But the novel is more than that too, as it centers upon the young hearts of two inheritors of the tradition—in tension with it and yet also embracing it. In and through the stories of faith and families, neighborhoods and communities, it is at its core a reflection on the relationship of education to vocation, offering a tale of two answers to the question, *Knowing what I know, having heard what I have heard, having read what I have read, what am I going to do?*

One son lives with his father, a man determined to create a

homeland for the Jews. Within his community, this yearning has taken on its own urgency with the news from Europe that millions of Jews have been murdered in an ethnic cleansing ordered by Hitler. Passions run deep, but nowhere more so than in the heart of this father who spends his energies arguing for a safe place for his people. The other son lives with his family: mother, brothers, sisters and father, who is the *rebbe*, the rabbi of the rabbis among the Hasidim of Brooklyn.

The fathers disagree, deeply and profoundly, theologically and politically, about what the news from Europe means. Both are articulate and passionate men, and their sons have learned at their knees. The adolescents are unusually bright, full of life and loves, and are the best of friends. That their fathers see the world differently does not matter so much—until the Hasidic father forbids his son to see his friend, the other son. It seems harsh to separate the boys, but for the rabbi it is a matter of his most important beliefs; for him it is a blasphemy to even imagine "creating" a homeland for the Jews—that is the work of the Messiah! And so, for fidelity to the family's faith, the father requires his son to step away from the friendship.

But finally the issue is settled after the United Nations votes to partition Palestine, creating the longed-for home for the Jews. History, past and present, tells us that it was a more politically and socially volatile matter than the U.N. acknowledged at the time, with its rhetoric of "a land without a people for a people without a land." The Palestinian people, with their centuries of residence as shepherds and shopkeepers, were left out of the equation—a politically shortsighted decision that has ever since tragically rippled through the Middle East and the rest of the world. But that reality is not part of the storyline of *The Chosen*, which has its own traumas to address.

One of the most perplexing issues is the pedagogy of silence. The Hasidic father seems a wise man, a kind father, a respected leader in his community—and yet, he has chosen to live in silence with his son for fifteen years. Apart from teaching him the Torah as a member of the synagogue, the father has not spoken to his son since the boy's earliest years. How could it be? Is he really an ogre beneath his beard, behind his lively smile and eyes? Why silence?

After the U.N. vote, he explains, inviting his boy and his friend to come into his study. The ban on their relationship is lifted and he blesses them in their friendship. But he wants them to understand the meaning of his silence. As hard as it is, as painful as it is, for him it is a means to a more human life, a more holy life.

The rabbi tells of his affection for his son, of how when his son was a baby he used to bounce him on his knee, to play games, to take delight in the company of his first child. As his son began to read, the father noticed that he would not just "read a book, but would swallow it." He would read stories of people who suffered and feel nothing of their suffering; instead he would be so proud of having read the book, newly aware of his growing intelligence.

> I went away and cried to the Master of the Universe, "What have you done to me? A mind like this I need for a son? A heart I need for a son, a soul I need for a son, compassion I want from my son, righteousness, mercy, strength to suffer and carry pain, *that* I need from my son, not a mind without a soul!"[1]

And so he decided to raise his son in silence, as he himself had been raised, to feel the pain of the world in his own pain.

It is quite painful to hear him tell his story of struggling to form the soul of his son. While acknowledging the difficulty of his choice and the potential terrors implicit in his choice—for the love of his son, to lose the love of his son—he was at the same time so fearful of seeing his son become "a mind without a soul!" None of us, child or parent, older or younger, can read this without weeping. And none of us can conclude that the father's choice was cheap.

KNOWING AND DOING

This story has weighed on me for many years, shaping much of who I am and what I care most about. It was more than twenty-five years ago that I began a lecture series in the university neighborhood of Pittsburgh, set in the beautiful Heinz Chapel that is located between the University of Pittsburgh and Carnegie Mellon University.

Working with others in the city, we called it "Knowing and Doing: Crucial Questions for the Modern University" and commissioned a provocative poster, black and white for starkness, of a student standing on very large books, Grand Canyon–like, looking down into the world. Each time we had a lecture, these posters were distributed around the neighboring universities. We brought in some top-quality speakers: J. I. Packer, John Perkins, James Sire, John Stott, Nigel Goodwin, Os Guinness, Alden Hathaway and others.

Each in his own way spoke to the question of the responsibility of knowledge within the academic community, perennially challenged as it is by the fiction that one can know but not do, that one can in fact "get all A's and still flunk life." What is the point of learning, after all? The question is not new. In Dostoesvky's story of the university, *Crime and Punishment*, he explores whether it is enough to write a brilliant paper proposing a horrific idea—that some in society have the authority to decide for others whether or not they should live— and be applauded by one's professors because the argument is intellectually compelling. That story became reality a century later in the appointment of Peter Singer to an endowed chair at Princeton University, where he has famously argued that parents ought to have at least several months after the birth of a child to decide if in fact they want to keep the child. And all this from the ironically named Center for Human Values, which he directs.[2]

It was in Stott's address, taking up the question of the series, that I first heard the story of *The Chosen* as one with meaning for learning. With his characteristic insight, Stott told the story of the Hasidic son being raised in silence and of the father's lament, "A heart I need for a son!" But then he went on to the conversation of the father with the two boys, and the rabbi's words, "A mind without a heart is nothing." I can still hear Stott say those words in his deeply Oxbridge voice, and they still ring true—for everyone everywhere. Knowing still has to mean doing.

Recently my wife, Meg, and I were asked to lead a seminar on parenting for a church in downtown Washington. The people of this church have chosen to locate themselves in the center of the city, taking on its hopes and dreams, its complexities and challenges. From a small living room gathering only a few years ago, they have grown to over five hundred people, both singles and married couples with small children. The pastoral leadership wanted their congregation to understand parenting as a vocation. From the first, I had been deeply involved with the church, teaching about the relationship of worship to work, of liturgy to life, and I am implicated in who they are and who they want to be. We agreed to lead the seminar, with one caveat: it had to be called "Still Stumbling After All These Years," as it would be false to imagine otherwise.

For our first session, I introduced Potok's story and showed some of the film, asking the question, *If not silence, then what?* These were young parents who had passion for the city and the world, and they wanted their children to care about their city, and to care about cities all over the world, to eagerly engage the questions of their neighbors and friends, to find their way into vocations that are marked by responsible love for both the local and global character of life—perhaps in a word, to not be afraid of life.

If we have ears to hear, the film asks a hard question, and we talked for a while about it. While we may decide that the pedagogy of silence is flawed, even fundamentally, the more haunting question remains, *If not that, then what?* If we could offer the most cogent critique of silence as a means to teach a child to hear the pain of the world, that it is by its very character dehumanizing and debilitating, then what is the alternative?

There are no easy answers, and there are only more questions. How do we learn to become people who have minds and souls at the same time, in the same bodies, in the same persons? How do we avoid fragmenting ourselves so that we read stories of suffering but are insensitive to their meaning? To hear but not care? To see but not respond? That is harder, and because it is, a superficial response to the pedagogy of silence is impossible.

As Mark Schwehn has argued so well in *Exiles from Eden*, "Epistemologies have ethical implications . . . ways of knowing are not morally neutral but morally directive."[3] The ways we learn shape our souls, for blessing or curse, consciously chosen or not, and are rooted in epistemological commitments which are not morally neutral. Each and every time, they are morally directive. *The Chosen* is a story situated within a worldview, a vision of life and learning that is formed by assumptions that grow out of the Hebrew understanding of reality, of certain beliefs about God and the cosmos, about human nature and history. And so the rabbi's response to his son's boyish brilliance is not done in a vacuum, historically or morally. He knows that being smart is not good enough, that mastering the material in and of itself is not enough.

The question this chapter will explore grows out of this story of Jews in Brooklyn, of families hoping that their children will learn to love what God loves, to feel what God feels. To learn to live in the world with the ears of their hearts open to the cries of groaning people—even as they at the same time find deep gladness in the honest love given between human beings. Both matter, groaning and gladness together, for people who love what God loves and who feel what God feels.

What is it in the Hebrew vision that so profoundly connects

knowing with doing, learning with life—so much so that generations would decide to teach the most far-reaching, heart-probing
lessons with the pedagogy of silence?

A COVENANTAL EPISTEMOLOGY

With unusual wisdom, Louise Cowan's essay "Jerusalem's Claim
Upon Us" takes up for one more generation the age-old question,
What does Jerusalem have to do with Athens? Comparing and con-
trasting their different visions of history and human nature, she
notes the analysis of Matthew Arnold a century ago in his essay
"Hebraism and Hellenism." Arnold argued, Cowan says, that "the
object of the Greek way of thought is to know rightly; the object of
the Hebrew is to do rightly."

She offers this rephrasing:

> The highest calling of the Greeks is to pass by appearances
> and "hit the mark" of intellectual truth, whereas the supreme
> obligation of the Hebrews is to walk in the way of the Lord
> and on his law to meditate day and night. It has been the
> complicated task of Christian culture to bring these two im-
> peratives together.[4]

Impeccably fair and wonderfully rich, this University of Dallas
professor's article walks through the history of Western learning,
sifting the contributions of both worldviews, refusing to make a
pejorative point. While Cowan sees them as complementary understandings of life under the sun, her thesis is that it is the Hebrew
vision that

> passed down to us something radically new: not myth, but
> history, a movement forward in time, and therefore, the sense
> of an ending. Further, their dominant paradigm was not the
> lonely masculine hero, as in classical culture, but marriage,

man and woman standing side by side as partners—Adam and Eve, Abraham and Sarah, Isaac and Rebecca, Jacob and Rachel.[5]

Weighing back and forth the Greek and Hebrew conceptions, Cowan portrays the classical picture where "the gods are children of earth (Gaia) and sky (Uranos), and though mortals are thoroughly second-rate, they are called upon to be as like the gods as they can." She then says,

> In striking contrast to the Greek, Hebrew literature assigns immense significance to humankind, made in the image of God, though it enjoins a necessary humility in the face of the creator's majesty and power. It affirms that mortals are not simply offspring of nature or of Mother Earth but children of the God beyond gods—and obligated through the very fact of their existence.

To sum up, she argues that this deity who "fashions a cosmos out of love"—not the *eros* of the Greeks but the *hesed* of the Hebrews— makes a covenant with the human race, calling forth "a creature like himself, in his own image, one that could know and understand and love."[6]

Taking these ideas together, Cowan sets forth the contours of the Hebrew vision of the way the world is and ought to be. Several themes stand out. Not only to know rightly, but to do rightly. History, a movement forward in time. Man and woman side by side as partners. Obligated through the very fact of their existence. To know and understand and love. Woven as strands, they become a tapestry of the way to be holy and human, which in the end is the gift of "the covenant with the human race" that makes sense of the Hebrew understanding of life. Not forever lost in the cosmos, wondering who they are and how they are to live, but rather created in covenant to know and be known, to love and be loved. They were

called to know and to do, to see themselves as actors in history, as
male and female partners together in the image of God, as responsible for history, having as their central calling to know and understand and love God, each other and the creation—a spectrum of
relationships full of complexity, mystery and wonder.

Written into that vocation is an epistemological challenge, a
way of knowing that is not and can never be morally neutral, but
is always morally directive. We must not only *know* rightly, but *do*
rightly. And we must know and understand and love—at the same
time. Taken together this is the heart of the Hebrew way of knowing.

Listening carefully, we begin to make sense of the moral vision
set in motion in the pedagogy of silence, in Potok's story of a father
and his son yearning together to learn to hear the pain of the world.
Why would it matter so much to a Jewish family whether or not a
son has "a mind without a soul"? That a child be both intelligent
and compassionate? Only if there is an epistemological vision that
so prizes the relationship between knowledge and responsibility,
between knowing and doing, that anything less is seen as less than
human, less than holy.

And, in fact, that is exactly the way it is seen. If at the core of the
calling to be human is the task to know and do rightly, to act responsibly in history, to coherently connect knowledge with understanding
with love, then there must be a reason for being that makes sense of
human relationships and responsibilities in those terms, a context for
seeing what one believes and how one lives as a seamless whole.

For the Hebrew people, this comes from their understanding of
covenant. They are the covenant people, called into being by the
covenant God who in the beginning created a cosmos where human
beings are to live faithfully, making covenant with him, each other
and the world (Genesis 1–2), a cosmos where coherence is both
plausible and possible. And generation by generation, God continued to "covenant" with his people—with Noah, Abraham, Moses,

David—and of course, in the Christian vision, the life, death and resurrection of Jesus is the covenant incarnate, the covenant made flesh, living for a while among us.

But what is a covenant? What is it to covenant? Words like *agreement* and *contract* begin to explain, and yet they are insufficient to communicate the rich character of the word as it comes to us in the Hebrew scripture.[7] First of all, there is no definition that is once for all given. For the Hebrew people, whose theology unfolded over time as they saw God work in history, the word could only become clear as they interpreted their experience in its light, listening carefully to what God said, but also watching carefully what God did. God spoke in history and God made covenants with particular people in particular places, but the meaning could only be understood as the word was lived out before their eyes.

From beginning to end, the word *covenant* represents the reality that God is holy, holy, holy—and expects his people to be so, too. Covenants reveal a God who is gracious and compassionate—and expects his people to be so, too. A covenant was a call to live rightly, to act justly—images that imply a "north star," which is the character of God himself. This is who I am, this is who you are and this is the way you are to live. The word is dynamic, not static. But it has content, weight and substance. It is not an ideal out in the heavens, a covenant to be idealized in some otherworldly realm but never truly understood in the flesh-and-blood, push-comes-to-shove of everyday experience. Rather, it is only understood in history as God reveals himself to his people, time and again calling them to be like him in the world, to care for the world as he does, to know and understand and love as he does.

RELATIONSHIP, REVELATION, RESPONSIBILITY

Three realities mark covenants wherever they are found in the Hebrew scripture: relationship, revelation, responsibility—the first and the last mediated by the second. Whether it is the creation covenant with Adam and Eve or the Davidic covenant with the shepherd-become-king centuries later, each time a covenant is made, a relationship is offered, a revelation is given, a responsibility is expected. It is the very fabric of life in the Hebrew world, as Cowan saw when she contrasted the Hellenic and Hebraic visions. It is the God who "fashions a cosmos out of love" who calls a people into covenant, saying, "I want to know you and to be known by you. This is who I am and who you are. This is the way you are to live. Now, what are you going to do? How are you going to respond? With faithful love, with heart and mind and soul and strength—or will you falter?"

Relationship, revelation, responsibility. The words define each other, even as they define covenant. Inherently, implicitly, they are woven into human life and history, because there is no other world in which to live. If it is not the covenantal cosmos, then it is a cosmos in which we are lost—and in Percy's perceptive image, we *are* lost in that cosmos.

The Hebrew God makes himself known in history, by great grace choosing persons and peoples for himself, taking initiative born out of love with sons of Adam and daughters of Eve, establishing relationships where we are known, understood and loved. He does not leave human beings cowering in their shame in the garden, but seeks them out with a heart-searching question, "Where are you?" (Genesis 3:9). He does not leave Noah wondering whether the rain will ever stop, whether the flooding will be forever, but promises, "I establish my covenant with you: Never again will all life be destroyed by the waters of a flood" (Genesis 9:11). He does not leave Abraham hoping against hope, but instead promises generations so numerous that they will outnumber the stars in the heavens, assuring, "Do not be afraid, Abram, I am your shield, your very great reward" (Genesis 15:1). He does not leave his people adrift in the wilderness, free from the Egyptians, but free for what? Instead he says to them, "I am the Lord your God" (Exodus 20:2). He does not close his ears to the desires of his people for a king, but chooses a most unlikely boy, the youngest of Jesse's sons, to lead them: "And from that day on the Spirit of the Lord came powerfully upon David" (1 Samuel 16:13). In each of these examples and countless more, the God of Abraham, Isaac and Jacob connects to his people through covenant, saying with word and deed, "I know you, I know all about you, and I choose to love you. I will be in relationship to you."

But with that relationship comes a revelation. This is who I am. This is what I am like. This is who you are. This is how you are to live. He is the one who knows and understands and loves, and therefore makes his ways known—so plainly that we are without excuse (Romans 1:18-20). As with the relationship, the revelation is always a story of grace. In every generation, there are human beings who find favor in God's eyes, and they are people who refuse to go their own way, who choose against autonomy as the way to true happiness.

Noah was someone like that. Years ago, when our son Elliott was a little boy, we read to him from Peter Spier's wonderfully illustrated story, *Noah's Ark*. Unusually imagined, Spier chose to tell his tale through pictures, having words only on the first and the last pages. The opening scene is of a horrible world, full of bloodshed and terror—and then on the opposite page, across the valley, Noah tends his vineyard. Having read the book several times, beginning with the words, "And Noah found grace in the eyes of the Lord," we went on to read the story by its pictures. One day Elliott surprised us, piping up that he wanted to read it himself. Very proudly he began: "And Noah found grapes in the eyes of the Lord!" Noah did find grace, as well as grapes—and God revealed himself to him, explaining that a judgment would come, that the rain would fall, and that he should build an ark for his family and for the creatures of the earth.

God is the one who charts out for Abraham a vocation to embrace and a place to live. He is the one who makes sure that his chosen ones, the slaves of Egypt, know the whys and wherefores of how to live as they set out on pilgrimage for the promised land, giving them ten words by which to live and die (Exodus 20; Deuteronomy 10–11). He is the one who does not leave his people perplexed by their time and place, wondering how to bring together worship and war-making into a coherent vocation (1 Chronicles 17). The God who fashions a cosmos out of love is not the god who is made in our image, not the god who can be manipulated, made into whatever and whomever we like. To be drawn into relationship to him is to know him, and to be known by him. He is the holy, holy, holy one, and the whole earth is full of his glory (Isaiah 6).

A relationship initiated—by grace. A revelation made—with power and clarity. And a responsibility, an ability to respond, built into the very structure of the cosmos, into the very sinew of the human soul, of men and women made in his image, made to image him in the world.

Always and everywhere, the revelation requires a response.

Take care of this world, explore and love it, have dominion in it, be faithful stewards of it—for me, for you, for the future of the world. Name the animals as you begin to understand them, and give order to what you know. Take delight in each other, bone of bone, flesh of flesh; become as one, and enjoy your nakedness. Eat of every tree in the garden, except one. In all this, you are responsible, able to respond to each and to every word I have given you.

But if you choose to be less than responsible, knowing what is right but choosing not to do it, then there will be consequences of the most grievous kind, consequences that will affect generations to come.

What will you do? How will you respond?

The rest is history, full of joy and sorrow, blessing and curse. But it is always a history of responsibility, of people making true choices for which there are real consequences that ripple out across time—so much so that centuries and cultures later Václav Havel, the brilliant Czech playwright and politician, would sum up the human situation with these words: The "secret of man is the secret of his responsibility."[8]

Though the words are historically situated in a moment in Hebrew history, Joshua's charge to his people echoes across the ages: "Choose this day whom you will serve" (Joshua 24:15 ESV). It is a line in the sand for every generation, perennially asked and answered in every time, in every place. But it is particularly so within the covenantal character of the biblical story, where the dynamic of relationship/revelation/responsibility is sustained in time and space, generation by generation. Noah, Abraham, Moses, David—on each occasion that a covenant is made, a question is set forth: What will you do with what you know? How will you respond to what you have heard? The question only makes sense, metaphysically and morally, if we are in a universe where choices are real, where in fact we are able to respond, and therefore responsible.

In and through the imagery of covenant, it is the character of God himself that gives the imagery reality and meaning. Omnipotent and omniscient, just and merciful—a thousand times, yes. But the covenant, at its very core, reveals the God who knows rightly and does rightly, who knows and understands and loves. There is an epistemology at the center of the covenant that makes moral sense of the biblical story; as Cowan writes, of a "history, a movement forward in time, of a man and woman side by side as partners, obligated through the very fact of their existence." While each phrase is pregnant, full of meaning, it is the last one that holds the key. To be "obligated" requires that one know the reality of one's situation, of one's moment in time, in relation to God, to others, to the world. To be obligated means that one understands one's responsibility, one's accountability, and then acts upon it.

To see it in contrast, being "obligated" stands against the idea that we are autonomous, that we are able to make it up as we go along, doing whatever we want whenever we want.[9] It is not a new idea; in fact it is as old as the first stories in the Hebrew scripture of a man and a woman created able to respond, and therefore responsible. In the tragedy of tragedies they together determined that human happiness in history would best be served by choosing to go their own way. They knew what was right, but chose not to do what was right.

It is their obligation, their responsibility, their accountability to God and to history that makes theological sense of the story. Otherwise it is on the level of a fairy tale, with a point worth pondering but bearing no metaphysical or moral weight for us.

In the early 1990s, America went to war for a short time. We called it Desert Storm. I was teaching undergraduates on Capitol Hill then, and was responsible for our international policy courses of study. As we had for years, we chose issues that at that moment were the issues of the city and the world, and therefore allowed our students the opportunity to learn from the debates all around them—in fact, to learn from the people who were the active players in policy formation. That year we took up the debate about Desert Storm. What was it about? What is our responsibility? How will we know if we have won? Good questions, and hard questions.

Havel was just becoming a more internationally known figure at the time, having come from prison to the presidency of Czechoslovakia and then the Czech Republic. I remember that the Librarian of Congress invited him to come lecture at the Library, located just blocks away. In fact there were several days given to Havel and his thinking, which is some indication of the weight of his vision. Dignitaries from all over the world were invited to engage with him.

In the plenary address, like plenary addresses he had given the world over by that time, Havel spoke about responsibility for history. As a citizen of Czechoslovakia, he had seen it pillaged by the Nazis in the 1940s and then the Communists in the 1960s, and he knew that decades later his people saw themselves as victims. But he also knew that there was no future for his people if they could not set that identity and history aside and instead take up responsibility for the future. It was that theme that became his, all over the world, always asking, "What are the conditions in which human beings can take responsibility for the world?"

The speech that night ranged across history and the world, but once again he made this point, not as a Christian and perhaps not even as a theist, but as a human being who has read history very carefully: If we lose God in the modern world, then we lose access to these four great ideas—meaning, purpose, responsibility, accountability. An astounding claim, but over the years since then I have come to that speech many times, sure that Havel understood the consequences of convictions in ways that most are afraid to follow through on. And yet this has far-reaching implications for who we see ourselves to be and how we understand our lives and world.

What Havel saw is what Cowan saw, that human beings are "obligated through the very fact of their existence." *Obligation* is a rich word and is another way of saying that meaning, purpose, responsibility and accountability are bound up with our deepest commitments and beliefs about God, the human condition and history. How could it be otherwise?

THE RESPONSIBILITY OF KNOWLEDGE

What is the relationship of ideas to life, of theories to practices, of knowledge to responsibility? Almost always, we assume a connection, that the one implies the other.

Aren't the best stories always this story? Don't they always explore this question? Think through Shakespeare. *Romeo and Juliet?* *Hamlet?* *Much Ado About Nothing?* Or Dickens. *A Christmas Carol?* *Great Expectations?* *David Copperfield?* Or Dorothy Sayers. *Whose Body?* *Unnatural Death?* *Gaudy Night?* Imaginative, unique, compelling, but each one built out of the dynamic relationship of knowledge to responsibility, and it is that that draws us in.

Alfred Hitchcock was a master at this. His film *Rope* is a twisted tale reminiscent of Dostoevsky's *Crime and Punishment,* the classically heart-searching novel about a student whose brilliant essay is applauded within the academy but leads to the most horrific murder. Set in an apartment of newly graduated friends who take their professor's ideas more seriously than he ever intended, a serious question is at the heart of Hitchcock's story: Is the professor responsible for his theories? Are his students responsible for trying them out?

Knowing and doing are at the core of every examined life, but putting the two together is the most difficult challenge we face. At our best we long for integrity, for what we know and what we do to be coherent, because we believe they belong together intrinsically.

Why else do we care about *what* someone knew *when?* Our newspapers, courts, even family conversations are full of the assumption that if one knows, then one is responsible.[10] *If you knew, then why didn't you do?*

With an eye for reality and a rare creativity, the films of Hitchcock explore this question persistently, *Rope* quintessentially. *Rear Window* tells the story of a man confined to bed with a severely broken leg. While spending his hours and days at the window looking through a telescope, he is sure that he sees a crime committed in an apartment across the courtyard. The terror of the story is bound up in the question, *What is his responsibility? What should he do with what he knows?*

In *The Confession,* a priest hears the most horrible words, "I have killed someone!" But then this taunt is added, "You must not tell because you cannot tell—after all, you have heard me in the confessional." The murderer then presents to the police "clues" that indicate that the priest is the surprising suspect. The question? What will the priest do with what he knows? Especially now that he himself is implicated in the crime?

Vertigo also explores the psychology of crime, drawing in an innocent man as an accomplice who slowly begins to understand what has happened. In the complexity and heartache of love and death, he strains over the implications of his responsibility. Hitchcock even titled one film *The Man Who Knew Too Much,* which plays off of the drama of spies and kidnappers with a murder in the offing. The question? Can he be responsible for having been in the wrong place at the wrong time and seeing what he should not have seen, at least, what someone did not want him to see? A storyteller whose work will long outlive him because he spoke so truthfully about the human condition, Hitchcock rarely missed the opportunity in his films to ask, and answer, the probing questions which are implicit in the relationship of knowing to doing. We love his work, even in its terror, because we see ourselves in it.

All of us—friends, parents and children, teachers and students, employers and employees, political leaders and their people—at some point are faced with the question: *If you knew, why didn't you do?* How could you be so irresponsible? East or West, Northern or Southern Hemisphere, rich or poor, conservative or liberal, our supposition is the same: there is a responsibility for knowledge. In quiet resentment, in public outcry, the response is always, *We expected otherwise from you. And now we find that though you knew what to do, you failed to do it.* From the most personal to the most public of our relationships, from marital unfaithfulness to corporate scandals—how else do we explain the outrage, the disappointment, when we find that one more time in one more situation with one more person, there was a disconnect between what someone knew and what they did?

What *does* it mean to "know"? Cultures have answered the question very differently. In *The Meno,* the Greeks wrestled with whether virtue—to live the way a human being ought to live— could be taught. It is a question shaped by critical concerns, philosophically, politically and pedagogically, and good people who care about good societies have been debating the question ever since. The Enlightenment was born out of certain commitments to a way of knowing and living; Bacon's "knowledge is power" shaped centuries of civilization. At their best, those beliefs brought forth a responsible engagement of history, developing the resources of the earth for advancements in health and education. At their worst, they resulted in an uncanny willingness to disconnect oneself from the so-called forces of history. We see this, for example, in the question at the core of *The Last Butterfly*, and of Eichmann's life and death. A child of the Enlightenment, the scientist and philosopher Michael Polanyi asked a haunting question after the Holocaust, and was so troubled by it that he changed the direction of his life: How can people be brilliant and bad at the same time? How could they have gone to our best universities and acted so horribly, so inhumanely? How dare we call this "enlightenment"?[11]

What *does* it mean to "know"? If we were to take the Hebrew scripture, from Genesis to Malachi, listening to and learning the way that knowledge is understood, it would come to something like this: *to have knowledge of* means *to have responsibility to* means *to have care for.*[12] If one knows, then one cares; if one does not care, then one does not know.

Like the word *covenant,* it is defined in life, not in abstraction. There is no ideal of "knowledge," a reality existing somewhere, somehow beyond the way that it is understood in the ordinary experiences of human life. The Hebrew word *yada,* "to know," offers the richest vision, though as a word it is one among several that are embedded in the covenantal epistemology. Its first use, not surprisingly, is in and of itself a picture of the relationship/ revelation/responsibility dynamic.

God invites Adam and Eve to live in his garden to be the stewards of his world, and sets before them the meaning of that vocation. Do this, and this—and don't do this. A yes, another yes, and a no. Take care of the garden, eat of all the trees—except one. That tree represents the knowledge of good and evil, and for Adam and Eve it was a test of their faithfulness, of their willingness to respond responsibly.[13] What would they do with what they knew? The great Princeton theologian of a century ago, Geerhardus Vos, in his reflection on Genesis 2–3 and the tree of the knowledge of good and evil, maintained that the "Hebrew 'to know' can signify 'to choose'"— and so, he argued, responsibility is written in from the very beginning, etymologically and theologically.[14]

Even having chosen wrongly, horribly so, the next use of the word describes the sexual union of Adam and Eve, a knowledge that grows out of an intimacy born of love and commitment. "Adam made love to his wife Eve, and she became pregnant" (Genesis 4:1). The word *yada* is translated "made love to," because the reader would not know what "know" means in that context. It is clear that it is a million miles from the detached, disconnected, dispassionate "knowing" of the Enlightenment, the epistemology that shaped Eichmann's vision of vocation. Rather, there is something wonderfully tender, something much more human here.

The book of Exodus is full of this word, and it is plain that translators have tried to help us understand it. After four hundred years of Joseph's family living in the land of Egypt, they had become "exceedingly fruiful," and a new king "to whom Joseph meant nothing, came to power" (Exodus 1:7-8). The New Living Translation says, "who knew nothing about Joseph." The pharaoh knew about

Joseph; the problem was that he did not care anything about Joseph, or the promises made to him by earlier rulers. Realpolitick required a different valuation, and the children of Israel became slaves.

Centuries later, "The Israelites groaned in their slavery . . . and their cry for help because of their slavery went up to God. God heard their groaning and he remembered his covenant with Abraham, with Isaac and with Jacob. So God looked on the Israelites and was concerned about them" (Exodus 2:23-25). *Yada* is translated "was concerned about them." Outraged at the injustice, Moses murders an Egyptian overlord and runs to the desert where he is confronted by a burning bush from which God speaks:

> Do not come any closer. . . . Take off your sandals, for the place where you are standing is holy ground. . . . I am the God of your father, the God of Abraham, the God of Isaac and the God of Jacob. . . . I have indeed seen the misery of my people in Egypt. I have heard them crying out because of their slave drivers, and I am concerned about their suffering. (Exodus 3:5-7)

Again, *yada* is translated, "I am concerned about their suffering." Implicit in the meaning of the word itself is concern and care—if I know, then I care—because when God sees and hears, he responds.

Sent back to Egypt to address the pharaoh, Moses announces the judgment of God on the hardheartedness of the king. "This is what the Lord says: By this you will know that I am the Lord: With the staff that is in my hand I will strike the water of the Nile, and it will be changed into blood" (Exodus 7:17). Here *yada* means that God will be known by what he does. That relation is also expected of his people, the people of his covenant. And so after the Israelites flee Egypt, and at the foot of Mount Sinai where God gives tablets of stone to Moses, he explains more fully their meaning with these words: "Do not oppress a foreigner; you yourselves know how it feels to be foreigners, because you were foreigners in Egypt" (Exodus

23:9). "You yourself know how it feels" grows out of the word *yada*;
in effect, God commands his people to feel what they know.

In the second giving of the law, Deuteronomy, Moses sets forth
in broad scope and great detail what it will mean to be the people
of God. "Now, Israel hear the decrees and laws I am about to teach
you" (Deuteronomy 4:1). Obedience is commanded, idolatry is for-
bidden and he asks the people to ponder the wonder of it all—the
God of heaven and history has spoken to them! "Has anything so
great as this ever happened, or has anything like it ever been heard
of?" (4:32). Moses comes to a crescendo moment, summing up
with a very pastoral word: "Acknowledge and take to heart this day
that the Lord is God in heaven above and on the earth below. There
is no other" (4:39). It is "acknowledge" that translates *yada*, giving
us one more window into its meaning. Moses is urging his people
to avoid becoming "minds without souls," but instead wants them
to take to heart what they know.

As they sojourn through the wilderness and finally enter into the
land of promise, they become a people. Moses dies, looking across
the Jordan, hoping with hope. Generations come and go, commandments are kept and broken, kings and kingdoms are established and lost. A worldview is being formed, not only by the words
of God given to Abraham, Isaac, Jacob and Moses, but by the practices of the people. As always, the way that belief and behavior are
formed over time is complex; but it is clear that the way we live
shows what we believe.[15]

And it is the way that God's people live that is the focus of the
collection of wise sayings that we call Proverbs. They are not so
much statements of creed or confession, but of a worldview become
a way of life—or to put it the other way, of a way of life become a
worldview. The epistemological vision that threads its way through
biblical history is plainly part of this book's account of why and how
to live in the world: if you know, you care; if you don't care, you don't

know. And so, "The righteous care for the needs of their animals, but the kindest acts of the wicked are cruel" (Proverbs 12:10). *Yada* here becomes "care for," as once again the reader would be perplexed by the word "know." "The righteous care about justice for the poor, but the wicked have no such concern" (29:7). It is no surprise that "care about justice for the poor" emerges from the translators' desire to accurately account for a way of knowing that grows out of the covenantal epistemology. In both of these remarkable passages, the relation of knowledge to responsibility to care is assumed—if one has knowledge of, then one has responsibility to, then one has care for. No disconnect here between knowing and doing.

Over time, the way that Israel lives becomes more and more of a problem. Even with the Proverbs' purpose to set forth a vision for "doing what is right and just and fair" (1:3), the people of the covenant are increasingly marked by just the opposite: they do what is not right, not just, not fair. And God in his faithful love, *hesed*, sends prophets to call the people back to the meaning of the covenant. *Remember who I am. Remember who you are. Remember how you are to live.*

The first of these voices is Isaiah, who begins with these sober words, "Hear me, you heavens! Listen, earth! For the Lord has spoken: 'I reared children and brought them up, but they have rebelled against me. The ox knows its master, the donkey its owner's manger, but Israel does not know, my people do not understand'" (Isaiah 1:2-3). "But Israel does not know." What is it that they do not know? The commandments? Not possible. The ways of the Lord? Not possible. Even the ox and the donkey know, even they *yada*. But the people have rejected the covenant, they have separated knowing from doing. They may *know* rightly, but they do not *do* rightly. They do not understand the moral meaning of the covenant—that it is the gift of life to them, making it possible to be human and holy at the same time.

The prophet Jeremiah adds his voice to Isaiah's, lamenting the loss of knowledge, calling the people to an integrity of heart, to do what they know, to move outside the compartmentalization of faith that is the perennial temptation of people of faith anytime and anywhere.

"Woe to him who builds his palace by unrighteousness,
  his upper rooms by injustice,
Making his own people work for nothing,
  not paying them for their labor.
He says, 'I will build myself a great palace
  with spacious upper rooms.'
So he makes large windows in it,
  panels it with cedar
  and decorates it in red.

"Does it make you a king
  to have more and more cedar?
Did not your father have food and drink?
  He did what was right and just,
  so all went well with him.
He defended the cause of the poor and needy,
  and so all went well.
Is that not what it means to know me?"
  declares the Lord. (Jeremiah 22:13-16)

Plaintively, it is *yada* that is offered as the *telos* of life for the people of God—socially, economically, politically. True knowledge is your very reason for being.

Like a prism in the sun, *yada* is a multi-faceted word that, in its near one thousand uses in the Hebrew scripture, is translated variously as know, knows, knew, known, knowing, knowledge, acknowledge, understand, teach, realize, show, experience, care for, concern, concerned about, have sex with and learns. From beginning to end it is a word for life, ranging across the spectrum of human relationships and responsibilities—and not surprisingly, its meaning includes both joy and sorrow, the way things ought to be and the way things more often than not are.

That was true then in the life and literature of the Hebrew world, and it is true in our day as well—sometimes painfully so. In *Seinfeld*'s cynical world, the point was that there was no point, and "Yada yada yada" was the response. As silly as Seinfeld meant it to be, for those with ears to hear, it did have meaning. After the Fall, where the covenant is first broken in the Garden, everything is broken, the whole cosmos is affected—and so is *yada*, so is knowing. *Yada, yada, yada.*

How could it not be? Because *yada* is a common word used by common people, and therefore it does not and cannot always communicate a high view of men and women, or a true sense of stewardship for what one knows and how one lives. In a fallen world, even the best of life, the best of work and the best of sex has some element of brokenness. And sometimes, sorrowfully, they even take on a vicious quality, for example, the story of Lot's neighbors in Sodom, pounding on his door, insisting that he produce his guests "so that we can have sex with them" (Genesis 19:5). Our word *sodomy* comes from that moment when *yada* is self-centered hedonism. In the book of Judges, there is a horrible story of rape, and once again a wounded and distorted *yada* tells the sad tale (Judges 19:22-26). The griefs and groans of men and women the world over are bound up with knowing and being known, with the experience of knowledge as care and knowledge as abuse. In and through it all, God's own knowing is the North Star, offering light to our path, showing that it is possible to know and understand and love—all at the same time.

WHY DID YOU CARE? THE STORY OF LE CHAMBON

Why do we care? Anytime, anywhere, it is a weighty question—and sometimes even more so.

When our older children were almost adolescents, I invited them and their friends at Rivendell School to see the film *Weapons of the Spirit*. With unusual seriousness, the *Washington Post* saw it as "a kind of spiritual quest," and I thought it would be good grist for the mill of young minds. "The question at the heart of this modest, compelling film is this: how in the middle of great evil did a great good take place?" The reviewer explains,

> Pierre Sauvage's documentary about the extraordinary French village of Le Chambon-sur-Lignon during the Nazi rule in World War II is like a murder mystery in reverse. It's an examination of crimes that didn't take place, of atrocities averted, and in such a way that history itself seems to have been subverted by their absence.[16]

And so after school one Friday afternoon we made our way to Georgetown and took it in—with the plan that we would walk around the corner for pizza and conversation afterwards. Looking back, every effort I made like that was probably more of hope, longing for my children to see, to begin forming eyes of the heart that could make sense of both the glory and the shame of the human condition. We live much of our lives with hope.

We watched and then we ate. Using the most simple terms, I wondered what they thought of what they saw. Did they understand the ideas and issues of the Holocaust in their young hearts? Born in the last years of the twentieth century, would they empathize with people who had been born a half-century earlier under very different circumstances than theirs? I did not want to overwhelm them, even as I hoped that they would take it seriously, asking questions about the story but also about themselves.

Why do we care? It is never an easy question, and there is never an easy answer. But even for these young people, I wanted them to begin thinking through the responsibility of knowledge. Habits of

the heart form early, with tens of thousands of choices made, more
often than not under the radar of our consciousness. As we move
from childhood to adulthood, our visions about what matters and
what does not matter, about what is important and what is not
important, come into maturity with commitments and judgments
in place. Yes, I longed for my children to know about the world, but
also to care about the world—and to see that the one should imply
the other.

Why did you care? That question runs through the film, asked
and asked again of the Le Chambon villagers, descendents of the
Huguenots, the French Protestants who centuries earlier had been
horribly persecuted for their faith. The filmmaker took his camera
throughout the town, interviewing men and women forty years
after the Holocaust. Almost no one wanted to talk. Characteristically, the response was something like this, "What else could I have
done? I'm not a hero, and I don't want to say more." But of course
they could have done something else. Most of Europe chose to do
something else.[17]

In one of the ironies-become-providences of history, the great
French novelist Albert Camus lived in Le Chambon during these
years. And while the definitive story is not yet written, it is clear
that he wrote the novel *The Plague* while living among a people who
decided to step into history with rare courage and unusual grace.[18]
With surprising moral vision, their knowledge of the Jewish persecution led to an instinctive sense of responsibility, and they opened
their basements and barns to five thousand people during the Holocaust years. Reflecting on this miracle of responsible kindness,
the filmmaker insists,

> If we do not learn how it is possible to act well even under the
> most trying circumstances, we will increasingly doubt our
> ability to act well even under less trying ones. If we remember

solely the horror of the Holocaust, we will pass on no perspective from which meaningfully to confront and learn from that very horror. If we remember solely the horror of the Holocaust, it is we who will bear the responsibility for having created the most dangerous alibi of all: that it was beyond man's capacity to know and care.[19]

All of this mattered supremely to Sauvage. For him, it was never mere history, a philosophical abstraction—with chills, we learn that he was born in Le Chambon, a baby born to Jewish parents. That the Chambonnais cared was a matter of life and death for him, and years later he wanted an answer to his question, which in its own way was the question at the heart of Camus's novel.

Staying in an old granite house named Le Panelier, Camus would walk the streets of the village, seeing what there was to be seen, writing his story of a holocaust in the lives of a physician and a priest, the central characters of his novel. How should they respond to the plague that has come to their town? First a death, then another, and then many, many more, and the two men debate, "What is our responsibility?" The physician sees it as evil, and spends himself on behalf of the people who have been afflicted by the plague. The priest sees it differently, reading it as "God's will" and concluding that to fight the plague is to fight God. While Camus never explicitly connected *The Plague* with Le Chambon, it is impossible to account for the former apart from the latter.

In the image of Simone Weil, true learning is learning to pay attention, seeing things as they really are. That is why she takes up the parable of the Good Samaritan, grounding her argument in the story Jesus told in response to the question from the expert in the law, "And who is my neighbor?" (Luke 10:25-37). Camus's novel is at its heart a twentieth-century retelling of that parable. A religious professional who is able to justify his indifference—skewing the truth about both God and human beings as he does so—is not unlike the religious professionals of Jesus' story who for theological, historical and sociological reasons do not "see" a neighbor in the beaten, bruised man on the road to Jericho. And the counterweight of a physician who sees neighbors wherever he looks, and responds to the need—he is not unlike the Samaritan who has eyes to see the man as a neighbor, offering help with remarkable generosity. Camus makes this point, speaking to us in the words of the narrator of his novel:

> There always comes a time in history when the man who dares to say that two plus two equals four is punished with death. . . . And the issue is not a matter of what reward or what punishment will be the outcome of that reasoning. The issue is simply whether or not two plus two equals four. For those of our townspeople who were then risking their lives, the decision they had to make was simply whether or not they were in the midst of a plague and whether or not it was necessary to struggle against it.[20]

Two plus two equals four. Simple math it is, but only if we have eyes that see.

With uncanny insight, the Hungarian Jew Michael Polanyi made the same point, arguing that "two plus two equals four is a moral equation." At the height of his professional expertise during the years of the Holocaust, his peers saw him on a Nobel Prize path in chemistry; but the horrors of that time affected him deeply, so much so that he left his laboratory and gave the rest of his life to one question, which became the question of his life, *How is it possible to be brilliant and bad at the same time?* Or more historically, *How dare we call this the Enlightenment?* For Polanyi, the simply arithmetic was a matter of seeing the truth about the world, believing that mathematics and moral meaning are finally the same. To say it differently, the equation is about reality, about things as they really are.

Camus came to the same conclusion. The story he wrote is a metaphor for a way of knowing that implies responsibility. Simply said, his vision was informed by the lives of a village of Christians who saw themselves implicated in history—and he decided to write a story about what he saw. For Camus, it was about paying attention to what was happening in Europe, and in Le Chambon—to the reality of life as it was.

Why do we care? Because we see ourselves in relationship, "obligated by the very fact of our existence." And now knowing what we know, we are responsible, for love's sake, for the people and places that are ours—if we have eyes that see.

5

Come and See

The most determinative moral formation
most people have in our society is when they learn
to play baseball, basketball, quilt, cook or learn to lay bricks.

STANLEY HAUERWAS, "DISCIPLESHIP AS A CRAFT"

*A*ll happy families resemble one another; each unhappy family is unhappy in its own way." This opening line in *Anna Karenina* assures all of us that Tolstoy lives in the same world we do. We see ourselves in his art and know something more truly about ourselves because of his art.

Seen by many as our greatest storyteller, it was Tolstoy's ability to open windows into the human heart, glorious ruins that we are, that makes him a novelist whose work is read by every generation. The best stories are timeless, where everyone everywhere says *yes*. And Percy's wisdom is timeless too, that "Bad books always lie. They lie most of all about the human condition." In Tolstoy we have story upon story of pilgrimages through love and life, of people finding their way in the world on journeys of all kinds. Percy, a "pilgrim in the ruins" himself, saw the thread of pilgrimage in every good story, considered it in fact the criteria for what makes a story good.[1]

One of Tolstoy's best is *Two Old Men*. Set in nineteenth-century Russia, the book tells the tale of two men, Efim and Elisha, who decide that before they die they must make a pilgrimage to Jerusalem. I first read it when I was on my way to Israel where I had the task of reflecting on what it meant for a group of modern pilgrims— and it seemed a story just for me.

After months of planning, Efim and Elisha collect what they will need and began to walk. In a day before planes, trains and automobiles, this was a major undertaking. But walk they did. After another long day on the road, they come to a village that seems deserted. No one is about, and seeing a small hut, they look in to see what has happened. They enter its darkness and smell death. As their eyes adjust to the lack of light, they see bodies on beds. With trepidation they come close, and see that the people are still alive, but barely.

One of them wants to stay and help. He encourages his companion to go on beyond the village, "And I will catch up with you." But as Elisha opens doors and windows, and offers them food and drink, he begins to see that their needs are more complex than he first imagined—and that it is not only them, but the whole village that is suffering. He finds his friend and tells Efim that he wants to stay longer, encouraging him to make his way on to Jerusalem— "And I will find you."

The story goes on, but the short story is this: The one man stays in the village, helping the villagers find their way again to happiness and health, never going on to Jerusalem, eventually returning home; the other man makes his way to Jerusalem, but is dissatisfied by what he finds—and does not find. He visits the places meant to inspire, but he never is inspired. Always looking for his friend, expecting him to come too, before long he decides that his pilgrimage is over and he returns home to Russia—again, walking across a continent. At one point along the way, he comes to a village that seems strangely familiar to him. And then he realizes that it is where he left his friend—but everything seems very different now. Men and women, older and younger, are busy at work and play; animals are healthy, and the crops are growing, and so he asks, "What has happened?" In simple innocence, the villagers explain that a man stopped along the way and gave them back their life.

The story concludes with both men finally at home, sharing a bottle of vodka and telling the stories of their pilgrimages. Tolstoy has no desire to tell a black-and-white story, with a good man and a bad man; it is more nuanced than that, as life is. The last lines tell of their joy in meeting together again.

If we have ears, then hear; eyes, then see—and a nose, then smell. In Simone Weil's insight into sacramental learning, the one man paid more attention than the other. He could "smell" something that implicated him, and began to understand that his pilgrimage was the village, full of sorrow and hope as it was.

This business of seeing ourselves as implicated is central to the covenantal epistemology. That we see ourselves as responsible, for love's sake, is what the responsibility of knowledge is always about.

THE HOPES AND FEARS OF ALL THE YEARS

In the post-9/11 world, Washington changed. More barriers to buildings, more security in airports, more concern about the rest of the world—and for some, more of a sense of being implicated in history, as responsible for the way things turn out.

I remember one day walking from the Capitol to the Senate office building and seeing Todd Deatherage. We both are committed to the wisdom of William Wilberforce and his friends of two hundred years ago, men and women with diverse vocations who chose to live near each other in the neighborhood of Clapham, then a few miles from London, now part of the city. This was their credo: Choose a neighbor before you choose a house. They thought that the needs of the world were too complex for fragmented living, and knew that if they were to see the renewal of the social fabric of English life, including the abolition of slavery, they would need to be a community, living near enough to have an honest life together. Remembering this story, we live life like this too: celebrating holidays together, caring for each other's children, making sure that our spouses are well when someone is traveling, listening to the dreams and heartaches of life and labor. All this and more is written into our unfolding vision of vocation, of a life together.

Long a chief of staff in the Congress, Todd then served in the same position at the State Department. That day he was hand delivering to every senator an important document that would be headline news the next day, so in the spirit of keeping peace, he wanted those who needed to know, to know.

In the course of the conversation, we lingered over Israel and the policies of the United States in the Middle East; not surprisingly, the State Department's special briefing for senators involved that part of the world. Our foreign policy in relation to Israel is not administered in the State Department, but in the White House—meaning that as far as Israel goes, public opinion shapes the decision making, not necessarily what is in the long-term interest of the United States or Israel. So Todd's work took place within that political dynamic, and given the integrity of his vocation, he knew that he needed to both satisfy the hopes of the administration, but also the needs of the people of that region—both Israelis and Palestinians.

Before we were finished that day, he told me of his plan to go to Jerusalem on a political pilgrimage. The government of Israel was building the great wall of separation between the two peoples, marking off a "safe place" for Israelis to live without the fear of Palestinian suicide bombers. Not a small matter, for anyone. The point of tension, though, was that the wall was to run through centuries-old Palestinian neighborhoods, so that generations of people who had coherent lives of home, school, business and church/mosque were now forced into fragmented existences—the wall making what had been their normal lives now horribly abnormal, even impossible.

A month later he took his trip and spent a week literally walking along the wall, talking with people whose lives were entangled in what this new barrier meant, Israelis and Palestinians. The stories were heart wrenching. For people committed to lives of doing justice, loving mercy and walking humbly with God, it is never easy to craft a public policy that makes everything right for everyone. We know that at our best we still fall short—and someone somewhere will be hurt, falling through the cracks. Todd is not a romantic about the past, present and future of the Middle East; but neither is he a cynic or a stoic. He is committed to putting his shoulder to history and doing what is possible, working for a proximate justice.

For several years that calling kept him in the State Department as the chief of staff for the internal think tank, giving counsel to the secretary of state on issues far and wide. Over that time he made many trips to the Middle East, developing a deepening wisdom about what is needed for a sustainable peace in the region as a whole, but also in Israel, divided as it is between Jew and Arab. Our little community of friends met week by week, hearing news of important speeches and consultations, as well as the stories of the trips he took. It was increasingly obvious that his heart was becoming fixed upon that part of the world, and he yearned for a political commitment to a common good.

When it came time for him to leave the State Department, he and Gregory Khalil—someone he had met in his trips back and forth to Israel—who was a Palestinian, a human rights lawyer and the son of generations of people who call Bethlehem home, decided to form a new organization to argue for something that almost no one wants, almost no one believes.

What is that? That any long-term solution for Israel means that one must be for *both* the Israelis and the Palestinians, at the same time. It is a short-term fiction to believe otherwise, but most people do. So the work of the Telos Group is very difficult, even as it is very important, because for the most part—for complex historical, sociological, political and theological reasons—neither the church nor the world wants to believe that thesis.

For Tolstoy's men on pilgrimage to Jerusalem, it was in *seeing* that the one understood the meaning of his journey, just as it was in *not seeing* that the other missed the meaning of his journey. Central to the Telos Group's mission is the conviction that it is in seeing what is going on that people will begin to understand the realities of the situation and begin to see themselves as responsible, willing to care about justice for all, not justice for "just us." Their strategy is formed by a profound incarnational commitment. They invite leaders of various communities to come with them to Israel to see places of importance to both the Israeli community and the Palestinian community, and to meet key spokesmen for both. Almost no one else does this kind of hard work, as it is obviously easier to choose one story over against the other.

One visit may be comprised of a group of Catholic bishops from around the world, another a group of Latino or African American leaders, still another a small group of business leaders from the Aspen Institute, and yet another a group of young evangelicals—but each time there is a disciplined commitment to giving flesh to their words, showing that the hopes and fears of all the years are only addressed when both histories are honored, when both futures are guarded. And it is no surprise that when people see and hear, meeting real people with real lives, that a transformation often takes place. Relationship, revelation, responsibility. When we learn like that, we begin to see ourselves as implicated.

IDEAS HAVE TO BECOME LIFE

My friends know that I am a great lover of books, perhaps too much so. But truth be told, over time I have come to believe that books only take us so far. They can open windows into life, offering ideas about the world and our place in it that can be transforming—but we need more. As human beings we have to see words made flesh to understand them.

One of the reasons that I have long loved Robert Coles's work is that he understood this so deeply and well. His *The Call of Stories: Teaching and the Moral Imagination* is a great book, principally as it allows the reader to read through the heart and over the shoulder of the unusually gifted psychiatrist and professor that Coles is, telling about his use of literature to awaken the moral imagination of his students at Harvard. In undergraduate courses like "The Literature of Social Reflection," he asked students to read Jane Austen and Leo Tolstoy as well as Walker Percy and Flannery O'Connor; but in graduate courses like "Dickens and the Law," he invited law students to read the novels of Dickens with him, exploring the meaning of the law. (As he noted in proposing the course to the dean, the curriculum as a whole never addressed that question.)

But if this book is a critical gift, it is also important to see it in relation to his *The Call of Service,* the companion volume, where he sets forth a vision of learning that takes place in life. For Coles there is a profound coherence in the two books; never one over the other, but more the two complementing each other—words becoming flesh, allowing us to see in the stories of the one the ways that people live in the complexity of the narrative world, and in the other to see the importance of lives of commitment being worked out in time and place. For Coles, the deeper thread throughout is his passion for a kind of learning that awakens the moral imagination, allowing us to see ourselves as responsible for the way the world is and ought to be.

The Gospels are like this too. Story after story, we meet people with names and histories, but also we meet imagined people who seem as if they too live in the same world we do. Either way, Jesus is teaching that ideas have to become life, eventually, for everyone everywhere—whether the story is of Levi the tax collector or of the Good Samaritan. Both are important; they need each other. In the best of learning, in the truest learning, words have to become flesh, and more often than not it is in storied service that the eyes of the heart are awakened.

The covenantal epistemology is a way of knowing that sees the world through the lens of relationship. *I know you, and I love you.* From the patriarchs on, God calls a people into being, naming them as his own and calling them to live in the world, remembering to remember the most important things. The God of the prophets became angry with his people because they failed to see themselves as the chosen people; they resisted the relationship to the God who chooses because he loves, and who therefore expects his people to choose to love too, responsible to love others as he has loved them. It is a profoundly personal knowledge, one that assumes relationship, and then responsibility for what the relationship means. Relationship, revelation, responsibility—the heart and soul of the covenant lived in and through the vocations of Adam, Noah, Abraham, Moses, David—and of course the same is true for the generations of people who saw themselves as belonging to God, known by him and loved by him.

The Hebrew vision of life, grounded in the God who has "fashioned a cosmos out of love," is covenantal. There is no other word that so captures the meaning of life lived before the face of God, responsible for love's sake to God for history, for the way the world is and ought to be. The biblical vision is that the covenant becomes incarnate in Jesus. Wisdom and justice, sovereignty and mercy, compassion and kindness, anger and patience, all characteristics of the Holy One of Israel, become flesh in Jesus.

AND WORDS HAVE TO BECOME FLESH

For years, I thought that the Gospel of John was the least accessible and the most mysterious of the Gospels, and I stayed away. But then I read it again, with more of life lived, and read and re-read it over ten years, going further in and further up into the story of the Word becoming flesh and living for a while among us. What became clear over time was that chapter after chapter, conversation upon conversation, was one more window into that reality. The Word was becoming flesh, again and again.

Come and see.

In the first chapter of John, the Word becomes flesh, and we read of Jesus taking up his vocation among the people of first-century Palestine. Walking the roads, entering the villages, meeting people, his first words are, "Come and see." And in fact in the first two conversations he has, "come and see" is his response to those who want to know him. We have their names, first Andrew the brother of Simon, and then Philip and Nathanael. Attentive, intrigued, they ask their questions, wanting to understand more, and Jesus simply says, "Come and see."

Good books have been written about the nature of the incarnation, and more will be. It is not a small thing to get it right. What does it mean that God enters into history in the person of Jesus? The Abrahamic religions have several central truths in common, but at this point of God becoming flesh there are deep divisions. "Not for a moment," Judaism protests, arguing instead that God is one—even as they still hope for a Messiah, someday and sometime. And while Islam believes that there was a great prophet named

Jesus, it is incensed at the idea of incarnation. Pushing the boundaries into the pluralizing world at large, those who call themselves atheists and pantheists do not believe that an incarnation of God happened in history. And yet it is the heart of mere Christianity.

But if that is the central reality of Christian faith, *come and see* is profoundly instructive. We do not learn the deepest lessons any other way. Moral meaning is always learned in apprenticeship, in seeing over-the-shoulder and through-the-heart of those who have gone before us, of those who have something to teach us. Theologian Stanley Hauerwas maintains that we learn brick laying only through apprenticeship, just as we learn to hope only through apprenticeship—and he is right. We do not learn anything that matters any other way.

Books are a gift, but they can never teach us to live. We have to see the words made flesh. I have taught five children to throw a Frisbee, and every time it has meant me standing over their shoulders, my arm along theirs, my hand over theirs, then throwing. It never works the first time. Either the Frisbee quickly falls in a hard drop to the ground, or it never gets free of their tight grip. But finally I move away, and standing a few feet from the child, I invite the throw, "Just try it." It may take days, or even weeks, but they learn, watching me take the Frisbee into my hand, placing my fingers along its edge, bringing it back to my waist, and then . . . off it goes.

As much as I like books, no one has ever learned to throw a Frisbee by reading a book about it. Books may help with technique along the way, and they may add depth and breadth to the experience, but learning is only possible when the child allows the teacher to show the way, to put hand on hand, arm on arm.

Brick laying . . . hoping . . . Frisbee throwing? Yes, over-the-shoulder and through-the-heart. We can only learn the things that matter most when we come and see.

Words have to become flesh.

The story of Nicodemus in John 3 is intriguing, for many reasons. On the one hand it is a conversation between two remarkably gifted teachers. The text calls Nicodemus "the teacher of Israel," and he comes at night wanting to seriously talk with the man who is widely known as "rabbi," the teacher who has been speaking in the Temple courtyard to all comers, local residents and cosmopolitan visitors alike. "The teacher of Israel," Nicodemus, has heard, and he has been drawn in—but he does not understand what it is that Jesus is saying.

"What do you mean by these words?" Nicodemus asks, and Jesus responds, "How is it that you, the teacher of Israel, don't understand?" And he goes on to explain that Nicodemus, like everyone who wants to understand, will have to be "born again," which is very perplexing to Nicodemus—"To enter again into my mother's womb?" They talk for some time, coming to that famous summary of salvation history, "For God so loved the world . . ." It would be easy to see that as the meaning of the conversation, the *summum bonum* of all that matters most. But where the text takes us is to the person who knows but does not do, to a disconnect in the responsibility of knowledge.

It is a hard teaching of Jesus: people hate the light because they want to do what is evil. But to press the point, Jesus goes on to say that those who understand what is most important do so because they "do the truth," they put the truth into practice. Yes, they give flesh to the word, and to their words—and that they do so is critical to understanding the meaning of the words.

We are not, finally and fully, brains. We are not, most of all, rational creatures, as if it is our reason that most completely explains our humanity. Everything is broken, and therefore our rationality and reasonableness is "bent" too. Our minds are less than what they ought to be. Not only do we not reason as we ought, and therefore we do not "see" as we ought, but we do not see because we do not *want* to. Instead we love the darkness of our imaginations, the deceptions and distortions of a good life rather than a true good life. We want to do what we want to do when we want to do it. In effect, Jesus says to Nicodemus, "The reason you do not understand what I am saying is that you do not do the truth. You do not live as you ought to live; instead you love to live as you love to live—even in the name of your religiosity, of the seeming holiness of your life. I am calling your heart into question. The reality is that you do not do the truth. You know, but you do not do."

There is not a week that goes by where in a conversation with someone somewhere this dynamic of the human heart fails to play itself out. And over many years, after many conversations, my conviction is this: moral commitment precedes epistemological insight. We see out of our hearts. We commit ourselves to living certain ways—because we want to—and then we explain the universe in a way that makes sense of that choice. It is why Augustine's long-ago question still rings true: you cannot really know someone by asking, "What do you believe?" It is only when you ask, "What do you love?" that we begin to know another. We see out of our hearts? Yes, because we live out of our loves.

In my experience, final objections to faith are never primarily intellectual, as if epistemological difficulties make coming to faith impossible. To an honest question wanting an honest answer, I will give my life. But what I have seen is, in the end, it is always a matter of one's heart leading the way, one's loves shaping one's vision of the world and the way that a person will live in it. It was for Nicodemus, and it is for us.

Words have to become flesh.

The story of the Samaritan woman in John 4 is its own wonder, offering another take on the meaning of incarnation. After too many frustrated conversations in Jerusalem, Jesus teaching but people not understanding, Jesus decides to return to Galilee. A holy one of Israel—a teacher of Israel like Nicodemus, for example—

would first walk north before crossing the Jordan so that he would not have to compromise himself by coming into contact with the Samaritans, whose land was in the direct path between Jerusalem and Galilee. Rewriting the rules of holiness, Jesus walks due north, not crossing the Jordan, and at midday finds himself at a well in Samaria. Fully God and yet fully human, he is thirsty and tired—and he asks a woman at the well for a drink.

It is not a long conversation. A need for a cup of water, and she offers him a drink. He tells her that there is a kind of water available that would make its recipient never thirsty again. She understands his metaphor and wants water like that, not surprisingly. He tells her to call her husband, and she responds, "But I have no husband." Seeing into her heart of hearts he says, "You have had five, and the one you live with now is not your husband." The more I read the story, the more tender it is to me.

I know of no other conversations that are more sensitive than those about relationships in general, and about sexual intimacy in particular. Our deepest hopes and fears are inexplicably bound up with our sexuality. But we hardly talk about that part of life with anyone—unless we hire them to hear our hearts, wounded as we are. But here the Word becomes flesh to the woman, and she sees something that she has never ever seen: a man can know her and still love her. She has been known by many men, but not loved by any. Time and again she has tried, opening her heart one more time, hoping to find a man who will know her and love her, whom she can know and love, and it never works out. We do not know why that is true for her, but we do know these stories well enough from the worlds we live in to know that this is a story for Everyman and Everywoman.

What is most surprising perhaps is that her response to being known by Jesus is to run back into the village, saying as loudly as she can, "Come meet this man! He knows everything about me—

and he loves me." Not words abstracted because he wants my body, as the surprisingly candid lines in the film *All That Jazz* long ago put it, explaining a character's willingness to bed anyone he wanted: "Do you believe in love?" The response: "I believe in saying, 'I love you.'"

But the words of Jesus give life. He promises a kind of water that actually gives life, drawn from a kind of knowing that becomes loving. "You need to come meet him, too." And the text says that Jesus came and lived for a while among them, incarnating words like holiness and mercy, wisdom and compassion. The people of the Samaritan village could see what the words meant as they were incarnated in their midst.

Words have to become flesh.

Some time later, Jesus returns to Jerusalem for one of the Jewish feasts and walks by the pool called Bethesda (John 5). Known by those who suffered as a place of mysterious waters, the lame, the blind, the paralyzed all gathered, hoping for healing. One man had been lying there for thirty-eight years. Jesus asks him, "Do you want to be healed?" It seems a strange question to our ears.

As I have heard it, the covenant incarnate says to the man, "I see you, I know you, and I know that you know something of me. But will you respond?" If we take Havel's insight into the human condition seriously, that "the secret of man is the secret of his responsibility," then we hear this conversation differently. Jesus is the Word made flesh, and he enters into the history of human affairs and human beings as the one "whose property it is always to have mercy," in the words of the Book of Common Prayer. As he walks through the five-roofed colonnade of Bethesda, Jesus knows where he is and what he is about—in a word, he understands his vocation.

But he also understands the human heart in its glory and shame. Sometimes, very strangely, we choose to love our wounds. Not so much that we openly embrace them, but so much that we cannot imagine living life without them. They have come to mean so much to us. We see ourselves in their light, or darkness, as the case actually is. And of course in the heartache of human life, it is out of our wounds that we wound others.

For reasons beyond what we are given in the text, Jesus stops to talk with the long-suffering man, "Do you want to be healed?" The man explains that he has tried to respond to the strange stirring of the waters of the pool, but can never get there in time. Others make it before him. It is amazing grace that finds him in his desolation, and he hears, "Get up, take your bed and walk." It is an invitation to respond from the one who knew that the man was responsible, able to respond. When all is said and done, what happens is a profound mystery that is finally beyond our explanation—and we can only be amazed at the grace given.

Words have to become flesh.

For Mary, Martha and Lazarus, Jesus has been a friend, even as he has been a teacher. On his way to Jerusalem one last time for the final Passover before his crucifixion, he hears the news of Lazarus's illness (John 11). In the mystery of providence, Jesus does not respond immediately. A few days later, he makes his way to Bethany, which is only a few miles outside of Jerusalem.[2]

He is the covenant made flesh, and therefore we see him entering into relationship more fully and deeply as he shares in the weeping over Lazarus's death. He reveals the truth about life, death and resurrection, perplexing as it all is for Martha. She hears, but does not understand. And of critical importance, Jesus groans deeply in response. Not only does he offer honest sympathy, grieving with those who grieve, but he is also angry at the destructiveness of death, at the skewing of the goodness of life as it was meant to be.

For me to be drawn into faith, it is crucial that God be like this, so it matters that the incarnation show this to be true of God. Even if we do not fully understand the whys and hows of this story, it matters supremely that God is not a passive responder to life and death—and that he does not expect us to be.

Finally, Jesus walks to the tomb and calls, "Lazarus, come out!" It is many things, perhaps especially a great mystery, but it is also an invitation to respond given to someone who was responsible, someone who by great grace was able to respond. Lazarus had not lost his humanity in his death—he had not become an automaton. The secret of his humanity was still his responsibility, as mysterious as it finally is. The words fall flat if there is no ability to respond, to be responsible. Relationship, revelation, responsibility—always and everywhere the heart of the covenant, especially the covenant incarnate.

Words have to become flesh.

Jesus spends the night before the crucifixion, Passover night, with his disciples, and several chapters of John are given to that (John 13–17). The story of the washing of his disciples' feet is instructive on many levels, but for our purposes it is one more window into the deepening relationship that he has with these chosen people. *I know you, and I choose to love you—so sit down, and I will wash your feet.* A sign of affection and respect, of honor and love, he serves them with remarkable humility.

In his gift to them, he explains more of himself and his mission, revealing his own raison d'etre more fully—*I want you to know who I am and why I have come, to know where I have come from and where I am going.* What is especially intriguing about this account is that Jesus so very plainly says that his vocation is situated within the story spanning creation to consummation, intuitively understanding why it matters because he is the Alpha and Omega of the story itself.

Stories do matter, and believing the true story of human life under the sun will give meaning to our vocations, as denying it will prove the implosion of our vocations.

Why not then "eat, drink and be merry, for tomorrow we die"?

(see Ecclesiastes 8:15; Luke 12:19). From the prophets and poets of ancient times, quoted by the writers of both Old and New Testaments who were attentive to the important cultural voices of their day, on through to the contemporary rock star Dave Matthews—prophet and poet that he is—who offers these same words in his song "Tripping Billies"[3]: in every generation the most honest people have always understood that if there is not a story to make sense of my story, then why not "eat, drink and be merry, for tomorrow we die"? The teaching of Jesus is never disconnected from the tensions of life, from the questions and concerns of real people in the world that is really there.

When Jesus finished washing the disciples' feet, he asked, "Do you understand what I have done? What it means?" Then he goes on to say, "You should do just as I have done to you. For a servant is not greater than his master. Now that you know these things, you are blessed if you do them."

The central themes of the covenantal epistemology are written into the story. Jesus initiates a deepening of the relationship, revealing more of himself in the process, and then sets forth their responsibility—which is summed up by the crucial connection of knowing with doing. This is the covenant made flesh.

Words have to become flesh.

The final story here is in the last chapter of John's Gospel, the story of the disappointed and perplexed disciples returning to their fishing (John 21). Having watched the crucifixion of their Lord and not understanding what his resurrection meant for him or for them, they decide to take up what they know how to do—fishing in the Sea of Galilee. All night long they labor and catch nothing. As morning comes, a man on the beach tells them to keep trying, to put their nets on the other side of the boat. We can all imagine the rolling of the eyes. "What does he know about fishing and this lake?"

But then John himself recognizes that it is Jesus who is speaking to them—and Peter is Peter, so he strips off his clothes, jumps in the water and swims to the shore, exuberantly wanting to see the one who knows him and yet still loves him. But before they have their longer conversation, heart to heart as it will be, Jesus gives his closest friends a glimpse of the resurrected reality that will be theirs. Two of the most common and most ordinary human activities, working and eating, are sanctified in the story, made holy by Jesus, showing all with eyes to see that in the new heaven and new earth these will be an integral part.

He could have shown them anything, he could have done anything. The resurrected Lord that he was, he could have done something noticeably "religious" for them, like baptism or the Eucharist. He could even have preached to them or prayed for them.

What he chose to do was honor their work and then eat with them. "Bring your fish, too!" It is obvious that as Lord of heaven and earth he could have insisted that they eat the fish he provided— and that would not have been a bad thing. But what he did instead was acknowledge that they had been working through the night, and in truth had been working their whole lives. *Bring yourselves, the work of your hands, into this resurrection breakfast, and add your fish to mine—because we are in this together.* The master-and-servant relationship continues, even as he has made them his friends. But then, simply, he invites them to eat with him. Not sacramental remembrances, as critical as those will be over time, but ordinary food, the stuff of everyone's life. Working, eating—these are central to human vocation, in every culture and every century.

Do we see Jesus, the Word made flesh, showing the meaning of the covenant to his loved ones? He calls out to them, initiating relationship once again, knowing their frailty and fears. He reveals that he is Lord of heaven and earth, of every square inch of the whole of reality, even the depths of the Sea of Galilee. And then he invites them to respond with their labor and their lives, seeing even the most ordinary things of life as sacramental, made new as they are by the reality of the resurrection. They are signposts in a strange land of the world that someday will be.

Words have to become flesh.

WENDELL BERRY, THE COVENANTAL COSMOS AND A *VOCARE* EVENING

A couple of years ago, I invited a group of folks to our home for dinner. We call these *Vocare* evenings "conversations about calling." That night fifteen people with vocations in the business world sat around our table, ate a wonderful meal and talked about an essay by Wendell Berry, the moral essayist whose prophetic voice ranges across the literary world.

By intention, we had older and younger together, believing that twenty-five-year-olds need to hear from fifty-year-olds that visions of vocation are worth pursuing in and through the bruises of the marketplaces of life. Yes, come and see.

So a bank president, a World Bank consultant, two senior executives in an international corporation, a restaurant owner, a Department of Commerce chief of staff, a USAID staff person and a few folks just starting out into the vocations of the marketplace were all together pondering the meaning of Berry's essay "Two Economies." In earlier conversations, we had discussed the essay and decided it would be worth a more prolonged conversation because his vision of an economics of mutuality was remarkably rich. The essay sets forth "two economies," a lesser economy and a greater economy.

Berry believes that wherever we look in the world there are lesser economies: farms, villages, cities, regions, states, even nations. In my world, that would mean that Virginia, northern Virginia, the Washington metropolitan area, the Chesapeake Bay region, even the United States, are lesser economies. But a lesser economy could also mean the Detroit automobile industry or Wall Street or the music industry of Nashville or farmers in the San Joaquin Valley of California or a family ranching operation in Wyoming. Each create metrics by which they will judge the worth of their respective economic visions and plans, and so in the end they can judge whether they in fact have been successful.

Berry argues that economic success is a more complex calculation because there is always a greater economy, too. It is the world that is really there, whether we like it or not, whether we want it or not, whether we approve of it or not. He says that for him the greater economy is "the kingdom of God," but that people are free to call it what they want. What he does not give freedom for is whether there is a greater economy, or whether the greater economy is in fact the final arbiter of all economic visions. Eventually every lesser economy has to "play" in the world that is really there, and so show whether its economic metrics reflect a true understanding of human nature and history, whether they are true to the world that is really there.

For hours we talked about Berry's vision. Not everyone agreed, but we all wrestled with the meaning of his argument, especially trying to understand what it meant for people making real decisions in the marketplace, whether that was as a local businessman or a global executive. Unless ideas have legs, they are not worth much.

It is important to understand this about Berry: he writes for everyone, translating his own deepest convictions in language that the whole world can understand. He is not writing for a parochial audience, for people who necessarily think like he does, who believe like he does. And in everything he writes—poetry, novels, essays—he sees the world in terms of the covenantal cosmos, of relationship, revelation and responsibility. But he is a translator, using images and words to connect to the wider world.

Like Tolstoy, Berry is writing about the truth of the human condition, situating human beings in relation to God and to history. It

is not that he ever uses the term *covenant*—he is not typically
making a theological argument. But it is in his assumptions about
life and the world, the way he sees who we are and how we live and
even the way he understands God that his deepest beliefs are manifest. Characteristically then, these make their way onto the pages
of his work, as they do for every writer, for every artist.

After the dinner, a few of us were so taken by the essay that we
decided to visit Berry on his farm in Kentucky. He and his wife,
Tanya, have lived along the Kentucky River for most of their lives,
farming land that is generations old. They have formed their own
lesser economy, growing the food they eat, sharing with family and
neighbors in a common good. And in the rhythms of his life, farmer
that he honestly is, he is also a writer and gives himself to that every
day as well.

We wanted to talk with him about a particular question, one that
grew out of the "Two Economies" essay, but one that was deeply
rooted in a business plan that would have consequences for people
all over the world. For six hours we talked, continuing on over a
dinner that his wife prepared, and then finally we took a walk into
his fields. Of all that he said, this seemed most important: "If you
want to make money for a year, you will ask certain kinds of questions; but if you want to make money for a hundred years, then you
will have to ask other questions." It is always in the visions we have,
and in the questions we ask of them, where the reality is seen. Or,
in light of the thesis of the "Two Economies," we only know the
truth of the lesser economy when it stands up over time, when it
proves to be consonant with the greater economy, when it shows
itself true to the way economic life must be if humans are to flourish.

In everything he has written, Berry writes about the world of real
people, of real politics, of real economics. He is not a romantic for
a moment. What he does argue for is the importance of people and
place, maintaining that when we casually walk away from either we

lose something that is crucial to our humanity. To many in the modern world that seems sadly idealistic—wisdom for a world that does not exist. For some, the Berryian vision is for a time out of mind, a world that has long passed away. That is not fair to him or to the world. But there is a tension here, and I have said to him on a few occasions, "If what you were arguing were simply nice ideas for nice people who live in nice places, then I would not be interested. But what you are saying is true, and so it is our responsibility to figure out what it means for where we are."

These are the truest truths of the universe: We do not flourish as human beings when we know no one and no one knows us; we do not flourish as human beings when we belong to no place and no place cares about us. When we have no sense of relationship to people or place, we have no sense of responsibility to people or place.

Perhaps the saddest face of the modern world is its anonymity, to live as if I am known by no one and belong nowhere. From road rage on freeways to the casually cruel crime of the city to the existential angst of being lost in the cosmos, when we are not in relationships that matter, it is almost impossible to see ourselves as responsible to and for others. Of course, the reverse is starkly true as well. Simon and Garfunkel saw this a generation ago, artists as they were, feeling the way the cultural wind was blowing—"I am a rock, I am an island." In the world that is really there, rocks do feel pain. Poetic lament as it is, "It's laughter and it's loving I disdain," in the end that is the point of their song: Human beings cannot deny the need for friendship, the need for belonging. When we are disconnected from people and place, we lose something crucial to our humanity.

Berry is writing about a covenantal cosmos, about life in the world where knowing and being known is critical if we are to flourish. This one theme runs through the body of his work: We must learn to live incarnationally, committed to particular people and particular places. If we are to have honest lives, we will have to incarnate who we are and what we believe with those people and in those places. While this is primarily seen in his novels and poetry, he makes the same argument more didactically in his essays. In the book *What Are People For?* he writes,

> Toward the end of *As You Like It*, Orlando says: "I can live no longer by thinking." He is ready to marry Rosalind. It is time for incarnation. Having thought too much, he is at one of the limits of human experience, or of human sanity. If his love does put on flesh, we know he must sooner or later arrive at the opposite limit, at which he will say, "I can live no longer without thinking." Thought—even consciousness—seems to live between these limits: the abstract and the particular, the word and the flesh. . . .
>
> Love is never abstract. It does not adhere to the universe or the planet or the nation or the institution or the profession, but to the singular sparrows of the street, the lilies of the field, "the least of these my brethren." Love is not, by its own desire, heroic. It is heroic only when compelled to be. It exists by its willingness to be anonymous, humble, and unrewarded.
>
> The older love becomes, the more clearly it understands its involvement in partiality, imperfection, suffering, and mortality. Even so, it longs for incarnation. It can live no longer by thinking.[4]

Words have to become flesh, whether in the lives of the Port William Membership in Berry's novels or in every community in every place, if we are to understand them. Love longs for incarnation.

There is a profound, dynamic nexus between knowledge and responsibility, from the ancient Hebrew imagination to the incarnation in the Gospel of John, across time to the writer who has been called the most serious and most prophetic in America today. How can there not be? We only get one world to live in, and that world is the covenantal cosmos created by the God of heaven and earth. Against the flawed hope of postmodernism, there are not countless narratives and countless universes to choose from.

In every century and every culture there is an integral connection between knowing and doing, and it is most fully expressed in love. For glory or shame, we choose to live in love—or not. But there is also a greater economy, the kingdom of God, and in it we live and move and have our being—or not. Our flourishing depends upon our seeing these truths as true to the way the world really is. If we are to understand our place in the world, we have to find a way into that vision, somehow somewhere. Come and see.

6

Vocation as Implication

At crucial moments of choice,
most of the business of choosing is already over.

IRIS MURDOCH, "THE IDEA OF PERFECTION"

*M*ost of life is very ordinary. We are children and we are
adults. We hope and we love. We work and we play. Most of life is
lived not globally but very locally, in houses or apartments, on
streets and in neighborhoods, in towns and in cities, and it is in
those places, among those people, that we live into who we are and
what we believe.

One of the reasons why I am drawn to the literary vision of
Wendell Berry is that he writes about this kind of common life. In
every course I teach I require my students to read him, looking over
his shoulder and through his heart as he unfolds a vision of vocation that is formed by the truest truths of the universe, and yet
in language the whole world can understand.

After years of schooling and getting the job he had long longed
for, Berry decided that his deeper identity was as someone from
Kentucky and that he should return home, a decision that has
shaped his life and literature. Buying into the family farm, he taught

writing at the University of Kentucky, but over time settled into the rhythm that has become his life: husband, father, farmer, writer, neighbor, friend, day after day after day.

It is not a surprise, then, that his stories are about people a lot like him. Imagining a small town on the banks of the Kentucky River, he has created a universe out of Port William, with its farmers and shopkeepers, fathers and mothers, sons and daughters, generationally twined together over a hundred years. He calls them "a membership": "The way we are, we are members of each other. All of us. Everything. The difference ain't in who is a member and who is not, but in who knows it and who don't."[1]

That Distant Land tells these tales as short stories, giving windows into the lives of people Berry's readers come to know and love. The Old Jacks, the Miss Minnies, the Mat Feltners, the Burley Coulters, the Mary Penns and the Wheeler Catletts, each one painted with a skillful brush, with complexity and nuance, richness and depth.

Take Wheeler, for example. The subject of several stories, we meet him as a boy on his way to becoming a young man in the story "Thicker Than Liquor."[2] As a child he loved his Uncle Peach, his mother's brother; they would play and laugh, full of pleasure together. But as Wheeler became an adolescent he began to see that Uncle Peach was an alcoholic and was drunk more often than not. Rather than being happy to be in relationship, Wheeler wanted nothing to do with him.

> Seeing how his mother troubled herself with Uncle Peach and mourned over him, Wheeler said, bullying her in her own defense as a seventeen-year-old boy is apt to do, "To hell with him! Why don't you let him get on by himself the best way he can? What's he done for you?"
>
> Dorie answered his first question, ignoring the second: "Because blood is thicker than water."

And Wheeler said, mocking her, "Blood is thicker than liquor."
"Yes," she said. "Thicker than liquor too."

Wheeler goes off to the university, then to law school, and returns home to begin his life as an attorney and a new husband.
Mother and son have an important conversation along the way, him
now a young man learning to see the world with both responsibility
and love. "'Blood is thicker than liquor,' Wheeler said to her, no
longer mocking, but gently stating the fact as he knew she saw it.
'Yes,' she said, and smiled. 'It is.'"

A hotel clerk in Louisville calls Wheeler one day, asking if
someone can come into the city and get Uncle Peach, who has
gotten drunk, horribly messing up his room. Instinctively, Wheeler
says he will come and help his uncle. And he goes off to love his
mother's brother, more because she does than because he does.

He finds Uncle Peach disheveled, and the room torn apart.
Cleaning him up, he gives him coffee and brings him home. But
before the train ride is over, Uncle Peach vomits again, horribly and
loudly retching in the crowded train car. Wheeler does his best to
clean them both up, and upon arriving at the station gets them into
the buggy and takes them back to Uncle Peach's home, enduring
more vomit along the way.

> Finally, after this had happened perhaps a dozen times,
> Wheeler, who had remained angry, said, "I hope you puke
> your damned guts out."
>
> And Uncle Peach, who lay, quaking and white, against the
> seatback, said, "Oh, Lord, honey, you can't mean that."
>
> As if his anger had finally stripped all else away, suddenly
> Wheeler saw Uncle Peach as perhaps Dorie has always seen
> him—a poor, hurt, weak mortal, twice hurt because he knew
> himself to be hurt and weak and mortal. And then Wheeler
> knew what he did need from Uncle Peach. He needed him to

be comforted. That was all. He put his arm around Uncle Peach, then, and patted him as if he were a child. "No," he said. "I don't mean it."

The story finishes with surprising grace, and has become a metaphor for life. When they arrive home, Wheeler decides to stay with Uncle Peach, rather than go home to his new bride. And so, after putting the older man to bed, Wheeler climbs in too. As the hours pass, he feels the terrors of Uncle Peach's mostly sleepless night, but eventually, "Wheeler went to sleep, his hand remaining on Uncle Peach's shoulder where it had come to rest."

In this short story Berry offers a window into life for Everyman, for Everywoman. There is no one who does not have, literally or figuratively, an Uncle Peach to love—a person, a place, a community, a culture. In the innocence of youth, Uncle Peach was loveable, but the older Wheeler got, knowing more of the world and of his uncle, the more difficult it was to love him. That Wheeler's mother loved her brother instructed her son, and he was willing to step into her love, for love's sake. But it was not until he began to see Uncle Peach as "poor, hurt, mortal," that he got into bed with Uncle Peach and put his hand on his shoulder through the night.

Can we know the world and still love it? Mostly we decide that we cannot—just like Wheeler—for lots of good reasons. Uncle Peach did not deserve to be loved, and there was no indication that he was ever going to change. Simply said, he was a mess, and whatever he touched became a mess. But in the midst of the mess, Dorie loved her brother, and taught her son to love him too. Knowing what they knew, complicated and complex as it was, they chose to love.

To do that with honesty and integrity is the most difficult task in the world. But there are people who make that choice. Not out of grandeur or great ambition, but in the spirit of Berry's vision: in the relationships and responsibilities of common life, they see themselves as implicated in the way the world is and ought to be. They see themselves as having vocations that call them into life, into the world—into a way of knowing that implicates them, for love's sake.[3]

And in the unfolding of my life, living where I have lived, working where I have worked, I have met some of those people.

JONATHAN GROENE—KANSAS BORN AND BRED

My first memories of Jonathan are from Bear Trap Ranch in Colorado, where he came for a summer after his first year at the University of Kansas. A native of Lawrence and the son of generations of Kansans, he loved being from the people and place that made him *him*. But as I got to know Jonathan, I also saw an unusual eagerness, a seriousness about things that matter and a softness of heart that led to a rare desire to learn all that he could.

That summer, with students like him from all over the middle part of America, he took up the calling to live between two worlds— in the rich image of John Stott—deepening and growing an intellectually grounded understanding of the Christian tradition and developing categories and lenses to make sense of the world around him. Over time he became a part of our family, eating meals with us, playing with our children, even helping us to bury a badly broken and now dead new puppy.

His educational interests eventually took him to other places, where he met Jennifer, and before long they were married on Lookout Mountain, straddling the states of Tennessee and Georgia. More schooling followed for both of them, and they moved first to Mississippi and then to Iowa, where they began having children. In school and yet needing to provide for his young family, Jonathan would day after day leave his books to take up the craft of carpentry, apprenticing himself to a skilled craftsman who trained him in the hammering of nails and the sawing of wood. He had always loved working with his hands; in fact, the harder the work, the more he liked it.

It was not very long before he decided that he would rather build houses than study history, and they moved back to Kansas, home to Lawrence. I remember smiling when I saw the T-shirt he had made to advertise his new company, "Steward of visions and resources," and I was sure that he was bringing his years of thinking about the world to bear on the way that he was going to live in the world.

Over the years his commitment to that kind of work has deepened as his children have grown from babies to adults. No longer a young man eager to take up the world, he is now fully at work in the world, a trusted and respected member of the community whose labor of love in building and rebuilding houses is prized by his neighbors. Being in business for himself, he has all of the usual hopes and fears built into his work: ups and downs in the economy, trustworthy and not-so-trustworthy employees, the daily reality of his reputation on the line.

Listening in over the years I know that Jonathan and Jennifer care deeply about both their local community and the wider world. It would be fair to say that they have made peace with living in Lawrence. They live in the tension of knowing that there is a lot of complex brokenness everywhere, and they often wonder about their responsibility. Sometimes that does take them to other places, to bigger cities, giving away their gifts for the sake of others, he in carpentry and she in counseling, while still living in Lawrence as they do, enjoying the graces of a small university town that still has a wonderful main street, where it is possible to know and to be known.

In a place like Lawrence, it is not possible to say one thing and then do another and still keep your head up the next day. The person you mistreated by doing bad work on his new kitchen may be your daughter's soccer coach or be married to your son's high school teacher. To have your vocation be embodied where other

people live, in their bedrooms and bathrooms, in their longed-for
new decks, more often than not requires a commitment to a
common good that is more lived than it is imagined. It is a simple
grace, really, to be trustworthy, to be known as someone who does
good work and who will stand by his work.

One of the great challenges for everyone is finding a place in the
world—seeing a lot, hearing a lot, reading a lot, and then deciding
where we will be and what we will do. *Knowing what we know, what
will we do?* How is it that our habits of heart become a life? How do
we grow our loves into a life? How do our deepest commitments
become who we are and the way we live? No one finds that easy; in
a thousand different ways we start and stop, wonder and try again.
The best story is that Jonathan has become the words he advertised,
living into his promise: a steward of visions and resources. And
Lawrence, Kansas, is a better place for it.

TODD AND MARIA WAHRENBERGER—MDS

Todd and I met on his first day of medical school. Not unlike Jonathan, there was an unusual eagerness in him; he wanted to learn.
So he too began coming over for supper, becoming a friend to our
whole family. Not far into the relationship, I invited him to join me
at a 7:00 a.m. Eucharist at an Anglican church in the neighborhood
of the University of Pittsburgh, where he lived and was in school.
Todd became a regular, often offering his musical gifts to all.

Over the years I have had many opportunities to watch a young
man begin to love a young woman. It is the eyes, I suppose, and
Todd's eyes began to light up when he saw Maria, another medical
student. Within a year they married, and kept at their schooling.
Maria seemed to be headed to a more academic track within medicine, while Todd had a public health passion. Rather than continue
on with his four-year program, he took a year off in the middle to
do a master's in public health; at the same time, he spent a summer

with a physician who had started a health clinic for a medically underserved neighborhood in Pittsburgh. Through that year, he and I met, along with some others, week by week studying ideas and issues that were foundational for forming a more meaningful vision of vocation.

Todd and Maria both went into residency programs, he into family practice and she into internal medicine. At the end of those years he became the chief resident and, with some other residents, began dreaming of another way to do medicine, something that would draw on passions they had been exploring together for years. One book they read was Denis Haack's *The Rest of Success,* and his writing gave them reasons to rethink what ambition meant and what a good life might look like. A year later they formed a health clinic on the north side of Pittsburgh, near the stadiums, in a neighborhood that was medically underserved.

As a wise friend has persuaded me, most things don't work out very well. Even with hopes and dreams, the vision of a common practice was not sustainable, and eventually Todd and Maria took more responsibility for the work. By that time they had decided to reorient their careers, together taking up more creative schedules so that they could become parents of two boys and practice medicine as well. They became more deeply involved in the congregation they had found as medical students, and it became a sustaining community for them as their young family grew and their careers developed.

The day-by-day work of physicians took them into a community of people who needed doctors who would know them and still love them. All of us are like that, really. We hope that those who serve us will really care about us. They are not romantics; they cannot afford to be—in their own lives they have known enough sorrow. Their choice to enter into the complexity of medical care for people who need it but often do not take good care of themselves is reflective of a deeper way of knowing, a deeper vision of responsibility, a deeper kind of loving.

Over the years Todd and Maria have invested themselves in the city, becoming known as good doctors who do good work. Being attentive to the wider world, they have gone to other places too, giving themselves away to people who rarely see a physician, who rarely have any access to medical care. To see them in their work is to see people who love what they do and who love the ones they serve.

That is the best part of a vocation—to love and serve with gladness and singleness of heart. When we take the wounds of the world into our hearts—not just for a day, but for a life—we long to see the work of our hands as somehow, strangely, part of the work of God in the world, integral to the *missio Dei,* not incidental to it. That is the life and the labor of Todd and Maria, husband and wife, father and mother, physicians together.

D. J. and Robin Smith—Tearing Corners Off of the Darkness

While I first met Robin when she was an undergraduate, I got to know her one summer when she entered into a month-long summer program of study called Knowing and Doing. There were lectures and readings, but there was also a lot of swimming and biking, with wonderful eating too. Politically serious, she found her first job at the Urban Institute, an economic and social policy research center and, remarkably, she is still there many years later.

D. J. moved to Washington after college, like thousands before him, looking for a job on Capitol Hill. He entered into an unusual community of men who chose to have a life together—Bonhoeffer-shaped—as they worked away at first jobs a few blocks away in the Senate and the House. In those years I had some responsibility for the life and times of the large townhouse on East Capitol Street where they lived, and I met him there.

I remember one week in D. J. and Robin's lives with a smile. Thoughtful people, gifted people, serious people, wonderful people, each one had scheduled a lunch with me within a few days of the other. I was teaching on Capitol Hill at the time, and so we met in Union Station, in the same little café both days. They were longer conversations, but in the end it was clear that he was interested in her, and she in him. Yes, I smiled, knowing what I now knew—and I encouraged them to talk with each other. They did, happily, and a few months later were married.

Robin continued on at the Urban Institute, working at some of the toughest questions of our common life. None were ever easy, as they involved history, politics and economics, always incarnate in a particular place with particular people. Because her own passions have been for "doing justice, loving mercy, walking humbly with God" for as long as I have known her, her analytical skills are never offered in the abstract, as if the research of the Institute is for ivory-towered policy wonks who live far away from ordinary people in ordinary places. For her, it always has to be worked at on the ground, in life.

D. J. kept at the Hill for a few years, earning his proverbial spurs by helping Congress move into the Internet age. That experience was the seedbed for the years that have followed, and he has taken that knowledge into a world of work that has him in places all over the face of the earth, mostly through the strange graces of websites and social networks. From contracts with military superpowers to the Brooklyn Hip-Hop Academy, from the Blood:Water Mission to International Justice Mission, he is a storyteller, deeply and professionally so. His great delight is to listen well and then help an organization tell its story through the wonders of the web.

They have little girls now, growing as the years pass, and together they have found a way to have a life as a family that is good for all. *Good* is a proximate word, of course, as it is not the same as *perfect*.

But for any honest person, none of us knows a life that is perfect. There are bumps and bruises we all know too well, and we find them not only at home but at work. The harder question is the same: Knowing what we know, what are we going to do? Knowing our frailties and the frailties of the world, what will do?

To choose to step into frailty—or, as Berry describes Uncle Peach, being "poor, hurt, mortal"—is what a vocation is all about. We are called to care, especially about complexity because that is the world we live in. There is never a question that comes to Robin at the Urban Institute that seems simple: "Ah, that one's easy!" There are too many factors, too many issues that have to be sorted out, often too much institutional injustice that has skewed the story from beginning to end. She keeps at it though, as she sees these as the questions of her life.

For D. J. it is the same, but different. He loves his work, and he is very good at it—not only the technical aspects, which matter very much, but the heart of it, which matters too. For him there is always a longing that his work address both that which is wrong and that which might be and must be. Whether it is kids in Brooklyn or political complexity in nations scattered across the globe, he wants the work of his hands to matter, to be part of "tearing a corner off of the darkness," in Bono's poetic image. We all do.

SANTIAGO AND NICOLE SEDACA—AT WORK IN THE WORLD

I can still remember Santiago sitting in the classroom of the American Studies Program, the interdisciplinary semester of studies on Capitol Hill where I taught for many years. Focused on public life and public policy, we had serious, motivated, academically entrepreneurial students from all over America come study with us. Our classes were often taught in a seminar style with pedagogical back and forth—and Santiago always had a hard question.

Even at that time he had a sense of what he wanted to do, so when he finished college he returned to Washington for graduate school, digging more deeply into understanding the nature of political economies. One job became another, and soon he was at work all over the world, coming alongside majority world nations who had needs for capital but even more for wisdom and knowledge.

Some years later he entered into another classroom of mine and brought a bride, Nicole. For years I led a little community that explored visions of Christian spirituality, learning from the wisdom of saints over the centuries by reading and reflecting on their writings. Santiago was Latin American and Nicole was African American, and their marriage seemed to bring together much of the world, wonderfully so. She entered into the State Department after finishing school, taking up the complex questions of international relations from the perspective of US national policy, even as he took them up from the perspective of a USAID-funded group that worked at many of the same questions, but from the position of an adviser to nations wanting assistance.

As I watched Santiago at work, asking questions about what he was doing, and where and why, I began to understand that his work was something like a plumber's or electrician's—except that he was working with nations to develop healthy infrastructures so that international aid would make political and economic sense. If a nation needed financial assistance but it did not have a working legal system or a working banking system, then any money would find its way into the proverbial toilet of history. Santiago's work was focused on building the infrastructure in nations all over the earth, spending days and weeks with nationals in their own nations, helping them see what was needed and then build it.

Why does it matter? All over the earth the rich can be heard. They can find ways, legal or not, to make their case and live their lives. But if courts do not exist, or are patently unfair in systemic ways, then it is the poor who suffer. The same is true for banks, which in the best of worlds work not only for the wealthy but for everyone. If a dollar or peso is given to a bank in trust, then it needs to be there with interest when the depositor needs it. The rich know what to do with their money and can always find a bank somewhere in the world that will take good care of them. But it is the powerless people who live in villages and cities the world over who are the clients of Santiago, as they are the ones whose lives depend on the healthy social ecosystems that are the focus of his work. Much of his day-by-day labor is with the unemployed and with small businesses, creating venues and structures in which they can find their way into international value chains that produce the goods and services that we consume in the first world. It is critical to link the poor to markets, and through that process to help them understand how countries need to change their production and distribution systems in a way that helps create wealth for everyone, not just the powerful.

And then a baby was born and then another, and as with families all over the world, Santiago and Nicole have made choices and then more choices, trying to find a way to be healthy together as a family. How do they take the lessons of international diplomacy and make them work in a home? What is the relationship of habits of heart that must be in place for a nation to work well and the habits of heart that are needed for one family to be healthy? Good questions, and no easy answers. But they have worked at answers and keep living into them.

And then came the day when they announced to the community that they were going to Ecuador for a few years, taking the global commitments they had and focusing on one region, Latin America. In one way it seemed a wonderful way for Santiago to go home and to take his young family with him, showing them what he loved. We sighed but knew that they should go.

Now they have come back, settling into the city as a family—but with hearts engaged by the whole world. Santiago continues in his work of building national infrastructures, and Nicole is a young professor in the same graduate program in which she studied, and gives leadership to the boards of the Institute for Global Engagement and International Justice Mission. Together they parent their little boys, teaching them to know the world and to love it—as they do. In a strange way, they live life at thirty-five thousand feet, and yet at the same time their vision of vocation keeps them attentive to life where people live. Living in tensions like that is life, for everyone, everywhere.

DAVID FRANZ—HOME AGAIN

St. Augustine argued that the question *What do you love?* is the most important of all questions. While other questions matter, it is the question of our loves that goes to the heart of who we are. What David Franz loves is Shafter, California, with all its local history and hopes.

The son, grandson and great-grandson of farmers, he has the soil of the San Joaquin Valley in his soul. He is a descendent of Mennonite immigrants who wanted to worship and work together in America as they had in Russia and found the fertile land of California a good place to make their home. David grew up loving where he was from, both the people and the place.

Shafter is also my hometown, and I grew up going to school with his uncles and aunts, and his parents. I first met David when I spoke on my work with the American Studies Program in Washington to people I had known most of my life back in Shafter. He was in high school at the time but later told me that when he heard about the life of our little community of scholarship and service, of junior and senior members learning together, he determined that someday he would join us. And he did.

Most of life is only understood in retrospect. While he flourished in every important way that semester, it was not until a few years later that I began to understand what those months had meant to him. He was awakened to learning, and began to see what he wanted to learn about and what he wanted to do with his learning. After he returned to California to finish school, I began to write recommendations for him to study in all sorts of interesting places. A summer at Notre Dame. A few months in Switzerland. A year on the Chesapeake Bay. And finally a graduate program at the University of Virginia.

With an ever-deepening sense of vocation, he began taking up the questions that have become his, the interdisciplinary nexus of sociology and economics, but with a great interest in what the questions in those disciplines mean for ordinary people in ordinary places. A first year grew into many years of study and finally a PhD in a good department from a good university. The doorways of the academic world were open to him.

One day he and I were having breakfast in Charlottesville. He had finished his degree the previous year, and he had been given a year-long fellowship to turn his dissertation into a book. We talked about what would come next, and with a twinkle in his eye, he told me that was thinking of going home to Shafter. I am sure my eyes lit up with perplexed pleasure as I wondered, *To do what?* And he told me of an unusual conversation with the city manager, someone whom I had known forty years earlier, who had a vision for the flourishing of his city that could use David's gifts and passions to help bring it about.

Over time the idea began to have legs, and to the surprise of colleagues in the academy, with his wife, Charis, and young family he moved back to the small farming community where generations of his family had made their home. His work there is focused on the renewal of education in the local schools, bringing the years of his study about people and places through the lenses of his disciplines and making that insight useful to the people and place of Shafter.

There is an echo of Berry himself in David's story, if we have ears to hear. From a farming family and community, off to higher education at different levels, with wonderful opportunities open to explore the world of work with his studies complete—and in and through it all an unsettled sense that "I am from somewhere and from some people, that my relationships to that place and those people give me a responsibility to and for them, and therefore my vocation will be found with them and among them."

There is a longer story here, as David is only stepping into this vision. There are difficulties in a small town, as there are in a large city. History, geography, politics, economics, race and class—always and everywhere these dynamics create complexity. What will happen over time is a story that is yet to be told. What is sure is that he loves where he is from and why he is from there. Because that is true, he wants honest coherence between his education and his vocation, so that what he has learned will be for the sake of where he has lived. That is a good life for anyone, anywhere.

Kwang Kim—A Global Citizen

We all have many conversations, and most of them slowly fall into the mist of the past. But some of them we remember, and I remember one from a weekend retreat some years ago, hearing a question at the Saturday evening campfire, "Can we talk?" The question became a conversation, and the conversation became a friendship.

Kwang Kim is the most global citizen that I know. Born of Korean parents from the North and the South, he grew up in Latin America: first in Argentina, then Brazil and finally Ecuador. He moved to Los Angeles for undergraduate study, then on to Boston for graduate school, and with years of learning to steward, he then began a career at the World Bank.

If there is a question at the heart of his life, it is this: *What should the world be like?* Is there a way we ought to live in the world, one that has implications for the way that development is done, whether that is in the Middle East, Latin America, Africa or in the

cities and societies of the Northern Hemisphere where there is still
such crying need?

Having spent the last twenty years thinking about the way we
help—the way large multinational organizations like the World
Bank assist the needy nations of the earth—Kwang is captivated by
the question, *What ought we to be doing?* Are there norms for development? Do we have any access to what it is supposed to be? Can
we ever know what development should be? Are there any oughts
and shoulds in this whatever world? Or are we only left with culturally relative "maybes" and "perhapses"?

Able to think and speak and write in many languages, Kwang
lives his heart out all over the world. His years at the World Bank
have taken him for periods of time to Pakistan, to Jordan, to the
Caribbean and to several countries of Latin America. Always the
passion guiding his work is to rethink the way development is done,
longing to be part of something more sustainable, where the hours
and dollars mean honest change for the good of those who live with
the programs and plans of the Bank.

Watching as I do, I am intrigued when someone sees seamlessly,
when someone's instincts are to find the connections between ideas,
when someone assumes that there is a coherence to the cosmos—
and that our task is to understand it. From my earliest conversations with Kwang, that was true. In the questions he asked and the
visions he pursued there was a thread that ran through everything
he took up. In a word, it was integrity. Not only for his life as a
human being, an Asian/Latino/American, but as someone with a
calling into the socio-political economies of the world, with their
almost unfathomable complexity. Even in the midst of that work,
Kwang wrestles his way to coherence.

That is not romanticism. He does not give an inch to pie-in-the-
sky. Rather, he works hard to master the information that each
situation presents, bringing his own vocation to the dynamics of

the assignment. Over time he has begun to see that there are in fact "true truths" about development, ones that are as meaningful to Latinos as they are to Pakistanis as they are to Arabs. But he also recognizes that development is broken, and Kwang has chosen a path to promote change from within. With his own necessary sophistication, having to speak the language of the Bank because that is the context of his work, he argues that humility and mutuality are the heart of good development programs.

The Bank can be the proverbial elephant in the room, requiring that everyone pay most attention to what it says and does. Among the nations of the earth, that does not make for a good future. Instead it breeds resentment on a large scale, and what might happen for good is more often than not frustrated by the tensions produced by arrogance in all its insidiousness. People want to know that they are being honestly served by people who are honest servants. And people as people want to know that everyone's ideas matter, so for an economic development project to work in Guatemala it has to be primarily the Guatemalan people that give shape and substance to the project. The Bank is an important partner, but it must be a partner—and it can do this by becoming an effective broker to the voices of the poor as it takes its place in the collage of local industrialists, the requirements of internal and external bureaucracies, and, of course, always amid the reality of global trends.

And it is this that Kwang gives himself to wherever his work calls him, month by month, year after year. Those virtues of humility and mutuality find their place in the serious, sustained debates about social structures that over time will either make or break the program, and that is always incredibly complex. But the structures do not exist or have life on their own. Rather, it is the virtues—a word formed by the Latin *vir*, or what human beings are supposed to be, are meant to be—that give life to the structures, bringing flourishing to aching people in aching places.

There is more to Kwang's life than the Bank though. For years now he has given time and energy to the renewal of North Korean culture, meeting monthly to pray with other Korean Americans in Washington, each one autobiographically implicated in the hopes of their homeland. The Washington group is only one of many like this all over the United States and Canada, each one full of eager, bright, motivated men and women who yearn together for a new day in Korea, where social and political and economic and artistic flourishing will become reality—because that is the way it is supposed to be, for everyone everywhere.

In the end, all of us are best known by the questions that keep us up at night and that wake us in the morning. *What should the world be like?* is the animating question at the heart of Kwang's life, making sense of his days and his nights. That is what a vocation is, and does.

CHRISTOPHER DITZENBERGER—
RECASTING THE PARADIGM OF PASTOR

It was the summer of 1988, and I had been drawn into the planning of the Williamsburg Charter, a part of the bicentennial celebration of the US Constitution. For most of a week, hundreds of people gathered in Colonial Williamsburg for the celebration and signing of the Charter—and Christopher Ditzenberger was there too, an intern with the Charter visionaries. That was the beginning of a friendship that has lasted for many years now.

As an undergraduate at Gordon College, he came to Washington to the American Studies Program. Committed to a pedagogy of responsibility, the program's vision was to engage bright, eager undergraduates with the complexity and possibility of vocations in the public square. We drew students like Chris into our life for four months, reading with them, encouraging them, critiquing them, all for the sake of nourishing a vision of responsibility for history.

He stayed in the city for several years working for a think tank and then took up years of theological study, first at Gordon-Conwell Theological Seminary and then at Virginia Theological Seminary. From those years he entered into the Episcopal Church, pastoring in rural Virginia for a time, then in South Carolina, and almost ten years ago he became pastor of St. Gabriel the Archangel Church in Denver, Colorado, moving with his wife, C. J., and their two children back to his hometown.

With his unusual blend of background, a vision for public life and a vision for the pastoral life, Chris entered into the ministry with passions for people to understand the world and their place in it—nurtured by the liturgical life of a congregation. Remembering the wisdom of Lesslie Newbigin, that "the congregation is the hermeneutic of the gospel,"[4] Chris gives himself away to his people with that hope in his heart.

This past year we have seen more of each other than we had for many years. Early one December day we were together with forty others from around Denver to meet over the vision of a book, *Work Matters* by Tom Nelson. Tom was also a friend, and when his book was on its way to the publisher, he called the Washington Institute to see if we could help him get it out to the wider world. We agreed on a strategy of traveling to cities with seminaries and meeting with seminary professors, area pastors and businesspeople with the hope that we might together come around the vision of recasting the paradigm about the meaning of work.

The credo for the Washington Institute is that "vocation is integral, not incidental, to the *missio Dei.*" Most of the time, all over the world, the church teaches otherwise, that vocation is incidental, not integral, to the *missio Dei.* It is always a compartmentalizing of faith from life, of worship from work, and it has tragic consequences for the church and the world.

Even with the heartache of his mother's death very fresh in his heart, Chris came to the breakfast. Afterward he told me he wanted to work on this vision himself, to dig more deeply as a pastor into the meaning of vocation. He had a sabbatical coming up in the summer; could he focus on this, and would we help? Over the next months we talked several times, and he put together a serious plan of study for his time of renewal and rest. At one point he wondered if we would help him with a retreat he wanted to do at the beginning, drawing in a group of other pastors from throughout Denver with whom he meets regularly, to launch his sabbatical. Of course we would, and months later we spent several days with him and his friends in the Rocky Mountains talking, thinking, eating, praying and talking some more. What would it look like for a pastor to so understand his vocation that he would be able to pastor people in their vocations, seeing their work as "integral to the *missio Dei*"?

The question matters, and the answer matters. Chris has chosen to live into this tension, not completely sure where his own deepening vocation will take him. Growing out of the commitments he has made to pursue this, he has also entered into a year-long learning community with folk from across the country, all focused on the same vision: Could we recast the paradigm? What would it look like in my congregation to rethink the relationship of worship to work, of liturgy to life and labor? To take part in this community each pastor must bring someone from the marketplace, so two from each congregation; the hope is that the conversation between them will make for something more honest and transforming.

Integral, not incidental? There is a difference, and it makes a difference. To see what we do as woven into the fabric of who God is and what the world is meant to be is the vision that has captured Chris's heart. He longs to so understand his work that he is able to pastor people in their work, praying and preaching in such a way that ordinary people doing ordinary things see the sacramental meaning of their labor, a common grace for the common good.

CLAUDIUS AND DEIRDRE MODESTI—A LIFE FOR OTHERS

There are people I want my students to meet. Given that deep within my pedagogy is the conviction that we learn the most important things over the shoulder, through the heart, it matters that my students see men and women who live what they believe—and do so with winsome moral seriousness. I want them to see commitment lived out, but I want them to see smiles and laughter too.

Native New Yorkers, Claudius and Deirdre came to Washington to study at Georgetown University as undergraduates. He was from a serious Catholic family in Syracuse, one of several brothers, all very Italian; Deirdre was from Staten Island, born of a German mother and an Irish father, and if there was a faith that formed the family, it was probably the editorial vision of the *New York Times.* Their families had grown them to be eager for the world, wanting to understand their place in it—not a small gift at age eighteen.

In those years at Georgetown, Claudius became a purposeful student, interested in all he learned. And given his history and the identity of Georgetown, it is no surprise that along the way he considered becoming a Jesuit; but through those years he began to love Deirdre too—and in the end she won his heart, and his vocation. Their undergraduate experience was rich in many ways, clarifying classroom interests that became callings, but also deepening honest faith for them, understanding more clearly what they believed and why. The following years brought more schooling for them both—he went to law school and she earned a PhD in clinical psychology—and they settled into the city of Washington.

Watching them over the years, it is clear that they live for others. They are openhearted about their lives, and their home has always been a place for people. Folk who walk in the door feel welcomed and wanted, and when it is time to eat, their wonderfully built table has room for all. Not surprisingly, Claudius loves to offer good wine, and Deirdre has a gift for creating sumptuous suppers; together they make good conversations about important things the habit of their home. A daughter, Elena, and a son, Liam, are now part of the story, coming into their own maturity, asking their own questions, and making their own commitments about who they are and how they will live. Different as they should be, it is also clear that they are their parents' children, learning to live as they live together as a family.

Their life for others extends beyond their home though. Since he finished law school, Claudius has always chosen public law, serving in a variety of settings over the years that are always one more version of doing public justice. After the Enron scandal that rocked the nation, with the complicity of major accounting firms fudging the numbers and creating a chasm of confidence in investment, Claudius was asked to give leadership to an effort that would bring more order to public accounting, and so for years now he has used his legal skill to oversee the financial records of major corporations. As the Hungarian scientist and philosopher Michael Polanyi argued, "two plus two is a moral equation."[5] If we fail to count rightly, we not only fail math, but we lie about reality—and we lose public trust, the heart of a good society.

Deirdre spends her days with the complex calling of woman and mother, attending to home but also to her practice as a psychologist. Early on it was clear that she had unusual wisdom about the human heart. By instinct resisting dualisms of different sorts, she brings a more coherent vision of human being in all its glory and shame, and it is *instinct* that is important to ponder here. Some of it is her family, some is her personality, some is her gift, some is her education, some is her community, but taken together she has eyes to see who people are and why they are. And over time she has become a trusted counselor, taking people seriously as she listens carefully.

People who keep at their callings for a lifetime are always people who suffer. The world is too hard and life is too broken for it to be otherwise. And that is true for Deirdre and Claudius. In their life together they have lived with heartaches in their extended family, and horrible sickness in their own family. They have known surgery after surgery, each one done in great hope and fear. It is true that at best we see through a glass darkly; the future is unknown for them, as it is for all of us. But they live with gladness and singleness of heart, which at the end of the day is the best that any of us can do.

Their life for others is a window into the meaning of common grace for the common good. From the hospitality of their table to the way they live in their neighborhood to the work that is theirs in the worlds of law and psychology, they have chosen vocations that give coherence, making sense of what they believe about God and the human condition, and have unfolded habits of heart that are a grace to the watching world.

George Sanker—Educating for Character and Competence

Sometimes questions are asked and you know from their urgency that they must be answered. That is my memory of the weight in George Sanker's words, "Can we talk this week?" I had given a lecture on the moral meaning of learning, and he was there, eager to take everything in. It was our first meeting, and I came to see that that was always true of George. At the time, he was teaching high school in Washington, D.C., and one afternoon we met in Union Station, the central thoroughfare of the city. Committed to the calling of teacher, he was well read in the deeper, wider thinking about education but particularly wanted to understand the meaning of character for education.

We talked, and kept talking.

As the years passed, his vocation deepened, even as his occupations have taken him to Charlottesville, Virginia, for more schooling, back to Washington to give leadership to a newly opened public charter school, then to Colorado to another school, and finally back to Charlottesville, where he now leads an independent school. Along the way I have been listening to the hope in his heart for a kind of learning that transforms people and their places.

In his own memory, it was coming along with his mother as she cared for the home of a wonderful family in Georgetown when he was just a boy that first opened his eyes to learning. Allowed to become a student in the more privileged neighborhood, mixing it up with kids who were expected to excel, he discovered his own gifts, latent as they were. As he grew, not only his mind developed, but his body too, and in his high school years he became a serious athlete. With a college scholarship, he went on for a degree that eventually brought him back to Washington, and to our meeting several years later.

The ways of the heart are complex, and we are wonderfully complex as human beings. Who are we? And how do we become the people that we are? The histories we are born into affect us. The social conditions of our lives affect us. The teachers we have affect us. But it is also true, as Thomas à Kempis once observed in his classic *The Imitation of Christ*, that "occasions [circumstances] do not make a man frail. Rather they show who he is."[6] Both sides of the story are true for all of us. A thousand little boys like George did not find their way into adulthood with a Jesuit education and a university degree, but he did. And as he began teaching, he began wondering what makes the difference.

That question brought him to me, and then a few years later it took him to the University of Virginia for graduate study. He wanted to focus on the nexus of sociology, education and philosophy, sure that there was more to learn about learning and about who we are as we learn. That is the vocation that directs his life.

One Saturday morning I drove into the city to take part in the opening ceremony of the charter school that George had been hired to lead. I remember thinking about the strangeness and wonder of it all: here was George back in the city of his birth, now opening a school for a host of boys and girls who were a lot like he had been thirty years earlier—so much possibility, so much eagerness, from the littlest kindergartners to the most wizened grandmothers.

And then there was a night several years later when he and I led a *Vocare* evening for educators throughout the metropolitan area. We call these "conversations about calling," always pressing into a particular vocation or question. That night we had chosen a monograph by Wendell Berry, *The Hidden Wound*, where he takes up the far-reaching character of racism in American life. The question we asked was this: tell about this "hidden wound" in your own life as an educator, especially the systemic issues that are often more subtle but are profoundly damaging to the soul of a school. We had newly minted teachers and long-practiced principals, from public schools and private schools, in the city itself and the suburbs as well. The question was not easy, and the answer was not either.

Then came the day that George told me that he and his wife were moving to Colorado to take up the leadership of another school. I sighed, groaning for myself and our city, still wanting to be glad for him and his family. As human beings, the reasons behind the choices we make are always complex, with a host of factors pressing for prominence, but one that seemed to drive George was the opportunity to try again with another school where the question of character formation would be central in the curricular vision. And truth be told, the deep blue skies of Colorado seemed to be calling too.

We make our way through the occupations of life, hoping and hoping that as we do our vocation becomes clearer to us, that over time we will come to know more and more about who we are and what matters to us, and who God is and what matters to him. George is one example of this, but his is only one story of this universal reality. We never know what the future will be, or what the meaning of our choices will turn out to be, until we step in and see, living into our hopes and our dreams.

While colorful Colorado was a gift in many ways, it was not so many years before he was invited to return to Virginia, and to Charlottesville in particular. There were parents who wanted a kind of learning for their community, and they wanted George to help them. The heart of their vision was for an education that taught children to become good people and good students at the same time, so with the sense of longer, deeper home the Sanker family had there in the shadow of Mr. Jefferson's university, they returned to the East.

In *The Abolition of Man,* C. S. Lewis's best-known public-opinion essay, about the state of education in mid-twentieth-century England, he argued that the most important questions of learning were being left out of the curriculum that was shaping British education. "We make men without chests and expect from them virtue and enterprise. We laugh at honor and are shocked to find traitors in our midst."[7] Think of a brilliant hedonist, someone who is incredibly well educated but whose life is marked by selfish egoism; in other words, someone who has a great education but who is without the character required to bring the intellect into healthy relationship to the imagination—which is what virtues are always about, which is what character formation is always about. What was sorely lacking were "chests," the mediating center where mind and passions could become alive together so that the student would become a whole human being. The stakes were not small for Lewis, or England; he saw the consequence as "the abolition of man."

A half-century later, Lewis's critique forms the contours of George's calling. He lives so that children will become men and women with chests, understanding that the way we educate the next generation will affect the way the world turns out. That is the *telos* that shapes his pedagogical praxis.

GIDEON STRAUSS—LIVING WITH HOPE

Justice has to be more than "just us."

Years ago I got a phone call from Gideon Strauss at the Christian Labour Association of Canada, asking if I would come speak to a gathering of union leaders from across the country. Mostly from the building trades, these were folk who argued with their lives for an alternative to the Marxist-influenced trade union practices in Canada. Deeply taken with a vision of public justice, from British Columbia in the west all the way across the provinces to the east, they were time-tested leaders with thousands of workers behind them, knowing that in the perennial tensions between labor and management, justice is more often than not defined as "just us."

I was intrigued, understanding something of their history and vision, but I asked Gideon to tell me about him: "Who are you, and where have you come from, and why do you care about this?"

Born into the alienated politics of apartheid in South Africa, he grew up in the same town that J. R. R. Tolkien had generations earlier—but it was not until Gideon entered adolescence that he began to understand the Mordor of his own moment: the moral meaning of apartheid, seeing its horror played out on the streets of his city with his growing-up-into-the-world eyes. Sure that he could not believe what his family and history taught him to believe, he protested, aware that to say no was to severely strain his familial and national loyalties.

How to push back against the injustice of the law? These are hard questions for anyone anywhere. Eventually he entered his country's compulsory military service as a conscientious objector, and his reading drew him into an increasingly wide literature that offered him richness and nuance for his deepening vision of engaging the world. Philosophers, theologians, politicians—each one offered intellectual complexity that accounted for the heart of his hopes. Into his twenties he decided to become academically equipped to enter into the professional ranks of those who were now debating the future of South Africa, and he completed a PhD in political philosophy.

When the long evil of apartheid was declared dead, South Africa as a nation was in a very vulnerable place politically, socially and historically. Who would they now be? How would they now live? Very gifted and passionate people stepped into that moment and gave leadership for what might be the future, beginning with the Truth and Reconciliation Commission. Because of the long horrors of the racial division, people of different races were on all sides of the institutional hatred and violence. If there were to be a new nation, it would have to deal with what had happened, and who had been wounded, before there could be a new day. The truth would have to be told, and reconciliation would have to be achieved.

Gideon gave himself to this for two years, traveling from township to township, translating for the commissioners. Because of his history, he was able to speak the languages that everyone understood, and because of his studies he was able to understand the weight of the words. And so for days upon days he listened to the sorrows of his people, translating their experiences in the first person: "You killed my father," or "Yes, I shot your son." He had to utter the most horrible words imaginable.

As days became weeks and months became years, Gideon came to the end of his ability to say more. To look someone in the eye who has known the most heart-wrenching evil, speaking as if "I was the one," eventually was too much. But for someone like him, passionate and committed in a profound way, what should he do? How to deepen one's vocation and at the same time find another occupation?

With his wife, Angela, he pondered the possibilities, eventually deciding to study with J. I. Packer and Eugene Peterson. Reading their books, the Strauss's saw that they both taught at Regent College in Vancouver, British Columbia, "and it was as far from Johannesburg as you can get in the whole world!" So with their two daughters, they moved to Canada, initially for a sabbatical, a rest from their weary life. While there, Gideon met people and ideas that renewed his vision of what might be done in the world. During his year of study at Regent, he was invited by the Work Research Foundation to join them as their research director, giving leadership to their understanding of the organization and its mission. It was in that time of sabbath that Gideon read my book *The Fabric of Faithfulness,* seeing its vision for vocations lived out over a lifetime, and it was that reading that led to my invitation to speak to the labor union leaders, committed, all passionate people, but worn down by their long efforts to keep at the vision that had first engaged them.

Often the longer we live, the more hardened we become. But sometimes some people still choose to enter in, knowing what they know of the world. Not naive, not innocents, but time-tested and able to step in again. Gideon keeps at it, now more than twenty-five years after his coming-of-age adolescent wrestling with apartheid, finding ways to deepen his love for the complexities of the world, whether they are political, social or economic, whether they are found in the academy, the studio or the church.

After many years of good work in Canada, he and his wife, Angela, moved to Los Angeles, first for her study. She wanted to understand the liturgical life of the church more fully, and entered into a disciplined apprenticeship of study and service. In the surprises of life, the move opened for Gideon a position of responsibility at the De Pree Center for Leadership, named in honor of the visionary business leader Max De Pree of the Herman Miller Corporation. Still committed to thinking through the hardest questions, his work is now focused on developing leaders for vocations within the social structures of the church and the world. Never a romantic, Gideon lives with hope, understanding that to try and try again is the heart of a good life, living between what is and what someday will be.

SUSAN DEN HERDER—A MOTHER AND MORE

Sometimes it seems as if I have spent my life welcoming new students into the classrooms of my heart. For reasons that are finally mysterious, some stay there and some go. That they are different is not a moral difference; equally good people respond differently. And it is not always obvious the first day. More often than not, it is weeks and months before I began to understand who a student is and to know whether there will be more of life together.

I do remember having lunch with Susan during her fellows year of study. We had spent a month in class reading the Word and reading the world at the same, focused for several weeks on sexuality. As we talked I began to see that she was someone with surprising instincts about life and love, about her faith and the world that was hers, as if it all mattered very much, and she had eyes to see why it did and how it did.

A recent graduate of Wake Forest University, she was only beginning to dig more deeply into the meaning of what she believed and how she would live. But it was her instincts that surprised me. If the challenge of the class was to take Christian convictions seriously, and at the same time to take the questions of the world seriously, Susan intuitively rejected any kind of compartmentalization and instead went straight for more coherence. She saw seamlessly and wanted to live seamlessly.

By the semester's end she had become a friend, and now ten years later, married to Nate, and mother to William, Molly and Isaac, she is only more so. We continue to talk about things that matter to both of us. Even this past week she texted me, wondering if I was home, and if so, could she bring her kids by? So we had lunch, me offering peanut butter and jelly sandwiches for all. As I told her little ones as they left, "Your mommy is very dear to me." And now they are too.

I watched her over the next years in life with a group of adolescent girls, helping them come to coherence, where what they believed about the world was more and more the way that they lived in the world. A few years later I was asked to teach for my daughter Jessica's class, a "summing-up of high school years" course, and agreed to do so—if Susan could join me as my co-teacher. I knew that if I could not be there, that she would be, and that it would be wonderfully rich and right in its own way.

When she and Nate began to spend more time together, I was drawn in, friend and professor that I was—and when the great day of their wedding came, they graced me with the task of giving the homily, outdoors in the beautiful Virginia countryside, amid farms and sky and mountains. Since I am not a pastor, I do not "marry" people, but sometimes am asked to speak about the meaning of marriage as part of the wedding. Musing with them on the reality that the best of marriages can be wonderful but not perfect, I offered them these words from Berry:

> What wonder have you done to me?
> In binding love you set me free.
> These sixty years the wonder prove:
> I bring you aged a young man's love.[8]

And then I said,

> Susan and Nate, we set before you today the vision of a long-loved love. Someday you may be sixty years old and writing poems for each other; by God's grace you will be. For however long your marriage lasts, as your community we long with you for a long love, hoping that at moments along the way—with creativity and care and commitment—you will bring to each other an aging love, full of the wonder it is that in binding love you set each other free.

A wonderful marriage, not a perfect one—like every good marriage everywhere.

As Susan has moved from just-out-of-college into marriage into motherhood, she has learned more about her vocation, living into her life as she has. What she began to see is that she loved to create with her hands, and so she spent time in a paper store, glorying in the tactile world of her work. As babies came, she wondered what they would mean for that love, and with her husband Nate's help, decided to build a home business of hand-printing stationary using a letterpress. This creative labor now sells in shops in her city and serves a growing circle of glad customers.

In our home we have a reading room between the front of the house and the back, and for those who love to read it always brings a smile. On one wall we have shelves from floor to ceiling, filled with books of all sizes and shapes. There are shelves of children's books, shelves of novels and shelves of biographies. But there is also a shelf for Leo Tolstoy, for Robert Louis Stevenson and for Charles Dickens—and one for Wendell Berry too, his essays, his poetry, his novels. Set in the middle of that shelf is a beautifully made card, letterpressed, with the words of one of Berry's poems, beginning with, "What wonder have you done to me?" A gift from Susan, yes, and seeing it I remember her ability to see into the meaning of things. Her studies, her loves, her marriage, her work, her children, together a vocation, she is making sense of life as she lives her life.

A JUST MAN

Ordinary people in ordinary places, each one is a story of a life lived as a vocation. None have arrived, and each lives with a keen sense that more could be done. Time and energy, ability and desire— together they are the contours of our lives, and when all is said and done, we have to sleep at night, making peace with who we are and how we have lived.

But it is true for all of us that sometimes the simplest grace is the most important gift. Take the remarkable story of *Les Misérables* and the decision of Bishop Bienvenu to keep his door open; as he said to his sister and housekeeper, "Someone may need to come in." And the whole world knows that that night, someone did. What most do not know is that in Victor Hugo's novel there is a lifetime behind that decision. If the stage play gives the bishop ten minutes, the novel tells the story of his whole life over almost one hundred pages, titling book one "A Just Man." From the calling to a pastoral vocation on through to becoming a bishop, we come to know an unusual man. If we hear Iris Murdoch's wisdom—"At crucial moments of choice, most of the business of choosing is already over"[9]— then we understand the pilgrimage the bishop made to be the man whose instinct was to show mercy. For years he had made choices, small and large, that shaped his soul, giving him eyes to see the world that was his as his to care for.

The someone who needed to come in was Jean Valjean, a wayfarer set adrift after almost twenty years in prison for stealing a loaf of bread. We know the responses of the bishop to his visitor, first the offer of a meal and a bed, and then amazingly, beyond comprehension, the offer of the silver candlesticks that had been "forgotten" after Valjean was arrested for stealing everything else.

"I have bought your soul for God," are the words of the bishop to his surprised guest. And the way that Hugo tells his tale, that is what has happened, not because Valjean is now fated to become good, but rather that he is transformed by the simple grace that was given.

If Berry has made a vocation of "telling stories shaped by the truest truths of the universe, but in language the whole world can understand," Hugo's *Les Misérables* is that story writ dramatic on the stages of every city and continent. Grandly and yet wonderfully, it tells the truth of the human condition in a way that draws everyone in. We see ourselves in the story: our own hopes, our own fears, the loves and longings of every heart.

But lest we forget, it is the story of "the miserables," of people who have stumbled along the way, economically, politically and socially. And it is the story of a man who sees his vocation as implicated in the lives of people like that. He has chosen to live a common life for the common good. And Valjean, very slowly, makes that choice too. Profoundly formed by the bishop's life, he begins to take up his new life with the same simple grace—not in the ministry, but in the marketplace. If the bishop's clerical calling implicated him in the lives of his people, then it was the vocation of business for Valjean that drew him into the welfare of his workers and his city. And because he saw himself in relationship to a people in a place, he saw himself as responsible for the way their world turned out, for the way it was and the way it ought to be.

7

The Great Temptations

They who know the most must mourn the deepest.

LORD BYRON, MANFRED

$\mathcal{B}$rowsing through a favorite used bookstore on Capitol Hill one day, I found a book by the German philosopher Nietzsche and brought it home. Reading in it that night, I came across these lines by the poet Lord Byron, "They who know the most must mourn the deepest." Intrigued, I returned to the bookstore, found a volume of Byron's poetry and read the longer poem from which these words came.

In a poetic meditation on the great temptation in Genesis 3, Byron muses over the meaning of the tree of the knowledge of good and evil, a surprisingly epistemological temptation, but one with a moral heart. It was not knowledge in the abstract, but knowledge with responsibility written into it. A poem, not a theological discourse—Byron argues that knowledge is weighty; that in fact it can be burdensome, thus "they who know the most must mourn the deepest."

It seems a strange turn of events in the Age of Enlightenment that knowing more, we mourn more. Promising "knowledge is power," the Enlightenment is also a reason for tears.

The longer I live the more sure I am that Byron was on to something, seeing the underbelly of the Enlightenment as he did. Knowing more has meant power, and power has meant progress. No one is ungrateful for skilled dentists and surgeons who have technological tools that make life more healthy and less painful. No one is angry about the gifts of electricity and plumbing. While where the power comes from and where the waste goes are honest concerns for honest people, the alternatives are the cause of strain and disease that bring massive heartache. These are true—and the examples could go on and on—but Byron saw something else. While modern medicine and modern technologies have their own moral and social complexities, Byron the artist was feeling the psychological pain of knowledge in his age, and any age. He knew that the primordial temptation to know more would bring its own wounds.[1]

Father Adam and Mother Eve felt this immediately, moving from the joy of being naked and not ashamed, to the sorrow of being naked and ashamed, hiding from God and each other. The knowledge that was now theirs was wounding, bringing pain in their deepest places. It is surprising that the promise of more knowledge—to know as God knows, in the words of the tempter— had the bitter fruit of anguish and shame. "Where are you?" comes the question from heaven. Their response? "We don't want you to know where we are, because we are ashamed of who we are."

From that first temptation on, human beings have responded in countless ways to the same question: *What will you do with what you know?* Or to put it another way, *Knowing what you know, how will you respond?* If that was the first question, answered with tragic consequences, human beings have answered it again and again, incarnate in times and places in every century and every culture. There is not a deeper question, there is not a more perennial question—and there is not a more difficult question.

Knowing more, we protect ourselves. Most of time we do not

want to be responsible for what we know—simply, sadly, it hurts too much. The *yada* of the Hebrew world may teach that *knowledge of* means *responsible to* means *care for*, but most of time we prefer a disconnect between the three. We do not want *knowing* to necessarily mean *caring*. Not because we are morally misanthropic, but simply because the one who knows the most mourns the deepest. More knowledge often means more pain.

In the story that Berry did not write, Wheeler Catlett never took his mother's love into his heart, making it his own. Blood could not be thicker than liquor—and so he never took the train to Louisville to step into the literal mess of Uncle Peach's life. He knew enough to know that he did not want to know more. Or in the novel that Hugo did not write, the bishop had spent his life caring for people not worth caring for and was worn out. At the end of his life, he knew the human heart and knew that he wanted no more—and so of course he kept his door locked, because someone might want to come in. These stories are the stories of everyone's life.

Byron understood this, and Nietzsche too. We all do. Over time human beings have, more often than not, responded to the dynamic relationship of knowledge and responsibility in one of two ways, each one being fully understandable if there had been no incarnation. Both offer a way to know that allow us to keep our eyes open, seeing things as they "really" are, but not requiring that we get so close that we are hurt by what we know. We have called these responses *stoicism* and *cynicism*. Both are ways to know that do not ask us to get too close to what we know; they allow us to protect ourselves from knowing too much, and therefore from caring too much.

THE STOICISM OF TOM WOLFE

"History repeats itself. Has to. No-one listens."[2] The poetry of Steve Turner echoes across history, and runs through the human heart. Day after day we see its reality, from generational dynamics in every family to political shortsightedness in every society. Not a fatalist, Turner psychologically and sociologically Turner underlines a sobering truth, that there are consequences for not remembering very well, and the consequences are ones that we do not want to have to think about.

We live in an increasingly global economy; it is the "flat world" that Thomas Friedman has written about so widely and so well. From chocolate to computers, we are profoundly interconnected. Air travel from one location to another in the United States is mediated via India, so a choice to fly from Portland to Denver pays a salary in Mumbai. A decade into the twenty-first century has shown that Wall Street is more than an avenue in New York City, it is also a global weathervane for economic life and death; the implosion of financial markets that brought about a global crisis began on Wall Street. What happens there affects people everywhere.

It is not new. A generation ago, Tom Wolfe, chronicler of American culture as he is, summed up the 1980s with his novel *The Bonfire of the Vanities,* a story situated on Wall Street and about its self-proclaimed "masters of the universe," the young traders who dominated the economic imagination of the time. They could do no wrong, at least as their trading abilities went. Entry-level salaries burgeoned into fortunes, and over time they began to see themselves as invulnerable, masters of the universe they were—until of course they fell on their faces, stumbling badly over their greed.

History repeats itself. Has to. No-one listens. Ten years later, Wolfe offered another novel, meant to sum up the 1990s as well as the twentieth century, titled *A Man in Full.*[3] Set in Atlanta—the new city for a new century—the man in full was "the last great white football player at Georgia Tech" who forty years later has made a fortune remaking the Atlanta skyline. His economic interests run across America, and his personal Gulfstream jet takes him wherever his business and pleasure require.

A long story full of families and friendships, business and politics, it eventually finds its way to the Bay Area of California where the businessman owns large frozen food warehouses. His accountant has informed him that it would be in his economic interest to sell the warehouses, and he simply says yes, taking the counsel of his trusted adviser.

Brilliant storyteller that he is, Wolfe then draws us to the last man hired at the warehouse, the one who drives the forklift on the midnight shift—and who is now going to lose his job. We find that he is a child of Haight-Ashbury in the 1960s—the iconic center of the flower-power, incense-burning, acid-dropping, tie-dye-wearing, peace-and-love-vibing counterculture—of parents who loved their lifestyle more than they loved him. The son was encouraged to do anything he wanted to do whenever he wanted to do it, and that did not mean taking school or life very seriously. Still an adolescent, he married young, had children and desperately needed a job that could take care of his young family. The simple decision in Atlanta has repercussions in Oakland that are tragic for the young man.

Some time later, he finds himself in the county jail with a long sentence ahead of him. Bored, wanting some distraction from the noise of inmate life, he requests a book from the jail library. The wrong one is delivered, and while he is disappointed, through the hours of the night he begins to read Epictetus, the Greek philosopher. Surprisingly he is drawn in to the ancient wisdom, finding in the Stoic philosophy a way to hold onto his humanity.

Jails and prisons the world over are rarely places of penitence, where rehabilitation of heart and mind is the order of the day. Horribly, they are more often the setting in which social stumbling becomes malicious intent, where small crimes grow into criminal lifestyles. The young man in Wolfe's novel wants to get out, to return to his family, and he knows he needs to stay clear of the worst ways of the jail. Night by night Epictetus is his teacher, showing him that it is possible to know about evil and suffering and yet not get close to it. Over time an apprenticeship over the centuries is formed, and the Stoic vision becomes his vision.

There is a push-comes-to-shove moment in the story, and against the best advice of Epictetus, the young man decides to step into the mess, rather than avoid it. A gross injustice will take place unless someone says "no"—and so he does. His choice changes everything. A longer story, and in the best Dickensian way, the last man hired, now fired, eventually meets the Atlanta businessman whose world has unraveled too. What do they talk about? Epictetus and his Stoic philosophy.

The last pages of the novel are unsatisfying, as if Wolfe understands that Stoicism did not work when it needed to work, and yet, and yet—the two men finish the story as business partners, offering Epictetus to the masses.

I once talked to Wolfe about this, telling him that I read his work carefully and enjoyed his novels, and that in my courses I assign his essays—but before the conversation was over I asked him about the end of *A Man in Full.* Sitting across the table, he was dressed as he always is in public, with a white linen suit and a carnation. I admit gulping when I said to one of America's great novelists, "Well, you see, the last chapter was unsatisfying." He looked back at me and said, "I don't finish my novels very well, do I?"

History and better readers than I will judge that, but what I am sure of is that his argument for Stoicism as an answer for a full life, a complete life, for being "a man in full," was disappointing. While I understand that there are horrors and heartaches that are beyond what anyone wants or imagines, it does not make a good life to think that we can have knowledge without responsibility, that we can know but not have to care.

Wolfe, like every Stoic before him, is simply a man trying to live in the world. While there are honest joys every day, if one has eyes to see, there are also honest sorrows too, if one has eyes to see. What we do with the two realities is what distinguishes us, and is what is distinctive about different religious visions. It was not for any small reason that Wolfe called his "summing up of a century" novel *A Man in Full,* as that title is itself full of meaning. Every account of human life, from varieties of theism to varieties of pantheism to varieties of materialism, has a vision of the human person at its heart—what is often called a *telos.* We believe certain things to be true of us as individuals, and true of human beings, and we live in that light. But we do not only live in that light, we theorize and imagine in that light as well. We develop economic and political visions, and we create artistic artifacts—sculpture, paintings, novels, poetry, music, theater and film—that resonate with what we believe to be true of human beings, in light of the *telos* that shapes our understanding of what is real and true and right.

The *telos* of the Stoic vision is *apatheia.* We are all that we need to be, all that we are meant to be, "a man in full," when we are *apatheia.* It is not a word that we use today, but it is close to one that we know—*apathy.* For the Stoic, there was nothing pejorative about the word; instead it defined the very meaning of being human. To be happy is the chief end of man and woman, the *telos,* and anything that gets in the way of that happiness is to be eschewed.

There are other words that are similar etymologically, each one rooted in the Latin *pati.* We know pathos, empathy, sympathy, passion and compassion, for example. Each of those words grows out of some effort to make sense of life, of a life where things are often not as they are supposed to be, where in fact there is disappointment, heartbreak and injustice. Knowing the world to be this way, knowing our experience to be this way, what will we do? How will we respond?

The Stoic response is *apatheia,* a way of knowing that does not require one to respond. One knows, but does not have to step in.

One knows, but does not have to be implicated. It is important to note that Stoicism is not malicious with its intentional indifference, but its willingness to look away at critical points is a problem for a good life and a good society.

As I see the world, there is an awful lot that is awful—sometimes grievously so. My story of the friend who was murdered on Capitol Hill is only one example; sadly the stories are legion, known only too well by millions and millions and millions of people, by every one of us, in fact. Who of us wants to get close to sorrow? Who wants to take sadness into one's heart?

The great Hebrew scholar Abraham Heschel, in his magisterial study *The Prophets,* argues that the prophetic tradition as a whole was a response to the stoicism of their time, whether that was formally taught and debated, or was more street-level assumptions by ordinary people living ordinary lives. Heschel sets forth a vision of life that is different, formed by the belief that God hears and responds to what he hears, that he sees and acts on what he sees. Not an unmoved mover, but the one who knows and who feels what he knows. When the prophets speak for God, their primary lament is that the people of Israel know but do not do, they know but do not feel. They are more Stoic than Hebrew—and God condemns their claim to be his people, because his people would be like him, knowing how he knows, feeling how he feels.

Another twentieth-century scholar, Benjamin B. Warfield of Princeton, intriguingly argues that the Gospels were a response to the stoicism of their time. Exploring "the person and work of Christ," he maintains that Jesus as God Incarnate showed the people of Israel that knowledge must be linked with the soft heart of true obedience born of a rich emotional life; that it was impossible to call oneself a Jew without a being a Jew of the heart, someone for whom knowledge is responsibility born of love—like the God of Abraham, Isaac and Jacob, for whom knowledge is most fully seen in love. His study of John 11 and the death of Lazarus (already noted in chapters 1 and 5 of this book) is a remarkably rich example of this, showing that Jesus' response to the death of his friend was a million miles from the Stoic *apatheia*. The Jesus of John's Gospel is the one who is angry at the curse of death, even as he cries with Mary and Martha. When the Word becomes flesh, he shows that it is possible to feel what we know, in sympathy, empathy and passion.

This is not a screed against stoicism. Again, if there has not been an incarnation, a moment in human history when God shows that we can know and still love, then stoicism seems a very good answer to a very hard question: Knowing the hurt of life, what are you going to do? Byron's insight is more than mere poetry, artfully capturing the truth of human experience as he does, "They who know the most must mourn the deepest." Yes, *knowing what we know, how will we respond?*

THE CYNICISM OF JOHN LE CARRÉ

Living in Washington, D.C., for many years now, I have come to the conclusion that while the world at large may criticize the city for its hubris, "the Beltway mentality" and all, the reality is that the city is cynical. It is a surprise to the innocent, but twisted virtues that vices are, hubris and cynicism nourish each other, the one the breeding ground for the other. Vices are always like that, skewing what it means to be human, becoming vicious in the end and destroying what might have been.

People come from all over America and the world wanting to put their shoulders to history. For six months or six years they may try, and then inevitably conclude that Washington is too much of a mess—and anyone who knows, knows that it is a mess. But the question which was first asked in the Garden, primordial and perennial as it was, is asked again of everyone who comes to town:

Knowing what you know, what are you going to do?

Many decide to leave, and they return to Des Moines or Austin, sure that they have tried Washington and found it wanting. In the globalizing political economy of the twenty-first century, others come from Egypt or India, and often they too return home, now knowing Washington and its ways, determined to make their future in their own society, drawing on the best and worst of what they learned. Others stay and commit themselves to the hard task of "doing justice, loving mercy and walking humbly with God," even as they know that Machiavelli got to Washington before Micah. And still others cynically work the city that is now theirs, making sure that they get what they want, sure that everyone else is doing the same thing.

For many years I taught on Capitol Hill, drawing students into visions of public responsibility. We read together, as they went off into the city week after week for internships in all kinds of settings, for-profit and non-profit, governmental and non-governmental, and we talked about this challenge. Often I would put on the whiteboard this syllogism:

Justice is an ideal.
Ideals are utopian and unrealistic.
Justice is utopian and unrealistic.

Hoping an honest conversation might act as an antidote, my burden was knowing that the city would do its best to eat them, with subtlety perhaps, but in the end there would be a devouring of their earnest motivations for vocations in the public square. Our teaching was hard work, and I always felt as if we were engaged in a struggle for the hearts and minds of our students, fighting for the way the world would turn out.

In the strange calculus of history and the human heart, the subtle temptation of cynicism confounds our best efforts at working toward a common good. Sometimes all we can do is name the problem, cancerous as it is to a good life and a good society. Some, of course, do not see it as a problem, instead embracing it as the reality of realities.

That is part of the long history of cynicism, of course. From the earliest Cynics like Antisthenes and Diogenes in the time of Socrates, it was an honest effort to see through theories and metaphysical abstractions in favor of on-the-ground life, the practice of living. Rather than being taught by the gods, mediated through social conventions as that must be, cynics saw life itself as the teacher, believing we learn from nature the way we are to live. *Look around you! See for yourself. Stop imagining a world that does not exist. Be real.*

Of course it is a perennial problem to theorize without a true concern for the everyday realities of human life. People in every age resist those who imagine a better world than the one in which we have to live, full of strain and struggle as it is. We cry out, "But you don't know!" rejecting the counsel as irrelevant because it is not grounded in the way things are.

But that is the point of tension too. *How are things? What is the truth about life? What ought we to expect of others, and of life?* We debate those questions all day long, in education and politics, in families and neighborhoods, in the marketplaces of life large and small. And whether we are Greek Cynics from long ago or very modern men and women who make our way into the realpolitick of the cities of this world, there is enough disappointment, malice and corruption to cause us to wonder whether justice is more than an ideal. *A nice idea, but please—we have to live in the world that is really there.*

And it was "the world" that intrigued the Cynics. Dissatisfied with being a *polites*, a citizen of a particular place, a *polis*, Diogenes preferred to be known as "a citizen of the world," a *kosmopolites*, or cosmopolitan. In the nuances of moral and political philosophy, grounded in the human heart as those visions always are, the Cynics did not disdain "places," but rather saw their place as cosmic, belonging to the universe.

Like most of life, there is a yes and a no to that sense of self, so very cosmopolitan as it is. To see oneself as engaged by the world, as responsible for the world, is right; to see oneself as unbound by ordinary relationships and responsibilities for a people and a place is a problem. In that view, one never has to commit to the common good, full of complexity as it is, as one can always stand outside, because it is possible to stand apart from the underbelly of history and not be implicated in its mess.

But it is a pregnant image, "a citizen of the world"—and it invites a question: What is the world, and what is it really like? One of the best chroniclers of contemporary geo-politics is the British novelist John Le Carré. From *The Spy Who Came in from the Cold* to *Tinker, Tailor, Soldier, Spy,* to *Smiley's People,* to *The Honourable Schoolboy,* to *The Constant Gardner,* to *The Most Wanted Man,* to *The Mission Song,* he draws on his own years of spying for England in the MI5 and MI6 to tell his tales of the intelligence service through the Cold War and its end; in the years since then he has taken up global corporate machinations as the subject of his work.

Every story is remarkably engaging and sobering. A very gifted writer, Le Cairé is brilliant, novel by novel taking up the most complex dynamics of the political economies of the modern world. If one story is Russia, post-USSR, with politicians full of malice doing business with kindred spirits in the West, another is Africa in all its hope and despair, with warring tribes set against global economic interests that profit when Africa suffers. Le Carré is a master story-teller, seeing the evil of the human heart played out in public and political arenas—and he expects his readers to come to the same conclusion that he has.

In a word, he is a cynic—about individuals and institutions, about persons and polities, about anyone and anything that has to do with power and money. And why not? There many good reasons to be cynical. Governments do betray their citizens, sometimes with tragic consequences. Nations do sacrifice long-term good for short-term gain, sometimes with intentional injustice written into the equation. People who *really* know what goes on in government and corporate bureaucracies have a very hard time not believing that everyone and everything is corrupt. They have seen too much. In Hitchcock's inimitable image, they are men and women who know too much.

Le Carré captures this insightfully and eloquently. There have been many nights over many years when I have set his novels down, sure that the world is a better place because Le Carré has written another story. His sensibility about the nuances of the human heart rings true to my own heart and to people that I know. His instincts about motives, true and false, seem plausible, given what I have experienced. But there is also a sense of shame too, as I read him. It is almost as if I have been a voyeur, looking in on life in a way that is illegitimate, a way that is intentionally perverse. Yes, I know that Bismarck, the Prussian politician, was painfully right about political life, about the human heart getting close to political realities, when he said that "if we want to respect sausage or law then we must not watch either being made." But as I read Bismarck, there is a hard-won realism that is different than Le Carré's cynicism.

Take *The Constant Gardner,* one of his novels, which also has become a film. It is about the world where global economic interests butt up against global health interests which butt up against global political interests. A complex and complicated world it is, and sausage-making is the reality that runs through the story. The British government has a part in the story, but a health crisis in Kenya does too, as does a British pharmaceutical company—and no one is clean, in fact, no one has integrity. The sausage has been made, and it stinks; it has made some people very wealthy, others have died from it. Only the naive refuse the logic of cynicism.

To keep going in the world, we cannot afford to be romantics. Even if we acknowledge that Pollyanna is fictional, we know the temptation and allure to imitate her. We do want all to be well, for all to be happy. "Life is good," the T-shirts promise, and we buy them by the truckload. Well, sometimes in some places, but not very often in the massive ghettoes of Nairobi, which is where Le Carré takes us in *The Constant Gardner*. And when money and power are to be had, there are few who say no. Almost no one.

But there are exceptions. And it is here that Le Carré's cynicism is more a protection of his heart than a truthful account of the heart. Whether conscious or not, intentional or not, the temptation to cynicism is always a way of keeping one's heart from being wounded, again.

Given my work and my city, I have watched scores of hundreds of twenty-somethings come to Washington, bright-eyed and bushy-tailed, ready for life, wanting to affect the way the world turns out. For most it does not take very long smelling the sausage being made. Before long, cynicism begins to grow as they see and hear more than they ever imagined.

But I have also watched many who are now older, seasoned as they are, who can remember a day when they too believed that justice was worth working for but who now *know* that it isn't, because it only exists in university bull-sessions. After all, they are not twenty-one-year-olds anymore! They *know* how the world really works. And of course they are very willing to tell twenty-one-year-olds that they'd better get on with the real business of politics, which is using it for one's own end. As one senior aide in the Senate told one of my students who had asked about the meaning of justice for a particular national debate in which his senator was a key participant, "Justice is crap! Grow up!" And for a half-hour he harangued her for even imagining that justice, inscribed though it might be on the buildings of Capitol Hill, had anything to do with Realpolitick, with the real business of politics. (Answering the question *What is real?* turns out to be more than an academic question, because how we define it has far-reaching consequences.)

There is much to be cynical about—and it is a good answer if there has not been an incarnation. But if that has happened, *if* the Word did become flesh, and *if* there are men and women who in and through their own vocations imitate the vocation of God, then sometimes and in some places the world becomes something more like the way it ought to be.

A VOCATION IN IMITATION OF A VOCATION

Over twenty years ago, Mark Rodgers and I decided to be neighbors, remembering the credo of the Clapham community in London two hundred years ago: "Choose a neighbor before you choose a house."[4] We first met in a project that connected politics and education, and not so many years later Mark and his family moved to Washington, where he took up the work of chief of staff in the House and Senate for the next sixteen years. So we invited Mark and his family to move into our neighborhood, and they did.

One afternoon, Mark and I were talking about family and work, our lives and the world. Over time, we had made many decisions that bound us up together; never particular political issues, but more the questions and concerns that make for a good society, believing together that the culture is upstream from politics. Mark is a visionary with an engineer's mind, and he has a remarkable ability to imagine and convene.

Long a lover of music, he is always interested in the next song by the next songwriter, characteristically eager and hopeful as he is. There have been times when he has brought together artists of every sort—musicians, filmmakers, playwrights, novelists, painters—and I have joined in, bringing my questions to the con-

versation. There have been other times when he has called, wondering if we could put together a meeting for Bono, who for years
called Mark his "angel on Capitol Hill." There was no one in those
years of Bono's lobbying Washington for the HIV/AIDS crisis who
was as helpful to the cause as Mark. And other times he has brought
people together between the worlds of politics, the arts and business,
pouring his heart out for common-good visions about the ways we
live together.

That day he told me of walking through the Senate, feeling imaginary arrows flying into his back from others who worked there,
hearing their "curses" as he made his way, "There goes Mark
Rodgers. We wouldn't have to care about Africa if he didn't keep
making it an issue. Our constituents don't really care, so why
should we?" He did not say it with an ounce of arrogance; more
with real weariness, feeling the weight of working on something
that most did not think was worth working on. Too often, winning
the next election is the only thing that matters, and if the people
back home are not motivated by the needs of Africa, it is hard to
expend political capital on such very far away concerns. There is
nothing romantic about trying to do the right thing and feeling the
indifference of those you work and live with.

And that is only one story of Mark's life. Year after year he has
kept at it, seeing ideas and issues that implicate him. There is leg-
islation that has changed the way we live as a people—in fact, that
has changed the way the world works—and the fingerprints of his
heart are all over the laws. There are songs and stories that have
been seen and heard by people all over the world that have his
name written into their production. There are projects that address
educational problems in the cities of America and animal rights in
every neighborhood of America that Mark has labored over.
Complex, difficult, sometimes unpopular, and yet each is important
for the way the world turns out.

Can we know the world and still love the world? Can we know the messes of the world and still work on them because we want to, because we see ourselves as responsible, for love's sake? Sometimes some people make that choice, like Mark has, and always it is a vocation in imitation of a vocation. At our best and truest, we stand in the long line of those who remember the profound insight of Thomas à Kempis in calling us to "the imitation of Christ." To choose to know, and still love, is costly; it was for God, and it is for us. In fact it is the most difficult task imaginable.

Hear these words then, imitators of the vocation of God as we are.

> God knew the worst about us before he chose to love us, and therefore no discovery now can disillusion him about us in the way that we are so often disillusioned about ourselves, and quench his determination to bless us. He took knowledge of us in love.[5]

God knows us and still loves us. That is the heart of the incarnation, and not surprisingly the heart of J. I. Packer's contemporary classic, *Knowing God.*

His vision has shaped my vision, not only of God, but of life. Packer begins with the contrast between knowing about God and knowing God. In his own way, he rejects the Enlightenment paradigm of objective and subjective knowing, arguing instead for a more truthful knowing that is both a knowledge *of* God and a knowledge *about* God—implicitly maintaining that they need each other to be an honest faith. But then he presses into the argument, maintaining that God knows "the worst about us" and for love's sake refuses to be disillusioned about us. It is amazing grace, always.

If that is true, then intellectual honesty does not require us to be cynics. It has happened in history: God knows and still loves. Knowing myself as I do, the words make me sigh; but they are also words that make it possible to live. I am known and I am loved—

like the woman at the Samaritan well: "He knows everything that I've ever done—and he loves me! You come meet him too."

The incarnation is not a call to life in rose gardens, somehow closing our eyes to the terrors of this very wounded world. With Wolfe, we can acknowledge that the world is a mess, a horrible mess, but we can resist the temptation to keep ourselves clean, to stay "happy" as *apatheia* allows. With Le Carré, we can tell the truth about complicity, about corruption, but we can still refuse to go along with the hard-edged judgment that every time in every place with every person things are as bad as they might be. Strange grace that it is, sometimes people decide that their vocations are in fact to know the world and still love the world; in fact, sometimes there are people who know the worst about the world and still love it.

Truth be told, mostly those people are unnoticed in this life. At the end of the day, we are ordinary people in ordinary places. The wisest ones have always known this, reminding us of this deeper, truer truth. In the final words of the wonderfully imagined novel *Middlemarch*, George Eliot says of Dorothea,

> Her finely touched spirit had still its fine issues, though they were not widely visible. Her full nature, like that river of which Cyrus broke the strength, spent itself in channels which had no great name on the earth. But the effect of her being on those around her was incalculably diffusive: for the growing good of the world is partly dependent on unhistoric acts; and that things are not so ill with you and me as they might have been is half owing to the number who lived faithfully a hidden life, and rest in unvisited tombs.

The best of us are like this, I am sure. Most do not work on the Capitol Hills of the world. Most do not get phone calls from Bono. Most of us come and go, and history does not seem to remember. Like Dorothea, we live hidden lives, still called to have an "effect" on the world around us, that things might not be "so ill." We hope and pray that we will be good people living good lives doing good work, in the end resting in "unvisited tombs" as we likely will. It cannot be, and will not be, otherwise—and that is the way it is for most of us most of the time.

LIVING FOR THE SAKE OF THE WORLD

Walker Percy offered the allusive image "hints of hope." Not a very grand vision really, and yet it is a vision that is true—for most of us most of the time. In the daily rhythms for everyone everywhere, we live our lives in the marketplaces of this world: in homes and neighborhoods, in schools and on farms, in hospitals and in businesses, and our vocations are bound up with the ordinary work that ordinary people do. We are not great shots across the bow of history; rather, by simple grace, we are hints of hope.

And while we may not be weighed down with the questions *What will I do today to stay free from stoicism? How will I steer clear of cynicism today?* the reality is that if we are to keep our commitments, sticking with what we believe is important, we will have to have reasons that make sense of vocations that implicate us in the histories and complexities of our communities and societies. To see ourselves as responsible, for love's sake, is both hard work and good work—and it cannot be done alone.

Several years ago at a *Vocare* evening of the Washington Institute—what we call "conversations about calling," where we sometimes discuss mothering, sometimes the law, sometimes international development, sometimes education—George Connors and Hans Hess came to one evening focused on vocations in business.[6]

We think that meals matter, as they have moral meaning. Stretched taut between the Last Supper and the Great Supper—with an invitation from Jesus to eat together week by week until he comes again—our *Vocares* always involve a meal. These two men have spent their lives watching sausage being made, working where they have. George has been a banker his whole life, and Hans has worked on Capitol Hill and now is a restaurateur. They do business together, George serving as Hans's banker.

If it is money and power that corrupt, making us be the cynics that we must be, then George is a counter-story, living as if another world is more real, more true, more right. After college he came to Washington and began on the lower rungs of banking, learning to make money while learning about people. As his skills developed, his responsibilities grew, and he began to have more oversight of his bank's policies. As in so many business ventures, good work one place turned into better work in another, and when a new bank was formed, he became the president of Washington First Bank.

Over the years, the bank has grown, and George's understanding of his vocation has grown too. He has surprisingly good instincts about money and people. Watching him at work, I am often amazed at his responses to the questions that are his, stewarding resources as he does. We often talk about what he does, not the particulars of his relationships, but more the character of his responsibilities.

For example, sometimes we talk about who gets money and why. Many banks, even against regulations, practice some kind of "redlining." (Laws require that anyone is in principle eligible for a loan and that certain neighborhoods cannot be "red-lined" and marked off as not worthy of a bank's time and money.) The sad history is that this is one of the primary faces of institutional racism, and in cities across the country—against the law—it is done. As a steward of the bank, George has a primary role in protecting its resources, but he is also committed to an honestly good society, and therefore to honestly good cities. He knows that the best businesses take risks, especially if something important is at stake. So while he has a 100 percent rating for his bank's performance, he has approved loans where other bankers would not. Sometimes a question comes to him that requires Solomonic wisdom. Because he refuses to be a cynic about his work and world, knowing what he knows, he chooses to enter into the complexity of the hopes for what a city might be.

He once told me of a conversation with the chairman of the board of his bank, someone with long experience in business and banking. George was asked, "So where are our legal fees?" Every bank he had known put aside money for legal fees, and in studying the books the chairman could not find outlays for lawyers. Perplexed, the chairman asked the president of the bank. No one's fool, George knows his work very well. His response? "I talk with people." And he explained that being at fault on a loan was not in the best interests of either a bank or a customer; both lose if a lawyer is brought in. So, sometimes with sleepless nights, George persists and persists, until the loaned money is finally accounted for. There are hard phone calls and even harder face-to-face conversations, but in the end he argues that a renegotiated loan is better than a lost loan. Not an optimist about people, but not a pessimist either, George steps into the city of Washington—full of power and money as it is—with a deepening sense of vocation, seeking a common good for both businessperson and customer. Simply, he sees his work as imitating the incarnation; knowing the way banking more often than not is, he works for what can be because he believes in what ought to be.

Hans is one of those customers. A Californian by birth, he has had an unusual pilgrimage vocationally. A physics major in college, he studied theology the next four years—and to the surprise of all, he then came to Washington to work on Capitol Hill. In those years the member of Congress for whom he worked asked him a question, and what he learned changed the course of his life. The congressman wanted to know why antibiotics given to children were increasingly ineffective. In his research, Hans discovered that one prominent line of study indicated that the problem was that our

meat supply was tainted, as the antibiotics given to make cows grow
bigger and faster were then of course in the hamburgers that America's children were eating. So when an antibiotic was needed, it was
not helpful; the medicine was already in the bodies of those who
needed help.

Like others before him, Hans thought he could make a better
hamburger. And with his wife, April, at work in the business world
herself, they spent a couple of years with hard pencils, thinking
through their vision. Ideas bumped up against ideas, bringing more
ideas into being, and then one day Elevation Burger opened its
doors in Falls Church, Virginia. Deeply committed to doing good
work for all, they began selling hamburgers that came from naturally
fed, organically produced cows, with French fries cooked in olive
oil to top them off. Arguing that "fast food doesn't have to be bad
food," they envisioned a business that would do well and do good
at the same time.

Over the years that they have been in business, their customers
have been loyal, and the interest in their model has grown. Being a
friend, I am always glad to see the store full of people, and I am glad
to hear of others wanting to open their own Elevation Burger fran-
chises all over the country and world. On the store's walls are
posters that artfully tell their story, explaining in ordinary language
that "ingredients matter," now the tagline for the company. It is not
meant to be a fancy place; burgers and fries are their chief handi-
work, an ordinary meal for ordinary people.

In the end, food is a matter of taste. Healthy food sometimes
does not seem very tasty, and if a restaurant cannot deliver on the
basic promise that its food tastes good, then it is unlikely that even
the most committed will be customers into the future. Children will
not clamor for "an Elevation burger!" that does not taste good.

So sometimes Hans and I talk about the challenge of making
eschatological hamburgers. If we believe that every meal in this

time in history is a foretaste of a Great Supper someday in the future, then what is important about what we eat now? The Marriage Supper of the Lamb will be a feast, and everything will be tasty and healthy at the very same time; there will be no trade-offs—a donut for breakfast and so of course an apple for lunch. Born of a human need and a strategic vision, his work is a foretaste of what someday will be.

What has intrigued me about Hans's business is that it is pretty close to Bismarck's sausage-making, very literally; hamburger is ground meat, after all. But I know from listening carefully that the company works very hard to offer a good meal to its public. Scrupulously so. They work to find suppliers who can promise good products, and they work hard to offer good service once the customer has an Elevation Burger on its way to where it belongs. As in any business, it would be more than easy to cut corners, just because it is always possible to do so. Who would know anyway? Doesn't everyone? The cynics of the world think so, but Hans and April have poured themselves out in hope, wanting to offer a common grace for the common good, in a bun.

But if cynicism is one siren calling, then stoicism is too. Why care? The question that came to Hans was one involving big business, big government, and a health crisis—about as complex as it gets, as Le Carré's novels show us. Why get involved? It is one thing to know about messes, but it is something else altogether to step into a mess. It is one thing to know about things being wrong, but it is something else altogether to decide that I am responsible to make it right.

Knowing what I know, what will I do? There are people who see themselves implicated in the way the world is and ought to be. For love's sake, they see themselves as responsible for the way the world turns out. Sometimes they are bankers, and sometimes they make hamburgers. But always and everywhere, they are people who have vocations in imitation of the vocation of God: knowing the worst about the world, and still loving the world. They are people who learn to live in the tension of life, living with what is and longing for what will be—keeping clear of the great temptations, for the sake of the world. Simply said, they become *hints of hope.*

8

Learning to Live Proximately

Having hope is hard;
harder when you get older.

WENDELL BERRY

Wyoming is where the deer and the antelope still play—and
it is home on the range for 500,000 people spread across its
grandeur, stretching as far as the eye can see, and farther.

I remember my first drive from Cheyenne to Chugwater on I-25.
After we left the capital city, we drove north for an hour and all we
saw was a huge sky, miles of grass and thousands of cows. Eventually we saw the sign for Chugwater, a small town of several
hundred in a county full of ranches and farms that are irrigated by
the largest privately owned irrigation system in the country. In the
1800s the Oregon Trail passed through the area, as well as the
Overland Stage Express, the local stop being called Horseshoe Stage
Station. Cattle drives from Texas often made their way along the
Rockies into the vast grasslands of Wyoming, ending along Chugwater Creek. And it became the home ranch for the Swan Land and
Cattle Company, which at one point controlled over three million
acres, about the size of Connecticut.

The Kirkbride family began ranching in Wyoming over a hundred years ago, in the 1880s, and generations later are still at work; raising cattle and caring for their neighbors are written into the meaning of their name. "Salt of the earth" only begins to get at the truth of who they are, but it does say something important about their life. They live by the seasons, with spring bringing longed-for green pastures; summer, a time for long hours at work with the cattle; fall, the gathering together of a long year's work; and yes, the long winter that is Wyoming. *Long* is the word, from beginning to end, year after year.

But that is what matters most in life, for all of us. The *long* obedience in the same direction. Keeping at it. Finding honest happiness in living within the contours of our choices. To wake up another morning, beautifully bright as a summer day spreads its warmth across the grass, or awfully cold as winter blows its way over the high prairie, and stepping into the world again, taking up the work that is ours, the life that is ours, with gladness and singleness of heart, as the Book of Common Prayer teaches us.

Dan Kirkbride was raised in a family of boys. His high school graduating class had sixteen students, all children of ranchers and farmers whose lives and labors were spread across the miles of the southeastern corner the state. A year behind him was Pam, a daughter of a farming family. Early on their hearts were twined together, and before they finished at the University of Wyoming, they were married. The next years were spent in Laramie, working for InterVarsity Christian Fellowship at the university there, and all over Wyoming. And after good years of service there, they packed up their hearts and house to move to Vancouver, British Columbia, where Dan spent a year studying at Regent College.

A surprising school, set on the campus of the University of British Columbia and between the oceans and mountains that make Vancouver a gorgeous city, its raison d'être has always been to draw thoughtful, eager, serious students from every continent into a kind of learning that will send them back into the world with the skills of heart and mind to more truthfully understand their vocations as service to God and history. Some return to their lives as painters and poets, some to the law and medicine, some to business, some to the church, and then a very few to take up the long-practiced family vocation of ranching.

That was the decision of Dan and Pam, now with a little daughter in tow. They settled in Chugwater, and Dan stepped into the saddle, so to speak, along with his father and brothers and their cattle, leaving the very cosmopolitan Vancouver for a very small town set in the long grasses of Wyoming. Soon another daughter came, and their family continued to form, as Kirkbrides had done for many generations. They found their way into a little church in town, one of two. As Dan said, "Well, there were two congregations—and we chose one." Habits of heart formed, long-held hopes in place, they were living into the years of their life together.

But one summer heartbreak came in the diagnosis of cancer in Pam. How could it possibly be? And yet it was, and it began to grow in the horrible way that cancer does, wreaking havoc in her young body. For several years every effort was made to fight it, yearning and traveling, hoping and praying—and yet, and yet, finally she died, leaving Dan with their daughters.

I remember driving along a dirt road with him a year or so later, wanting to talk about it but not sure what to say. These are the hardest moments of life. We know what we want to say, but we stumble over our hearts, not wanting to say anything that will bring more hurt. But I did say something, and I still remember Dan's response. Aching, and yet still committed. Wounded, and yet still sure of what he believed and what it would mean for his life.

By that time he had met Lynn. A mother of three boys, recently widowed herself after having cared for her husband as he suffered the horrors of cancer, they met in a grief-recovery group in Cheyenne. Dan had about given up hope of finding any grace there, until, one shining moment, in came Lynn with a plate full of cream puffs. He smiled, and his smile continues to this day.

They found their way into a surprising love, and finally made their two stories one story, their two families one family—and Chugwater became home for all.

The years came and went, as did the cattle. As must be, Dan's days have been spent caring for his cows, mostly on his own, hours upon hours, season after season. With his trusty dog along as companion, he has given the years of his life to the common good of Chugwater and of Wyoming and beyond, to the countless people and homes that are these United States. There are moments in his year when everyone joins in, the brothers and wives, the nephews and nieces, coming from other parts of the ranch—the bringing in of new cattle, the branding and doctoring, the round-up in the fall—but most of the time he has worked alone, finding his own peace on the prairie.

But life for all of us is complex, because we are complex. And our vocations are complex, because we are complex. *Vocation* has to be a big word, able to handle the whole of life. Spoken and unspoken longings, formal and informal responsibilities, first loves and second and third loves, relationships that matter most and ones that matter, but not quite like that.

Dan was a journalism major when he was in school, and he continues to write, now about the life and history of Wyoming, telling stories about the people and place that make his home "home." Along the way he decided to run for local office, as a county commissioner, taking up the cares of ordinary life for ordinary people. Roads and taxes, schools and hospitals, the stuff that is common to us all, making for a common good. And more recently, that sense of responsibility for people and place has taken him to the state capital, where he now serves as the representative for his part of Wyoming, a part-time work, before returning to the ranch and the rest of the year.

Lynn has long loved those whose needs are most easily forgotten and has given years to helping those with disabilities find their way into the workplaces of Wyoming. As most of life is autobiographical, Lynn's compassions and passions were formed by her brother's quadriplegia. Knowing him, she has loved a world of others, now serving on a national team with this at its heart.

N. T. Wright once wrote about vocation as holding together the most remarkable joy and the most remarkable sorrow.[1] He argued that that was true for the vocation of Jesus, and it will be so for those who follow him. There are few words so true. While unexpected happiness came to Chugwater in the marriage of Dan and Lynn, more heartache did too. One day the hard news came that while they were away from home, their house burned to the ground. Everything was lost—most poignantly every "thing" that had been gifts and reminders of their earlier loves and lives. How could this possibly be? One tragedy is too much, but again?

But they rebuilt their house and reformed their life together. A new house with new memories, a home for the Kirkbrides with a wide porch open to the world—and it has been that as many have come, from all over the face of the earth.

The kids have grown up, and their own callings have taken them far and wide. Several are gifted storytellers whose passions for cities and global health and development have taken them away from the grasslands of Wyoming; others have entered into the health care of their communities, a calling close to heart for Dan and Lynn and their whole family, whose lives have been so deeply affected by life and death. But it is also true that each seems to have a strong sense of home, wherever his or her dwelling is for the moment. With the great losses that have been theirs, they have found an honest happiness together.

There is no sense of great triumph with the Kirkbrides. They have suffered, and that is never far from any conversation—even as they have been surprised by joy in their life together. Early on they learned that childhood dreams do not always work out. Too early their young loves were lost. That is their story, and our stories are ours, similar and yet different. When we find that all that we hope for does not happen, that sometimes the worst things happen, what then? When we discover that our best hopes have been disappointed, what then? Some choose versions of stoicism or cynicism, deciding for very good reasons that "I have had enough."

But then, with surprising grace, some choose to keep at it, hard as it is—and slowly but surely discover different loves that become part of their different lives. Always and everywhere, they do so understanding that they are making peace with the proximate. With something, even if it is not everything. With something rather than nothing. They choose proximate happiness, knowing that a good marriage to a good person is a good gift. They choose proximate mercy for the disabled, knowing that doing something is better than doing nothing. They choose proximate satisfaction in work, knowing that even at our best we will not achieve all that matters to us and to the world. They choose proximate justice in the public squares of Platte County and Wyoming, knowing that some justice is better than no justice. And on and on.

Even if people still die tragic deaths, which in this life will happen; even if people still suffer disabling diseases and accidents, which in this life will happen; even if our good cattle are used for purposes that we do not believe in, which in this life will happen; even if our best hopes for political life are frustrated, which in this life will happen, to enter in with personal passion that longs for systemic change is something, even if everything that might be is still undone.

And so Dan and Lynn have lived their lives, loving each other and each other's children, raising healthy cattle and helping those who cannot help themselves, and standing alongside neighbors in their need for good neighbors. When the day is all done, more still could be done—but that is why we call it living proximately.

Living Our Lives Between the Times

It is so very hard to keep at it, knowing what we know. Even our deepest hopes are hard, because in this now-but-not-yet world we have to live with something less.

Several years ago I had to write an essay on the vocation of politics, and I offered "Making Peace with Proximate Justice." It is an old idea, one that ripples across the centuries, taken up by people who in their own times and places have longed to do what is right, knowing that all that is right will not be and cannot be done. There are few weeks that go by that someone somewhere doesn't talk to me about the essay, even people from very far away. To a person they are people who live in the world. Not fictional and imaginary worlds, but the one that is real. And the world is a hard place to live, but there is nowhere else to live. So if we are going to be honest, we have to live with what is proximate.

How do we do we do that, with any kind of integrity, knowing that there is always more that could be done? More that might have been done? We fall on our faces with a great groan, knowing that too often we fail to do what we believe we ought to do, to do what our hearts demand of us, to do what history requires of us.

It was Augustine of Hippo in the fourth century who first articulated the contours of these questions, so deep in the human heart. Not surprisingly, he has been called "the apostle of longing," understanding that it is our longings that tell the truest truths about us. To know someone is to know their longings, which is to know their loves. That is as true of Dan Kirkbride among his cattle and as it is of him as a county commissioner as it is of him as a father to his children. Our loves are complex, and they require beliefs about God, human nature and history that are rich enough and true enough to make sense of ourselves and the strains of our centuries.

Through the corpus of his writings Augustine argued that human beings are story-shaped people, stretched between what ought to be and what will be. In our imaginings, in our longings, at our best and at our worst, we are people whose identities are formed by a narrative that begins at the beginning and ends at the ending—the story of Scripture itself, of creation, fall, redemption and consummation—and from beginning to end we are torn by the tensions of our humanity, glorious ruins that we are.

Augustine put it this way. At the very beginning of time, human beings were *posse peccare, posse non peccare* (able to sin, able not to sin), then *non posse non peccare* (not able not to sin), then *posse non peccare* (able not to sin), and finally will be *non posse peccare* (not able to sin). Creation, fall, redemption, consummation. It is a long story, and a complex story, and it is our story.[2]

Living our lives between times is the human experience. Deep within us is the hope that it was not always this way, and equally deep is the longing that it will not always be this way. We cry out against the pain and the sorrow, against the injustice and the evil. And with the promise of all things being made new, on the one hand, and the wound of the world felt so painfully in every human heart on the other, we are in poignant conflict over the now-but-not-yet of history. Theological categories they are, and they have spanned the centuries; but that they are and have is because they are lines in the sand for everyone everywhere, stretched taut between what we know we ought to do and what, more often than not, we actually do. There are not cheap answers to this tension. Everyone who takes life seriously knows the reality of this strain. We awaken to it, and we go to sleep with it because it is life for every one of us.

Throughout history good people have tried to make sense of their own moments, socially, culturally, politically, working hard to understand what is possible, given the brokenness of life. Wherever and whenever people live, our deepest questions are always the same. Is it possible to honestly account for the ruin of the human heart and still live with hope? Can we form the habits of heart that allow us to know the world and still love it? Or are we fated to be cynics or stoics? The vision of proximate justice offers the possibility that we can find a way to be honest about the world, and ourselves, without giving in to despair.

Thousands of times in thousands of places people have stepped into history, wanting to change the way the world turns out. More often than not, the world wins—and we find ourselves falling into the wound of knowledge. We know too much, more than we wanted to know. Choosing versions of time-tested philosophies, consciously or not, we protect our hearts from what we know and the consequences of what we know. *They who know the most must mourn the deepest*, one more time.

But sometimes some people still choose to enter in, knowing what they know. Whatever our vocation, it always means making peace with the proximate, with something rather than nothing—in marriage and in family, at work and at worship, at home and in the public square, in our cities and around the world. That is not a cold-hearted calculus; rather it is a choice to live by hope, even when hope is hard.

Not surprisingly, Wendell Berry understands this about life, grounded as he is in the farmland of Kentucky, living within miles of generations of Berrys. Rather than proximate, he offers "partiality," seeing that unless we choose to live with limits, there is no honest happiness. Starkly and plainly, there is no other place to live, for any of us. We are always straining *against* limits, most of the time never content *with* limits—and that is as true for marriages as it is true for work as it is true for politics.

The older love becomes, the more clearly it understands its involvement in partiality, imperfection, suffering, and mortality. Even so, it longs for incarnation. It can live no longer by thinking. And yet to put on flesh and do the flesh's work, it must think.[3]

Our loves and our words have to be made flesh.

The story is true across the whole of life. We live between possibilities, between what ought to be and what will be, between what is and what can be. And always, our longings are complex because our loves are complex because we are complex. From the most public of responsibilities to the most personal of relationships—including marriage—this is true.

Most every year I give a wedding homily for young friends (as I did for Susan and Nate Den Herder, whom I mentioned in chapter 6). The days are always glorious, with months and years of long-held dreams finally incarnate in the family, friends, flowers and food of the very great day. These are always graces to me, and so I take them seriously, wanting to serve the young woman and young man in their celebration of hopes and promises.[4]

My wife, Meg, knows me well, and over time she has persuaded me that I say the same thing each time. Though the context is always different, and the histories and personalities and stories are always different, this is the same: with all the kindness that I can offer, I ask if they will be happy ten or twenty years from this day, if they have found their way to proximate happiness. Or will they require of the perfect day a perfect marriage, born of a perfect love?

In these homilies I have told stories about the coast of California and the mountains of Colorado, and have given them on the Great Lakes of Michigan and in the piedmont of North Carolina, but each time I have set forth a vision of proximate happiness as the worthy aim of a good marriage. It is no longer surprising that those who have been married for a while come to me, making sure I know that those words were just what they needed to hear. Why is that? After the wonders of honeymoon days, life begins, and love takes on a deeper meaning. As the theologian Stanley Hauerwas of Duke University puts it, "We do not fall in love and then get married. We get married and then learn what love requires."[5]

More often than not in my homilies I draw on the poetry of Madeleine L'Engle, hoping that a wiser, older voice can speak into the hearts of these almost-to-be-married folk about what marriage is and is not or, in L'Engle's words, what is required of us for a "long-loved love." As she says so well in one of these poems:

> Because you are not what I would have you be
> I blind myself to who, in truth, you are.
> Seeking mirage where desert blooms, I mar
> Your *you*. Aaah, I would like to see
> Past all delusion to reality:
> Then would I see God's image in your face,
> His hand in yours, and in your eyes His grace.
> Because I am not what I would have me be,
> I idolize Two who are not any place,
> Not you, not me, and so we never touch.
> Reality would burn. I do not like it much.
> And yet in you, in me, I find a trace
> Of love which struggles to break through
> The hidden lovely truth of me, of you.[6]

There have been days when those words have given life again to my marriage. Wounded, hurt, disappointed—or the wounder, the hurter, the disappointer—Meg and I have needed help to find our way back to love. L'Engle's honesty about the deepest longings that are ours is a gift to all, calling us to a touchable, certain, real happiness, if we

have ears to hear. To put it another way, she allows us to remember
that proximate happiness is worthy of our deepest longings.

On our bedroom wall is a reproduction of the painting by Edward
Burne-Jones, a British painter of over a century ago. Artfully capturing the yearnings of love, it portrays a man and a woman holding
onto each other amidst the ruins of a civilization. Simply called
Love Among the Ruins, its wisdom about the human heart speaks
into our life as husband and wife, reminding us that our best hopes
will be a "love among the ruins" of our own frailties.

In a move of over twenty years ago, this painting was the one
item broken. A whole house moved, and when the day was done,
one painting was cracked. My initial response was to restore it, but
over time I began to make peace with its brokenness, with its pic-
turing of proximate happiness in marriage. Years later it still speaks
in silence, and we continue to listen.

LEARNING BY INDWELLING

In my dropped-out years in the early 1970s, I spent a year in a
commune in the Bay Area of California. One of the posters of that
countercultural moment in the sun was of a very hip-looking guy
with exaggerated features walking along and the words "Keep on
keeping on." In its own way the picture was weighted with the
meaning of a generation in transition, no longer wanting what was
and not quite sure what was to come, a poetic and playful charge
to keep at it, wherever your shoes took you.

The words are hard to live by, and harder as we get older. But
some people do. For a thousand reasons known and unknown, they
keep on keeping on. When my parents were in their last years of
life, my father became increasingly sick and was unable to take care
of himself. My mother slowly entered into the vocation of his full-
time caregiver. While on the one hand it was true that she had been
that for the fifty-five years of their marriage, serving each other in

love as they had, the last few years of their life together were very
hard. She watched her friend and companion—a good neighbor to
people near and far and a good scientist, whose work rippled across
the country and around the world—become more and more disabled, almost completely dependent on her to care for him.

As we would talk on the phone across the country, with her in
California and me in Virginia, I would regularly ask, "Do you still
want to do this, Mom?" And again and again she said to me, very
simply, "It's hard to do this—but I want to do this. In fact, I'm glad
to do this." My father died the year of their sixtieth anniversary, in
their home, with my mother by his side. The last years were a long
ways from the hope and glory of their wedding day in Greeley, Colorado, at the end of World War II, at a time in their young lives
when the whole world seemed open before them. Promises made
in hope, words from the deepest places of the heart and a life to be
lived together—having no idea what the years would bring to them:
moving for study to Michigan, and back to Colorado, and then to
California, and then a decision with lifelong consequence to stay in
California after my father's studies were done. Along the way, they
had four sons, whose lives would become stories with unimagined
complexity, with the happiest of realized hopes alongside the crush
of disappointments. It could not be otherwise: we are a family like
every family, a normal family in an abnormal world.

Theirs was a long story of joys and sorrows, like human beings
in every time and place. We choose and then live, not knowing
what our choices will mean over the course of our lives. And the
deeper truth is that none of us know what the next day will bring.
We cannot know anything from the outside, in abstraction. In marriage, in work, in politics, from moving into a neighborhood to
visiting a new city or country somewhere in the world, we do not
know until we do. Across the whole of life, it is only as we step in
that we understand what we believe and what we love; it is only as

we begin to live into that that we understand what our beliefs and loves will require of us. Words always have to be made flesh if we are going to understand them.

True as this is, it is a hard truth to come by. In the waywardness of our hearts, we resist it, wanting ideas to simply be ideas, beliefs to simply be beliefs. We allow ourselves theories that have nothing to do with practice, in our lives or the rest of the world. In the yearning of my late-adolescent heart, wanting intellectual coherence as I had never imagined possible, I dropped out of college in hopes that I might find what I was looking for. It was then that I first began reading Michael Polanyi, whose seminal work *Personal Knowledge,* on the integral relationship of knowing to doing, of belief to behavior, recast the paradigm for those with ears to hear. Some of my teachers were reading him, and with my deepening criticism of the Enlightenment Project, I was drawn to his unusual story.[7]

Who was he? And why does his work matter here? Born into a Jewish family in Budapest, he was unusually gifted in the sciences, and by the time he was in his thirties he had moved to Berlin and was working in the same institute where Albert Einstein worked. By the middle of that decade, as Germany was becoming increasingly hostile to Jews, both men left, Einstein heading to the United States and Polanyi to the United Kingdom.

The next years were very hard for anyone who cared about life—we call it "the Holocaust," after all. Polanyi kept at his laboratory research, and those who watched carefully were sure that his insights would lead him to a Nobel Prize in chemistry. But by the time the war ended, his questions had changed. No longer was he most fascinated by chemical compounds; another question dominated everything else: how dare we call ourselves *enlightened?*

It was a surprising question, perhaps, for a child of the Enlightenment, especially for someone like Polanyi whose work was focused on understanding the nature of science and its chemical reality, a "project," so to speak, at the very heart of the modern world. But having lived through two world wars in his relatively young life, he was horrified that Europeans dared see themselves as "enlightened," as somehow more morally and intellectually mature than previous generations. Those who brought us into cultural chaos through the devastation of war had "gone to the best universities we have," he lamented.

How is it possible that someone could be brilliant and bad at the same time? For the rest of his life, Polanyi pursued that question. After several years of reflection, in 1951 he presented the prestigious Gifford Lectures at the University of Edinburgh, a series that became his magnum opus, *Personal Knowledge: Towards a Post-Critical Philosophy*. At its heart a critique of the Enlightenment Project and its epistemological hubris, the book calls into fundamental question the Cartesian dualism of objective and subjective knowledge, the split between facts and values. Polanyi was convinced that his own experience as a research scientist proved that so-called objective analysis was just that. As he put it, colloquially, the viewer is always viewing. The scientist does not leave himself at the door of the laboratory, Polanyi argued; in truth, he cannot.

For Polanyi, "personal knowledge" did not mean subjectivity, but something more deeply and profoundly human. Leaving behind the philosophically flawed assumptions of the Enlightenment, he began to think through a more truthful account of human knowing, one that honored the best of the scientific method but was more intellectually honest about its limitations.

One of his simple stories gets at this with unusually common wisdom. He offered his readers a little girl who has recently mastered the art of bicycle riding. Does she know how to ride a bike? Does she really know? "Of course I know how to ride a bike!" she insists, sure the questioner must be slow to not understand that "everyone knows how to ride a bike!" Pressing into the story, Polanyi asks a brilliant physicist to enter the conversation. Requesting that the scientist summarize the physics of bicycle riding on a page, the little girl is then given the paper: "Here is what someone must know to know how to ride a bike." Befuddled at the complexity of the numbers and letters, the little girl responds, "I don't know about this, but I *do* know how to ride my bike!" Polanyi asks: Which one is the more certain, the girl or the physicist? His point, and the argument of "personal knowledge," is that they know in different ways, and each is properly certain of their knowledge. The so-called subjective knowledge of the one is not less certain than the so-called objective knowledge of the other; each has a proper confidence.[8]

His work is remarkably rich, and worthy of more attention by those who understand the flaws of the Enlightenment Project—and perhaps even more so by those who do not, who still believe in its promise. Central to Polanyi's insight is that we only truly learn when we indwell what we want to learn. We cannot understand anything that matters standing on the outside looking in, whether bicycle riding or marriage or social histories with seemingly intractable complexity. It is only when we step in that we begin to know— and to see what love will ask of us.

Sometimes, though, love asks more of us than we are able to give, more than we imagine. As much as we see that "stepping in" is right, it is in indwelling our loves and longings that we understand them. We do not know until we do.

If Gary Haugen has become iconic for a certain kind of young person who is passionate about doing right in the world, calling a whole generation to join him in his International Justice Mission, it is important to remember that he too had to start—and he started very small. Initially it was just him, back from seeing the aftermath of Rwanda's genocide, talking with some trusted friends about what might be done. He had an intern with him that spring, one of my students, Kristin Romens.

When she finished her internship and study, she took up Gary's offer to join him in his new vision, spending the summer working with him to create an organization. Their very first project was in India and was focused on bonded slavery. Another recent graduate of the American Studies Program, Daryl Kreml, joined her, and together they went off to a village in India, hoping that justice might be done.

Over a few weeks they found hundreds of children in bonded slavery, working twelve-hour days under a taskmaster who treated them with mean-hearted indifference. All he cared about was their production of little cigarettes that would be sold in boutiques in the West, in places like Boston and San Francisco. With their laptops and cameras, Kristin and Daryl recorded the reality for their day in court. There is more to the story, and it is strange, true and wonderful, but in the end, hundreds of children were released. For twenty-two-year-olds, it was just about as good as it gets. Not shuffling papers in a cubicle-filled office building, but on the ground, flesh pressing flesh, doing justice and loving mercy.

And yet, and yet. I still remember the afternoon that Kristin came into my office a few weeks later in tears, still overwhelmed by all that she had seen and smelled. I was not surprised. She who knows the most mourns the deepest.

We talked that day, and more days to come, about getting "back on the horse" and trying again. Always bright, always motivated, always able, she took it all in with her characteristic seriousness of heart and decided to go to South Africa for a half year. A different place and different people, but she was determined to enter again into the complexity of the world, for love's sake taking responsibility for history—even bruised a bit as she was. That decision became another decision and then another, and over time Kristin's experience in India became a vocation in the world of the law, spending her life working out what she began as a just-out-of-college young woman.

At the end of the day, it was "only" a village with its many children. The aching reality is that much of India still suffers from the same injustice. But someone stepped in, something happened, and that was better than nothing. Hundreds of children were released from slavery, and their slave master was imprisoned. Proximate justice was done, and the International Justice Mission was born.

OF DICKENS, MARX AND KARMA TOO

Over the years I have watched a generation of young men and women take up their lives in the world. Some stay close over the years of life, and others go. But in different ways I have loved them all, longing for their flourishing.

My children take their own place among those I love. Through their adolescence and young adulthood they have each spent months and years around the world—Kenya, Romania, Switzerland, Costa Rica, Mozambique, Australia, China, England, Liberia, the Dominican Republic, Uganda, Guam, Egypt, Haiti and more— learning about its wonder and complexity and finding their own places in it along the way. Two have spent time in India, and at Christmas one year we went to see them. It is a beautiful country with millions upon millions of people and terribly complex. We did not see everything. But we did travel through the south, in Tamil Nadu and Kerala, and in our seeing and hearing and smelling were keenly aware that we were in a very different world.

For the week we were in Kerala, which is the state in the south-western corner of India, we spent days at the beach and in the mountains, and it was mostly glorious. Like all of the world, in the course of minutes and miles, there is both great beauty and great suffering, and though the particulars are unique along the Arabian Sea of India with its gorgeous coast next door to aching poverty, the same is true of Washington, D.C., with its monumental glory alongside its alienated underclass. Kerala has a long history: Hindu for thousands of years and then, since the first century A.D. through the witness of the apostle Thomas and the church that now bears his name, a lively Christian presence is part of the religious mix as well. More recently Kerala bears the imprint of Marx and Mao; some argue that Kerala has the first democratically elected communist government in the world. So in one small part of a complex society, there are competing ideas about what the world is and how we live in it, each vision a version of human flourishing, each one hoping to answer the long questions of the human heart.

Driving its roads, I was reading *A Christmas Carol,* a strange book for India, perhaps, but in truth a story for Everyman and Everywoman, especially so at Christmas. And as we went along the roads and streets of towns small and large, I looked up from my reading and saw signs with the sickle and hammer celebrating the communist vision, mostly banners in their characteristic red and gold colors. The sickle and hammer are iconic symbols of the ordinary work of our hands. Yes, ordinary work done by ordinary people all over the face of the earth. Everyone, every son of Adam and daughter of Eve, hopes against hope that our work really does matter.

The banners were themselves a debate between the Marxist and Maoist visions of human life, road by road, neighborhood by neighborhood almost competing over the two different accounts of the communist dream. Tragically, the reality was a *very* bad dream for people, for the hoi polloi of every city and country, resulting in the state-sponsored massacre of millions—whether in Russia, China or any one of the many places where communism ordered and disordered human life. And yet, for all they got wrong, horribly wrong, what they got right was that our work has historical consequence— a strange brew of eschatological hope embedded in a materialist universe. They promised that the work of human hands is written into the meaning of history, that there will be a new world someday that comes out of the ruins of our daily labor, of the sickles and hammers of ordinary people in ordinary places. We saw the literal truth of this while we drove through Kerala, passing people along the way with both sickles and hammers in hand, at work in the shops and fields.

Sickles, hammers and *A Christmas Carol*? One of the surprising notes of history is that Dickens and Marx were writing at the same time in the same city about the same thing: the consequences of capitalism without a conscience. We know Dickens' vision through the narrative universe he created in stories like *Oliver Twist, David Copperfield, Hard Times, Great Expectations* and, most dearly of all, *A Christmas Carol.* But as tender and prized as it is, most have never thought about the cultural context of the story itself and asked, What is its relationship to *Das Kapital,* Marx's magnum opus? And why were they writing together about the same thing?

Both Dickens and Marx observed the groaning and suffering of an industrializing Europe, the dissonance between the Scrooges and the Tiny Tims of this world. Both could see that capitalism without a conscience was a cultural dead-end that would lead the masses into alienation from each other and the world around them. The one did so as an artist, with his finger to the wind, artfully feeling the direction of his moment, the spirit of the age of mid-nineteenth-century England; the other did so as a political philosopher, with his brilliant mind at work on the social and economic reasons for the cracks in the capitalist dream that led to such alienation.

To say it very plainly, over the next century and a half, scores of millions lost their lives because of the misreading of the human condition and history at the heart of Marx's critique, and the world as we know it has been radically and wretchedly affected by his misunderstanding the nature of vocation and therefore occupation, of what life is about and therefore what our lives are about. In the early twenty-first century, there is almost global acknowledgment of this truth.[9]

But when I was twenty, that was not yet clear, and in my own late-adolescent longings I thought that Marx was close to the truth. He had a passionate commitment to a just world; at least it seemed so to me in my young idealism. He had a comprehensive critique of the world, and of our place in it, and I desperately wanted that too. But as tempted as I was by him, eventually I was drawn even more into another vision of the way the world should be—that of the kingdom of God. When push came to intellectual shove, the Christian vision for the way life ought to be answered my questions and addressed my hopes more fully than did Marx's—and it still does, more than ever.

Like everyone, I wanted a way to see the world that made honest sense of it. I yearned for the world to be the way it was meant to be, and I knew that I needed a worldview that could make sense of what I saw and heard all around me, a way of seeing that could help me understand the hopes and heartaches of human beings that were increasingly part of my pluralizing, globalizing world. In the end, Marx and Mao were inadequate for that; their visions were lies of the most fundamental sort, offering a fiction about who we are and how we are to live. But if those visions are untrue, then what is true? Who are we, and how are we to live?

These questions are not small, and the answers are even harder. The same week that I read *A Christmas Carol* one more time, I read the novel *A Fine Balance* by Rohinton Mistry. One of the finest storytellers writing about modern India, Mistry, like Polanyi, believes that one cannot stand on the outside and understand. Therefore he writes, "Walk, first, through the fire, then philosophize."[10] His novels are intricate and complex, drawing the reader into history and politics, sociology and economics, framed by the spoken and unspoken assumptions of karma.

Mistry was my companion before and after Dickens. A compelling story, even if an awfully sad story, it is the tale of two boys, a student and a widow who form a common life—hopes and sorrows, justice and injustice, embodied in the lives of these few people who are finally unable to imagine any meaningful change in the world that is theirs. In the end things will be as they will be; karma is karma. It is a stark contrast to Dickens on this point, where transformation is possible though hard won, where the Scrooges of this world can decide to change their life and the lives of those around them. What makes the difference?

On the last day of our travel in India, I asked a question of my son Elliott, who was there for the year, on a National Institutes of Health fellowship, studying the public health consequences of humans and cows drinking from the same water sources. Day by day we had seen much that was beautiful and much that was burdensome. Driving along we saw hospials often, and I noticed in passing that each hospital had a Christian symbol of some sort: sometimes named "St. George's," sometimes marked with a red cross, but each with a noticeably Christian history. I did not comment on it, and only at the end did I begin to connect the dots, finally asking Elliot, "Does Hindu culture produce hospitals?" I had my own thoughts about it, having studied pantheism of various kinds for many years, but I wondered what he thought after living there for some time. He said, "Not really. The view of karma is so strong. Everyone has their own karma to deal with, and one person isn't responsible for another person's karma." He went on to gracefully acknowledge kindness among Hindu people and the acts of generosity that he had seen in his months there. His observation about the meaning of karma and Hindu culture was nuanced, as it must be. Knowing that he had been a student of their culture in ways that I had not, and especially that he was there in a hospital setting in Vellore studying the etiology of disease—for him, the word is *zoonotics*, the phenomenon of human health meeting animal health meeting environmental health—I listened carefully, honoring his own decision to step into the complexity of a people and a place.

As I listened, I thought about the moral vision of *A Fine Balance* and the story it tells of human life, pondering its argument about what is and what is possible. No honest person debates the morass of misery all over the face of the earth. People cry out in their distress, in cities small and large, from circumstances of all kinds. If we have eyes that see, we know that people suffer for thousands of reasons, most of them incredibly and complicatedly related, with physiology and politics, economics and geography, metaphysics and morality all playing into the story.

What people differ over is the way we answer the question, *What do you do then?* Writing as a nineteenth-century Englishman with assumptions about hope and history formed by the Christian tradition, Dickens offers a way of knowing that leads to doing, that gives human beings a way to step into history. Mistry does not, because he cannot. They are not simply different people telling different stories; in reality they represent alternative accounts of the universe, and therefore of history and the human condition. Berry is right: there is "a greater economy," a covenantal cosmos where revelation, relationships and responsibilities shape each other, creating the conditions for human flourishing.[11] Mistry's karma cannot account for that. Differences do make a difference.

Love Interrupts

The rock icon Bono sees this as clearly as anyone. With his global glasses he watches the world, some days basking in its glory, some days immersed in its sorrow. While filling arenas on every continent with hundreds of thousands of fans, he has also stepped into the complexity of the HIV/AIDS crisis with remarkable passion and perseverance. When he speaks, presidents and prime ministers listen, and when he sings, the world sings too.

Poetically, he has written that it is grace that "makes beauty out of ugly things," because it is "more than karma, karma." On stages everywhere he has sung that song, simply calling it "Grace," and if we have ears to hear, we hear.[12] Asked by the French journalist Michka Assayas, "What do you mean by grace, and why is it different than karma?" Bono responded with surprising clarity, "The thing that keeps me on my knees is the difference between Grace and Karma." He continues, after being asked to say more,

> You see, at the center of all religions is the idea of Karma. You know, what you put out comes back to you: an eye for an eye, a tooth for a tooth, or in physics—in physical laws—every action is met by an equal or an opposite one. It's clear to me that Karma is at the heart of the universe. I'm absolutely sure of it. And yet along comes this idea of Grace to upend all that. . . . Love interrupts, if you like, the consequences of your actions, which in my case is very good news indeed, because I've done a lot of stupid stuff.[13]

Bono sees something profoundly true, even through a glass darkly. There are differences, and sometimes they matter, lines in the sand of life that they are. Not only is karma at the center of Eastern mysticism, but it is at the very core of Western materialism, *homo religiosus* that we are as human beings. We will worship something, making something or someone the cohering center of the cosmos. To explain his own life to himself, Bono needs something more than karma. To choose responsibility born of love, as he has, requires an alternative vision to karma; in fact karma cancels it out—and it is why Hindu culture does not produce hospitals.

To press the point, Bono's critique addresses visions of life in the materialist West as well as the pantheistic East. Evolutionary materialism teaches that we are first and last our DNA, nothing more, nothing less. The contemporary sociobiologist E. O. Wilson of Harvard has written widely in defense of this thesis, not unlike another Harvard professor of a previous generation, B. F. Skinner. Each a brilliant researcher with unique abilities to popularize their science—the one has spent his career on ants as did the other on rats—they have argued that we should learn from the little things of the world, and realize that we are "beyond freedom and dignity" in Skinner's inimitable phrasing.[14] To say it plainly, ideas like responsibility and accountability, meaning and purpose, are fictions (remembering the insight and argument of Havel). They are not true of ants or rats, and they are not true of the human species either. We are determined by the cause-effect nature of the universe, by our DNA, profoundly and with complexity—but not more and not less—and therefore we are metaphysically and morally stuck in moments that we cannot get out of, to paraphrase Bono one more time.

But are we? Is that it? Are we simply stuck? Some of us commit to and conclude with the philosophical determinism of the best of the East or the West, karmas of various kinds as they are; and there is a necessary resignation that comes with that. *Things are as they are, and we can do nothing about it.* And sometimes our pop-culture icons make millions celebrating this "stuckness" in anthems like "Born This Way" by Lady Gaga, celebrating in song the attitude that we are what we are and that's it. At our worst and in our wounds, we resist responsibility, the ability to respond. We feel the painful tension of knowing what is and what ought to be, and we cannot bear it—and we prefer being acted upon, sadly, rather than being actors. Sometimes the victimizer is another person, sometimes an institution or organization, and sometime the forces of nature, but in the end we are stuck—and we cannot get out.

For years now I have lingered over the words of a Hindu scholar to his lifelong friend Lesslie Newbigin, the bishop of the Church of South India and author of many important books, among them *The*

Gospel in a Pluralist Society. One day the Indian, the Hindu scholar, said to the European, Newbigin, something like, "I have finally read your holy book, the Bible, and it is a completely unique book. It is unique in its vision of history, setting forth a meaningful story from beginning to end, and it is unique in its vision of the human person as a responsible actor in history. The two go together."[15] In my first reading of those words, I remember chills running down my spine, thinking that the Hindu had seen so clearly, so profoundly something that most miss. To see that the way we view history shapes the way we view the human condition—and, importantly, the reverse is also true—is an astounding insight, with far-reaching implications for Hindus, for Marxists, for materialists, for Christians, for human beings wherever they are found.

At the end of the day, we have to choose a way of living that makes sense of life. I have looked the world over, even hitchhiking through some of it years ago, listening to people from every tribe and tradition. From what I have seen, I am sure of this: the vision of the "proximate" tethers us to the world that we all really live in. Wanting otherwise as we might, there is no other world in which we can be at home. To have good lives, we cannot spend much of life talking about utopian fantasies, about "wouldn't it be nice?" worlds. In the end they are fictions, false fictions, and therefore have very disappointing ends.

As anecdotal as he was in his narrative examination of London in the middle years of the nineteenth century, Dickens offered two stories that come into cultural conflict, that of Scrooge and Tiny Tim. Not social abstractions, as Marx was content to offer, but identifiable human beings with histories and personalities. By directing our attention to one businessman and one child, we are invited into a deeper reflection on the greater issues at stake, systemic as they were—and eerily, the very ones at the core of Marx's *Das Kapital* and the communist revolution over the next century, which sought to remake the world, socially, politically, economically.

Dickens captures us with his story of *A Christmas Carol*. It is one of the great stories, and therefore is told all over the world, year after year. It is about Christmas, after all, and it satisfies our deepest longings—that hope and kindness win. But as wonderful as it is, it is not anything other than a story about the world that we all still live in, one where we must be content with a proximate answer to our deepest longings. When morning finally comes, not all the capitalists and not all the children were reborn; something happened, but not everything. People still lived with injustice and indifference, in England and all over the world. Human beings still suffered and still groaned, living between what is and what one day will be, as we must.

Marx's new world it was not, nor was it the consummation of all things finally made right and well in the Christian story that Newbigin offered to the Hindu scholar—but one businessman began to see himself responsible, for love's sake, for the lives of those he knew. And his community began to change as he changed. *Knowledge* means *responsibility*, and *responsibility* means *care*. And two centuries later we are still listening to Scrooge call out his window, "It's Christmas Day! I haven't missed it!" and ordering a prize turkey for the neglected Cratchit family. We are still listening to Tiny Tim too, in his incomparable voice whispering a benediction of hope for all, "And God bless us everyone!"

The heart of the story is that an ordinary man with an ordinary life saw himself implicated in and through his vocation, and chose to do what he could. Through the slow *revelation* of the three spirits through the terrible hours of the night, Scrooge began to know as he had never known, and chose to enter into the history of his own time and place with his new sense of *relationship* to those around him shaping his sense of *responsibility* to them.[16] Not only did he offer the prize turkey to the Cratchits, an honest act of charity, but he changed the way he did business, beginning to account for justice and mercy in the business of business itself, beginning with a fair wage for his employee, Bob Cratchit. Dickens sums it up, "He became as good a friend, as good a master, and as good a man as the good old city knew, or any other good old city, town, or borough, in the good old world."

Love interrupts—and Ebenezer Scrooge's vision of vocation began to change. Knowing what he now knew, for love's sake he chose to be responsible for the way the world turned out.

COMMON GRACE FOR THE COMMON GOOD

We began in Beijing with the terrors of Tiananmen that became an address to the filmmakers of China years later. And over many pages many stories have been told of men and women who have eyes that see, understanding something of their responsibility for history. But in the end the question is played out on the streets of every city in every society: *Knowing what I know, what am I going to do?*

To learn to see oneself as implicated is the most difficult task of all—especially if it is a responsibility born of love. Duty only takes us so far; at some point we must delight in what is ours, in the relationships and responsibilities that are ours. It is duty and desire together that make for a good life, not only knowing what I should do, but wanting to do what I should do.

But how do we work this out? What does it look like in life? Simply said, it is in and through our vocations, committed to the common good—with gladness and singleness of heart—where this becomes real.

None of us are islands, despite the best attempts of some to argue otherwise. We are *we,* human beings together. Born into family histories, growing up into social histories, we live our lives among others, locally and globally, neighbors very near and neighbors very far. Context may not be everything, but it is true for everyone. Every story is a story of someone contextualized, of individuals and institutions, of persons within polities. Our relationships and responsibilities are always within this world of *both*; there is no other world to live in. Our lives, then, are always a tale of two realities, of men and women on the one hand, and of the world on the other: human beings in the worlds of education and the arts, in international development and human rights, in agriculture and craftsmanship, in health care and law, in business and banking, in politics and church, in marriages and families, in cities and societies. We are selves, but we are also situated within structures. That is our life.

It is Clydette Powell *and* USAID, with African politics to add to the complexity; it is Dan Kirkbride *and* his cows and community, with economics, politics and history thrown in, together making his life both very local and very national. And everyone whose story has been told is always one more story of people *and* the world. Twined together, our lives are always a story of both.

My neighbors and friends are another version of the same story. We meet at the neighborhood coffee shop, listening to each other's lives, hoping for each other's children, longing for all to be made well even as we feel the pain of so much that simply is not the way it is supposed to be, in our souls but also in our society. But every day we also live within the realities of organizations and institutions that shape our lives, called to responsibly love our neighbor in the context of the complexity of their lives. This is the way it is for everyone everywhere, including the people we have come to know on the pages of this book.

The question that came from the Chinese students was this: We have seen the worst of our nation, and we still love our nation—is there a hope that can take us into the future? We may be imprisoned, we may die, but we love China and want more than anything to be part of its renewal, to give our lives for its future.

Can we talk to you about this? Can you help us?

What do we say that is not cheap? It is one thing to hope for one's own flourishing; it is something else altogether to hope for one's nation to flourish. There is no more difficult task, holding onto individual and institutional responsibility for the way the world turns out—knowing the worst of the human heart and the corporate embodiment of that heart and still choosing to be responsible, for love's sake. But that task is ours. In our social and political situations, in our families and neighborhoods, we are called to form habits of heart that keep our loves alive, where duty becomes delight, where what we know becomes what we love—even in this terribly complex world, full of wonder and wounds as it is.

Can we? Is it possible? The challenge of the information age makes it seem almost impossible to imagine that we can do anything other than become numb. *We know too much.* The weight of "whatever" bears down on all of us, making us wonder if anything is real and true and right. *No one really knows.*

But the Hebrew vision that echoes across centuries and through cultures offers a different way to be human, where knowing becomes doing. And the Christian vision incarnates this conviction, telling the story of the Word becoming flesh, and of words becoming flesh in and though our vocations. This vision calls us to know and to care about what we know; in fact to love what we know. And strange grace that it is, it becomes possible to know without becoming disillusioned, to know the worst and to still love—not only people but the world in which we live. We will never do that perfectly, only proximately, at our very best. But in this now-but-not-yet moment in history, that is enough.

At the end of the day, not every Scrooge will have eyes that see. That some do is a gift, *a common grace for the common good.*

Epilogue

But Are You Happy?

What was the sense in saying that the enemy were in
the wrong unless Right is a real thing which the Nazis at
bottom knew as well as we did and ought to be have practiced?
If they had no notion of what we mean by right, then,
though we may still have had to fight them, we
could no more have blamed them for that
than for the colour of their hair.

C. S. LEWIS, "RIGHT AND WRONG AS A
CLUE TO THE MEANING OF THE UNIVERSE"

*M*y father was a scientist. For more than fifty years his vocation took him into laboratories, ones housed in universities and
ones in farms and fields. In fact, I was born in a high mountain
valley in Colorado where he directed the research for Colorado
State University on sheep and potatoes. Years later my mother told
me she was worried that her spring baby would have to compete
with the spring lambs for my father's attention when the day and
the hour finally came for my birth. In the end, we all came out well.

Our family moved to California when I was a little boy so my father could pursue more study, and I grew up within the world of the University of California, following my father as he worked to understand and care for California's cotton. When I was still a boy, we moved into the San Joaquin Valley, and the little community of Shafter, where the university had a research center. About twenty-five scientists in various disciplines worked together, all connected to the flourishing of California agriculture: plant physiologists, irrigation specialists, plant breeders, entomologists and plant pathologists, which was my father's work. I watered plants in his greenhouses, met his colleagues and assumed that, like sons have since time immemorial, I would follow him into his work, his vocation becoming my vocation.

That lasted until my freshman year in high school, when I took my first biology course. While I had access to test tubes of gross fungi which brought dismay to my classmates—not a small thing for a fourteen-year-old—the classwork itself did not capture me. I liked the teacher and knew that the material mattered, but I simply was not drawn in as I thought I would be, the son of a scientist that I was.

My questions were different and my passions were my own. I played football and swam, but by high school's end it was writing that had caught me. I started school in California, expecting the life of a journalist. But one day I read these words in a journalism quarterly, "The media today not only needs those that have the ability to communicate, but it needs those that have something to communicate." By the day's end, I decided to find a way to learn to learn about things that mattered.

I drove across the country in a Volkswagen bug and tried school again in a different place with different people. But after another year of wondering about the relationship between learning and life, I dropped out, returned to California and moved into a commune in Palo Alto. It was the high moment of the counterculture, and to a twenty-year-old it seemed like everything was important and possible—especially revolution. We could change the world!

I listened in for a year, hitchhiking back and forth between Palo Alto and Berkeley, hoping to find a better reason to learn and to live. The following year, I was in Europe with a backpack and a Frisbee, and one day I spent hours in the Tate Gallery in London. The work of the twentieth-century British painter Francis Bacon drew me in.

Though I have been a lover of the grandeur of skies and mountains and oceans my whole life, at age twenty I was beginning to understand that all of life was not glory—in sad fact, that much of it was awful, that there was much unhappiness in human hearts, and that superficial responses only aggravated the problem. The soul-wrenching canvases of Bacon captured that reality as well as anything I had seen.[1] If centuries ago a Hebrew poet wrote, "Out of the depths I cry unto thee" (Psalm 130:1 KJV), then Bacon was painting that anguish for my generation—but for Bacon there was no "thee" to cry out to, only the silence of the universe.

FROM INSTAURATION TO ALIENATION

My searching led me to months of reading in philosophical and theological anthropology, wondering, *What does it mean to be a human being? Who are we? How are we to live?* I was surprised to find that all over Europe—in England, Scotland, Ireland, France and Switzerland—I met people who gracefully opened their hearts to me, listening for hours to my questions. Often inarticulate and faltering, and yet bursting beyond all known boundaries, over the years these have become the questions of my life.

When I came back to the States and once again entered into my college's curriculum, I knew what I wanted to learn and began to work away at it. Among courses that caught me were ones in the history and philosophy of science. By then I knew that I was not going to be my father; his calling was his, and mine would be different. If the details of botany and biology fascinated him, the philosophers of science energized me. I wanted to understand the Enlightenment and the ways its vision of the human task had shaped my culture and century. Like the questions about the human condition, those ideas and issues still thread their way through my vocation.

In the fall of my senior year, I began to read Theodore Roszak, whose analysis of the 1960s, *The Making of a Counter Culture*, was seminal. With rare insight he understood the seismic shift that had taken place, even as the tremors were still rumbling through Europe and the United States. But it was his next book, *Where the Wasteland Ends*, that opened my eyes to the knife's-edge character of the modern world.[2] The "wasteland" was T. S. Eliot's image, of course, but Roszak's critique began centuries earlier; in particular, he argued that another and earlier Francis Bacon[3] had set in motion a way of understanding the world and living in it that over time had devastating consequences for human beings. It was named, presumptuously, the Enlightenment, and centuries later we look back on it as the Enlightenment Project. It offered a new way of seeing the world, a new way of understanding our place in the world.

The more I read, the more intrigued I was, and slowly, slowly I imagined a senior honors thesis comparing the two Bacons. I called it "From Instauration to Alienation" in which I attempted to make a connection between the world imagined by the first Bacon and the one painted by the second.

Those years were for me ones of visions and dreams of the way the world ought to be. Ideas mattered—and of course they still do. So the grand scale of Roszak's assessment drew me in as he was seeing the "ideas have legs" character of human life that was just becoming clear to me. Listening to William Blake's poetic lament of the industrializing world, Roszak pointed the finger at Bacon, ar-

guing that his *Novum Organon* was the culprit, that Bacon's commitment to "knowledge is power" had run rampant through the
Enlightenment era, ruining our world. What did he mean? What
could Bacon have said or done to deserve that judgment?

Central to his commitment was the belief that observation was
a philosophically neutral task, so that the "new knowing" implicit
in his Great Instauration could be done by anyone, regardless of
creed or culture. What was required was training in the discipline
of observation of facts—as they are and always will be. Summing
up his vision, his final words are these:

> And all depends on keeping the eye steadily fixed upon the
> facts of nature and so receiving their images simply as they
> are. For God forbid that we should give out a dream of our
> own imagination for a pattern of the world; rather may he
> graciously grant to us to write an apocalypse or true vision of
> the footsteps of the Creator imprinted on his creatures.[4]

There is so much in Bacon's vision that is profound and hon-
orable, and one would have to have a pejorative impulse to read
Bacon as anything less than that. His ambition was a good one,
wanting to honor God and serve the world through his labor. In the
years that followed, even those who disagreed with the theological
character of his commitments praised him as "founding father of
the modern era" (the French encyclopedist Denis Diderot), "ar-
chitect of modernity" (Kant) and "the father of experimental philosophy" (Voltaire).

What was it, then, that Roszak saw? The question itself is intriguing, as it is its own window into the problem of Bacon's understanding of "the promis'd land." Always and everywhere, we see out
of our hearts, and what we see and hear in the world around us
depends upon our beliefs about the world. As Polanyi argued so
perceptively centuries later, the viewer is always viewing, the

human being is always interpreting what is being seen in light of beliefs and commitments about reality; and so the most honest account of knowing acknowledges its deeply personal character.[5]

While Bacon was rightly concerned with the vanities of his day, and the way that they had compromised a truer learning and the possibility of exploring and understanding the world, his hope was based upon an epistemological fallacy: that it is possible to "see" unencumbered by one's history, culture, commitments and beliefs—in Bacon's language, "simply as they are." That kind of philosophical neutrality about the nature and meaning of life does not exist; it never has and it never will. How we in fact respond to Bacon is indicative of this reality, because our seeing is never neutral.

In Roszak's *Where the Wasteland Ends,* one image in particular was chilling to me. Roszak characterized the Baconian vision with the words "through a dead man's eyes."[6] For Bacon, and the Enlightenment tradition, which his work in part birthed, one's brain, one's heart, one's being, were "neutral," the "facts" were simply facts, to be seen as "through a dead man's eyes"—*simply as they are.* In their own terms, of course, the Enlightenment meant to set knowledge "free" from the distempers of the past, allowing for a truer knowing based upon a method of observation that would lead to certainty. All would agree, because all would see fact as "fact."

I must confess that my paper was evidence of a late-adolescent willingness to see things as more black and white than they truly are, and with my countercultural sympathies in place as well, I sided with the critique of Bacon, seeing him through Roszak's eyes—no dead man's eyes there, of course, as Roszak had an opinion and argued it persuasively and pejoratively. I wanted a villain, even an arch-villain, and Bacon would do.

With the very broad brushstrokes I was content with at the time, it seemed not so strange to draw a line between the seventeenth century and the twentieth, asking about the relation between "instauration and alienation." There was a certain ironic providence too—two Francis Bacons, after all. But it was very serious business to me and it consumed my final year in college.

I had been introduced to Bacon the painter in my humanities course, an interdisciplinary curriculum over four semesters that attempted to weave together history, art, philosophy, literature and theology into a framework for understanding the world. But it was not until I dropped out of college and in my "extra-curricular" years of undergraduate study when I read Hans Rookmaaker's *Modern Art and the Death of a Culture,* with Bacon's famous scream of Pope Innocent IX on its cover, "Head IV," that I began to see its importance. So, when I was in London, I went to the Tate, wanting to see Bacon's paintings for myself.

Having read some of the existentialist writers whose work was shaping the counterculture, I was aware of what one writer called "the striptease of humanism."[7] The hopes and dreams of the Enlightenment were dimming. One of my professors had given a brilliant lecture in the humanities course on the dashed promise of progress that Europe and the West experienced with the first World War, and then twenty years later, compounded by the second, told from the perspective of a British soldier. I still feel the chills that came to me at the end of class as I sat there contemplating what he must have felt. We were not getting "better and better" as the Enlightenment tradition had predicted when we were finally freed from the dogmas of faith. The war to end all wars didn't.

THE ARTISTS GET THERE FIRST

The artists, as always, felt it first. And so to the poets and painters, filmmakers and novelists I went, listening, looking, learning. But history is a complex story, and there is no one way into understanding a generation or century. A moment in time is part economic, part sociological, part political, part philosophical, part military, part theological—and always, in part artistic.

It was the profound despair of Sartre that intrigued me. What was he seeing about human life that made everything seem so bleak? At the essence of my being, simply, sadly, "nothingness"? NO EXIT written apocalyptically across the future? What was the anguish that made Camus write so searchingly about suffering and God, about human beings and responsibility, to conclude his questions with such futility? Was it really as harsh as Beckett saw it? We are born—and we die? Just a breath—and that's it?

Bacon's work was mostly mystery to me. He was painting about a world that I did not really know. I was from California and grew up in the best years of the Beach Boys, full of fun, fun, fun, and lots of sunshine—and yet it was one that I wanted to understand. As I walked through the Tate, I fought the urge to retell the parable of the emperor's new clothes. Is this just sophisticated foolishness? Will history see it more clearly, allowing the perspective of time to tell us that Bacon was playing with us—and that we paid him to do so?

But in the end, the more I listened to the world, the more I read and reflected, the more I was persuaded that he was a gifted artist feeling in his own body the anxiety of the modern world, the world in fact imagined by his forebear, the seventeenth-century Francis Bacon. To find that the painter was a direct descendent of the statesman and essayist was astonishing. To imagine the two in conversation about life and the world, about who we are and what it all means . . . well, that is what gave purpose to my final year of college.

In those same years I first read the poetry of Steve Turner, whom one reviewer described as writing for "people who feel that poetry has forgotten them." That seemed like me, and I began to listen. While he was a Londoner and I was a Californian, he saw the same world and had the same questions that I did. His poem "The Conclusion" was the first of his work that I read.

My love,
  she said
  that when all's considered
  we're only
  machines.
I chained
  her to my
  bedroom wall
  for future use
  and she cried.[8]

In most every way a thousand miles from Bacon's tortured canvases, and yet in Turner's poetic imagination it was clear that he understood the alienation of the Enlightenment world.

What he saw was that the mechanized, industrialized universe of the Enlightenment Project was a story with an Achilles heel. On the one hand, it has produced so much that is amazing and wonderful: from light bulbs to automobiles, from MRI technologies to handheld computers. We live by its gifts. And yet, pressed to explain more than it can possibly explain, it produces an unlivable world. We might theorize and we might conceptualize, but when push comes to shove, no one really wants to live in a world where we are just machines.

One might imagine that the human condition and history must mean that we are nothing but machines, after all—as some of our most famous philosophers and scientists insist. In fact, one might argue the vision with cultural force and with substantial institutional weight. The modern university-at-large lives by this assumption, and public education in most places assumes this understanding of life. But because we are still human beings living in the world that is really there, being machines, even very well-oiled sexual machines, cannot finally explain our longing to be loved, our yearning to be treated as human beings.

But Are You Happy?

Over many years now, it is this tension between the world that we imagine and the world in which we live that has most intrigued me. All of us live with this tension, because in the deepest possible way all of us long for coherence. We are not finally satisfied with incoherence, with dissonance between what we believe and how we live. And that is why I have asked, and asked again, *So what is it that you care most about? What are your deepest commitments?* Does the way we answer those questions offer a sense of vocation that gives coherence, that connects the things that matter to us? And of course then I am always interested to see how all this plays out in ordinary life, the day-by-day life of all of us. Sometimes it takes a while, sometimes many miles, to see with much clarity.

Take my conversation with Bill, for example. I did not become a scientist after all, but over the years I have been a professor, most interested in the relationship of belief to behavior. My work takes me all over America month by month, and I am often flying out of Washington's various airports.

One day I was on my way across the country, on a flight through Houston. Before we even began taxiing, the person in the seat next to me asked to borrow my pen—which was *okay*, really. But then I noticed that he was flirting with the stewardesses—and I thought, *Really? That's what you're going to do?*

I always have work to keep me occupied, and so I am not the kind of traveler who is looking for a long conversation on the plane. A book I want to read, an article I need to write; there is always something to keep me engaged on the long flight from East to West coast. But before we left the Washington airspace I could see that Bill wanted to talk—and yes, it was "Bill," as we were on a first-name basis from the beginning.

A native Washingtonian, a graduate of one of our most prestigious private high schools, on to undergraduate work and a law degree from one of America's best-known private universities, he had been at work in the city for many years. That afternoon, he was on his way to Las Vegas, where a client of his was hosting a weekend-long party in a villa supplied by one of the largest of the casinos. Apparently, his client, a fellow Washingtonian, was a big spender at the gaming tables, and the casino knew that keeping him in town was very good business—and so the villa, with expansive patios and pools inside and out. And yes, "beautiful babes" with $1,000 bottles of champagne—we mustn't forget that. Bill could hardly wait, because he was a "player," self-described, but nonetheless a man on a mission to have as much fun as could be had.

We talked about many things. His work as an attorney, his monthly dinners with very intelligent people who, like him, loved to talk about very important things, and we even talked about the world, especially about why things are not the way they are supposed to be. Very openly, he explained the universe in terms of the Enlightenment vision, the "through a dead man's eyes" philosophical commitment that is the intellectual backdrop to evolutionary materialism—that is, the most prized and trusted knowledge comes to us from science, as it alone can prove what is true. It offers facts, and the most basic fact is that everything and everyone is a complex result of time working upon matter in the framework of chance. He was as certain about that as he was about all the fun he was going to have with the babes and their bottles of champagne.

I asked some questions, and the conversation moved on into *why* things are so messed up. Without a blink, Bill argued that "the mess" we see—not "evil," as that assumes philosophical commitments that he would not make—is because the evolutionary schema has gone awry. In simple terms, no longer are "alpha males" like him in charge of the mating pool, so the DNA of the human race is now skewed. With genuine distaste, he told of the consequences of "B" and "C" and "D" males in the gene pool, wanting me to see what he saw, to feel the intellectual pain that he felt. I am sure that it did grieve him.

I listened carefully, and by now we must have been flying over Arkansas. What I could see was that he was just like me. He had the same hopes I did. He had the same fears I had. In every way we lived in the same world—the point of tension between us was that we explained the world differently. We saw the meaning of life, and of our lives, differently. But what I wanted to ask was a question to assure him that I knew we were the same kind of people. I wanted to build a bridge between his life and mine.

"Bill, a question for you, then. Have the choices you've made, made you happy?" He sat silent for a few moments. And then it seemed as if the universe flipped, and the garrulous, self-confident Washington lawyer—"player" and "alpha male" that he was—was simply an ordinary man on an ordinary day. He leaned over to me and said, "Not really. I've always wanted to find a woman who would love me—and I never have."

I thought of many things, in the flash of memory that sometimes speeds through our minds. Of the perceptively artful "Sigh No More," the song by Mumford and Sons, longing for "love as it was made to be." What would Bill think of their lyrics? Would he hear himself in the words?

> Love it will not betray you
> Dismay or enslave you, it will set you free
> Be more like the man you were made to be[9]

But then I also thought of my years of studying the Enlightenment tradition, of my growing discomfort with it as a final explanation for who we are and how we will live, and even of Turner's poem, "The Conclusion"—*and she cried.* There was at least a profound poignancy to the moment, if not tears.

What I did was affirm that that mattered a lot to me too. And after a few more words, I asked another question, "Do you ever go into court, Bill, and really believe that there is a right and wrong to be discovered and argued? Or are you only and always a mercenary? Does the highest bidder always win your services?" I was asking him about the possibility of a vocation to the law, and to the meaning of the law. Is the law ever about justice, or is it only "just us"? Is it ever a matter of truth and right, or is it only and ever a matter of the most powerful always winning? The story he had told of his life made it seem that his evolutionary materialism had answers for every question—and so words like *evil* and *truth* and *right* and *justice* were mostly meaningless. The survivors survive, and you do what you have to do to survive, which means that you always play to win— whatever the cost to your conscience or to the common good.

As we talked about the larger purposes and possibilities of the law, I told him of a brilliant Oxford and Cambridge professor who sixty years earlier had been asked by the BBC to give a series of radio talks on the meaning of the Christian faith. Sunday night by Sunday night, C. S. Lewis would record his ten-minute reflections on the nature of his faith, and these broadcasts were later collected into individual books, and later into one book, *Mere Christianity.*

The first talk that Lewis did was titled "Right and Wrong as a Clue to the Meaning of the Universe." I explained to Bill what Lewis had said, coming back into our several hours of conversation, and of course connecting it to my last question to him about the vo-cation of an attorney and the argument for right and wrong, for good against evil—and wondering how it is that his evolutionary materialism gave him a livable answer. Like every other son of Adam in history, Bill wanted to be loved. His worldview could make sense of sensory pleasure, even of machinery that works pretty well for a while. It could account for beautiful babes and expensive champagne, but not for love—just as it could not make sense of justice and truth and good. Together, they are clues to the meaning of the universe, for all who have ears to hear and eyes to see.

DIFFERENCES AND THE DIFFERENCE THEY MAKE

One of my father's best gifts to me was windows into the meaning of his life and into the vocation that was his. As an adolescent, I began to ask questions that I had never asked, especially about science, about what it could understand and what it could not understand, what it could explain and what it could not explain. He gave me categories to think with rather than easy answers to argue about. In his discipline he was said to be one of the best in the world, and his scientific skills mattered to him. They gave him tools to work with as he sought clarification on what, for him, were lifelong perplexities.

But for all that he believed about the value of science, and the scientific method, he was quick to say that most of life was beyond the purview of science. At its best, it asks, and answers, certain questions. But for most questions that matter and most answers that matter, science as science cannot address them; its method has no tools that can assess what is beyond the measurable, the quantifiable, the repeatable, the observable. It was a crucial distinction for him, and it became so for me.

Like many others in the years of the Enlightenment Project, known by many as the Baconian vision—which is the modern world as we know it—Bill missed the meaning of that distinction. Unusually bright, professionally able, remarkably gregarious, he found himself living in a world that his worldview could not explain. I doubt that he ever came close to the alienated screams of the modern Bacon, but I do think he longed for more than what his own answers offered—about love, yes, but also about life. In a deeper place he wanted to love and to be loved; but also he wanted in his work to be more than a hired gun, a mercenary who sold his skills on the courthouse steps. Like all of us, he wanted a vocation that could make sense of the hopes and dreams of his life.

Yes, of course that is true—because Bill is just like me, and you.

Prayer for Vocations

God of heaven and earth, we pray for your kingdom to come, for your will to be done on earth as it is in heaven. Teach us to see our vocations and occupations as woven into your work in the world this week. For mothers at home who care for children, for those whose labor forms our common life in this city, the nation and the world, for those who serve the marketplace of ideas and commerce, for those whose creative gifts nourish us all, for those whose callings take them into the academy, for those who long for employment that satisfies their souls and serves you, for each one we pray, asking for your great mercy. Give us eyes to see that our work is holy to you, O Lord, even as our worship this day is holy to you. In the name of the Father, the Son and the Holy Spirit. Amen.

Acknowledgments

Thank you almost seems small, and yet I am deeply grateful to my
wife, Meg, still the woman that I love to love. From our first days
together she has shown me that it is possible to know the world and
still love the world, which is never a highly theoretical proposition,
as eventually it must be that a man can be known and still be loved.
That she has is the great gift of my life. And for my children—Eden
and Charlie, Elliott and Becca, David, Jessica, Jonathan and Erika—
who each know the tender place where hope meets reality and have
lived with my longings that are always proximate.

When Meg and I first married we decided to live by the credo of
the Clapham community of two hundred years ago, "Choose a
neighbor before you choose a house," from our first dwelling in a
third-floor apartment to this present one on Burke Road, where we
have now lived for over twenty years. Our "cottage in the woods"
with its huge trees and perennially flowering yard is a place of quiet
in a busy city and a complex world. Others have joined into our life
over time, becoming our neighbors, and our life is richer because
of the friendships of Mark and Leanne Rodgers and Todd and Judi
Deatherage. In the swirl of a metropolitan world, we try to have a
common life, sharing in the things that matter most to all of us.

We are part of a larger life in the city of Washington, of good people who work at good lives. Some we see regularly and some irregularly, but they form the community that has kept us here for most of life now. Their names are legion, but some of them are Ray and B. J. Blunt, Beau and Rosemary Boulter, George and Liz Connors, Anne Cregger and George Patterson, Susan and Nate Den Herder, Hans and April Hess, Claudius and Deirdre Modesti, Clydette Powell, Gail Thompson, John and Susan Yates, Nancy Ziegler, and many more. We are known by our friends in more ways than one, and these friends both know us but also are signposts of the kinds of friends that keep a life alive for life.

For my colleagues in the work of the Washington Institute, I am grateful that they have in their own different ways made this work theirs too. As I write, they are Kate Harris, Bill Haley, Adam Joyce, Laura Merzig Fabricky, Jameson Bilsborrow, Sarah Phillips and Adam Thies. There have been others, and there will be others. That they have made the vision "Vocation is integral, not incidental, to the *missio Dei*" theirs too makes it possible for me to keep at it.

In the labor of love that has brought this book into being, there are others whose commitments and passions have forged my own, and while we do not live in the same city, they are gifts to me: Byron and Beth Borger, Andrew and Katherine Cornes, Don and Mary Guthrie, Denis and Margie Haack, David and Demi Kiersznowski, Dan and Lynn Kirkbride, Charlie Peacock and Andi Ashworth, and Christopher and Carol Wright. I want to specially note the gift of Os Guinness, whose interest in the responsibility of knowledge was catalytic for me. From early on I listened carefully and have taken his words to heart. And there are some whose own vocations have nourished me in unusual ways over the years of my life: John Stockton, Tod Moquist, David Freeborn, Patricia Boyle, Bill Hatcher, John Penrose, Brad Frey, Rick Wellock, Kenneth G. Smith, Jerram Barrs, Tom McWhertor, Jerry Eisley, Ron Lutjens, Paul Woodard, Bonnie Liefer, Sharon Parks, Stan Gaede, Rich Gathro, Jerry Herbert,

Bill Wichterman, Cheryl Jackson, David Naugle, David Turner, Scott Calgaro, Gideon Strauss, Dave Evans, Allan Poole, Morna Comeau, Bill Fullilove, Evan Loomis, Kwang Kim, Christine Buchholz, Graham Wells, John Lankford, Curtis Eggemeyer, D. J. Smith, Esther Meek, Gaylen Byker, Dan Haseltine, Charlie Lowell, Stephen Mason, Matt Odmark, Micheal Flaherty, Makoto Fujimura, Isaac Slade, Jon Foreman, Matt Kearney, Tom Shadyac, Jozef Luptak, Jena Lee Nardella, Mike Hamilton, Rich Hoops, Steven Purcell, Mark Roberts, Henry Tazelaar, Ed Hague, Jay Jakub, Bruno Roche, Shannon Geiger, Vince Sedmak, Jeffrey Lindeman, Cosma Gatere, Muriithi Wanjau, Robert Varney, Lou Guiliano, Dwight Gibson, Stephen Graybill, Steven Moore, Terry Stokesbary and Walt Turner. Thank you for the way you have lived your life.

This book takes its place alongside a long literature on vocation, differently imagined by different people. A remarkable resource is *Callings: Twenty Centuries of Christian Wisdom on Vocation*, offering a wonderfully rich collection by many authors over many years. More recently, Tom Nelson, Amy Sherman, Tim Keller and Katherine Leary Alsdorf, my friends and teachers, have each offered important windows into the question of calling and why work matters.

At a critical moment along the way, the vision and grace of Russ and Ruth Pulliam was the best of gifts, and years later I have not forgotten. For several years my thinking about all that has become this book was deepened through a grant from the Lilly Endowment, part of their remarkably visionary Programs in the Theological Exploration of Vocation. And when it came time to write, we found a quiet place along the La Plata River in the southwestern corner of Colorado. The poets and geographers describe it as the place where the mesas meet the mountains, and my longest, deepest memories of summer are of its great sky and gentle breeze.

And finally, there are people and places that have formed me, though the years have passed and the particulars of their lives and mine are no longer what they once were. But I do remember. When I was twenty I met ideas incarnate in men and women in the community of L'Abri, and they continue to run through my life, framing the way I see the world. I still believe that an honest question deserves an honest answer, and that has been the heart of my vocation as teacher. For some time I entered into the tutelage of the Ligonier Valley Study Center, when it still was, and my deepest convictions about the deepest things were shaped in those years. Meeting J. I. Packer and John Stott a few years later changed many things for me, and most of what matters most is different because of them. I spent years teaching on Capitol Hill at the American Studies Program, and the unique pedagogy of senior members and junior members together at work over the most complex questions of the modern world will always affect what I see and how I teach. And over the last years teaching for the fellows programs here in Washington, coming to love a whole new generation of the next generation, has only deepened my belief that the most important question is always, *What do you love?* What we believe and how we live is formed by the way we answer that question, so it is critical for teachers and students in every century and every culture. When education does not address the question of love, then it is at best only scratching the surface of life and learning.

The truest truth is that I am embedded in a life lived among others, some near and some far, but each someone whose love for the most important things keeps me keeping on.

Gratia orbis terrarum.

Notes

INTRODUCTION

[1]In the spring of 1989, thousands of students came to Beijing from all over China with the hope of engaging their government in a serious conversation about the future of the nation. In those same years of the late 1980s, communism was imploding around the world after several generations of a grand, if fatally flawed, experiment. The world was watching China, wondering what would happen. That young people were leading the longing for change was particularly dramatic; from the perspective of the students, they wanted their leaders to lead them into that change. After several weeks of peaceful protest in Tiananmen Square—the historic gathering place in China in the very center of Beijing—the government sent in tanks and soldiers, and many of the students were murdered. The ones I met were the survivors, people who literally crawled out of China over the next year or so.

[2]"If one film school anywhere in the world has shaped a whole nation, it's the Beijing Film Academy, China's most elite school for film direction, production and writing. Each year, it accepts about 500 applicants—primarily from China—out of 100,000." Tim Appelo, "The 25 Best Film Schools Rankings," *Hollywood Reporter,* July 27, 2011.

[3]Walker Perey, "Another Message in a Bottle," in *Signposts in a Strange Land: Essays* (New York: Macmillan, 2000), 364.

[4]Quoted in Jean Bethke Elshtain, *Real Politics: At the Center of Everyday Life* (Baltimore: Johns Hopkins University Press, 1997), 9.

[5]For more on the nexus of faith, vocation and culture, see this address, which explores the relation of *cult* to *cultivate* and *culture*: www.washingtoninst.org/165/a-church-of-great-grace-and-great-truth-the-call-to-the-convocation-of-anglicans-in-north-america.

CHAPTER 1: TO KNOW THE WORLD AND STILL LOVE IT?

[1]This quotation is often attributed to Bismark, whom I have credited it to, but it has also been attributed to lawyer-poet John Godfrey Saxe.

[2]This is the subject of chapter 7, "The Great Temptations."

[3]Lewis Lapham, "She Wants Her TV! He Wants His Book!" *Harper's Magazine*, March 1991, 44-55.

[4]C. S. Lewis, *Of Other Worlds: Essays and Stories* (Orlando: Mariner Books, 2002), 24.

CHAPTER 2: IF YOU HAVE EYES, THEN SEE

[1]Karel Kachyna, *The Last Butterfly*, 1991. In his review, David Mills observes that the film "has elements in common with *Schindler's List*"—for example, both demonstrate "the precious power of art to transmit emotional truths about history, if not the factual completeness of history" —but he concludes that "Moreau, as delicately portrayed by Courtney, is a more clearly heroic figure than Oskar Schindler. And this heightens the impact of Kachyna's ending, which offers nothing akin to Spielberg's relieving images of rescue. *The Last Butterfly* may not be real, but it's true." David Mills, "The Last Butterfly," *The Washington Post*, January 21, 1994, www.washingtonpost.com/wp-srv/style/longterm/movies/videos/thelast butterflynrmills_a09e21.htm.

[2]Hannah Arendt, *Eichmann in Jerusalem: A Report on the Banality of Evil* (New York: Penguin, 1965), 246-47: "For these crimes were committed en masse, not only in regard to the number of victims, but also in regard to the numbers of those who perpetrated the crime, and the extent to which any one of the many criminals was close to or remote from the actual killer of the victim means nothing, as far as the measure of his responsibility is concerned. On the contrary, in general *the degree of responsibility increases as we draw further away from the man who uses the fatal instrument with his own hands.*" See 22-25, 146-47, 232-33 and 289.

[3]Ibid., xvii.

[4]Ibid., inside cover.

[5]Ibid., 6: "There was only one man who had been almost entirely concerned with the Jews, whose business had been their destruction, whose role in the establishment in the iniquitous had been limited to them. That was Adolph Eichmann."

[6]Ibid., 135.

[7]Ibid., 146: "That Eichmann had at all times done his best to make the Final Solution final was therefore not in dispute. The question was only whether this was indeed proof of his fanaticism, his boundless hatred of Jews, and whether he had lied to the police and committed perjury in court when he claimed he had always obeyed orders."

[8]Ibid., 26.

[9]Ibid., 287-88.

[10]Ibid., 22.

[11]Ibid., 89-90.

[12]Ibid., 135.

[13]Robert Bellah et al., *The Good Society* (New York: Alfred A. Knopf, 1991), 44.

[14]For more on this, see the end of chapter 4.

CHAPTER 3: THE LANDSCAPE OF OUR LIVES

[1]William Barrett, *Irrational Man* (Garden City, NJ: Anchor/Doubleday, 1962), 54-60. Michael Landman in *Philosophical Anthropology* argues similarly, "As every man, consciously or unconsciously, has a *Weltanschaung*, or world view, he also has, prior to all philosophy, a view of man. It contains it without making any general statement about his nature, purely by the way he is depicted, by what is established as his predominant trait, what is expected of him. But occasionally it also is expressed in universal statements." Michael Landman, *Philosophical Anthropology*, trans. David J. Parent (Philadelphia: Westminster Press, 1974), 24.

[2]Alan Lightman, *The Diagnosis* (New York: Vintage Contemporaries/ Random House, 2000).

[3]Thomas de Zengotita, "The Numbing of the American Mind: Culture as Anesthetic," *Harper's Magazine*, April 2002, 33-40. The essay became a good book several years later: *Mediated: How the Media Shapes Your World and How You Live in It* (New York: Bloomsbury, 2005).

[4]Ibid.

[5]Ibid., 36.

[6]Theodore Roszak, *The Making of a Counter Culture: Reflections on the Technocratic Society and Its Youthful Opposition* (Berkeley: University of California Press, 1995) and *Where the Wasteland Ends: Politics and Transcendence in Postindustrial Society* (New York: Bantam Doubleday, 1973).

[7]Theodore Roszak, *The Cult of Information: The Folklore of Computers and the True Art of Thinking* (New York: Pantheon, 1986), 162-67.

[8]Todd Gitlin, *Media Unlimited: How the Torrent of Images and Sounds Overwhelms Our Lives* (New York: Henry Holt/Metropolitan Books, 2001), 115.

[9]Kenneth J. Gergen, *The Saturated Self: Dilemmas of Identity in Contemporary Life* (New York: Basic Books, 1991), 16.

[10]Ibid., 7.

[11]Neil Postman, *Amusing Ourselves to Death: Public Discourse in the Age of Show Business* (New York: Penguin, 1985), 155-56.

[12]Ibid., vii-viii.

[13]Nicholas Carr, "Is Google Making Us Stupid?" *The Atlantic*, July/August 2008, www.theatlantic.com/magazine/archive/2008/07/is-google-making-us-stupid/306868/.

[14]Nicholas Carr, *The Shallows: What the Internet Is Doing to Our Brains* (New York: W. W. Norton, 2010).

[15]Colin Gunton, *The One, the Three and the Many: God, Creation and the Culture of Modernity* (Cambridge: Cambridge University Press, 1993), 14.

[16]See chapter 4, "Knowing Is Doing," and the importance of the covenantal cosmos in the Hebrew vision of learning and life.

[17]David Lyle Jeffrey, "Can Humane Literacy Survive Without a Grand Narrative?" in *Rethinking the Future of the University*, ed. David Lyle Jeffrey and Dominic Manganiello (Ottawa: University of Ottawa Press, 1998), 56.

[18]Ibid., 54.

[19]Ibid., 61.

[20]Ibid.; Jeffrey's italics.

[21]Aleksandr Solzhenitsyn, *A World Split Apart: Commencement Address Delivered at Harvard University, June 8, 1978* (New York: Harper & Row, 1978), 1.

[22]Ibid., 47.

[23]Ibid., 49-51.

[24]Steve Turner, "Creed," *Up to Date: Poems 1968–1982* (London: Hodder & Stoughton, 1982), 139.

[25]Václav Havel, "It Always Makes Sense to Tell the Truth," in *Open Letters: Selected Writings, 1965–1990* (New York: Vintage Books, 1992), 94-95.

CHAPTER 4: KNOWING IS DOING

[1]Chaim Potok, *The Chosen* (New York: Ballantine Books, 1996).

[2]For more on Singer, read Michael Specter, "The Dangerous Philosopher," *The New Yorker,* September 6, 1999, www.newyorker.com/archive/1999 /09/06/1999_09_06_046_TNY_LIBRY_000018991.

[3]Mark R. Schwehn, *Exiles from Eden: Religion and the Academic Vocation in America* (Oxford: Oxford University Press, 1993), 94.

[4]Louise Cowan, "Jerusalem's Claim Upon Us," *The Intercollegiate Review,* Fall/Spring 2001, 14-15.

[5]Ibid., 16.

[6]Ibid. The contrast between *eros* and *hesed* is important, the one being the root from which *erotic* comes with all that it means in terms of romantic and sexual attraction, the other being the faithful, committed affection of a good parent.

[7]Geerhardus Vos, *Biblical Theology* (Grand Rapids: Eerdmans, 1948), 23. "The Hebrew word rendered by the above nouns is *berith.* The Greek word is *diatheke.* As to *berith,* this in the Bible never means 'testament.' In fact the idea of 'testament' was entirely unknown to the ancient Hebrews. They knew nothing of a 'last will.' . . . *Berith* may be employed where as a matter of fact a covenant in the sense of agreement is referred to, which is more than can be said for 'testament.' Only the reason for its occurrence in such places is never that relates to an agreement. That is purely incidental. The real reason lies in the fact that the agreement spoken of is concluded by some religious sanction." And an interview with Jean Bethke Elshtain by Tamara Jaffe-Notier, "Jean Bethke Elshtain and the Politics of a Social Covenant," The Damaris Project (www.dam arisproject.org): "Our culture embraces a dominant image that we enter into jobs and chosen communities because they serve our self-interest in some sense. We need to get away from the idea that all our relationships are reducible to social contract. The notion of a covenant is richer, deeper. It has roots in our tradition, going back to the Mayflower Compact. It's an ideal of a moral community that flourishes as long as fellow citizens think of one another as a brotherhood and sisterhood, when some kind of civic affection binds us. We have acknowledged it along the way, but that has faded as contractualism grew. Dr. Martin Luther King Jr. embodied the notion of a covenant. Abraham Lincoln's second inaugural address expresses the idea also. It is something that could not be invented outside of historical roots."

[8]Jean Bethke Elshtain, *Real Politics: At the Center of Everyday Life* (Bal-

timore: Johns Hopkins University Press, 1997), 9. "Freedom in this scheme of things is not the working out of a foreordained teleology of self-realization; rather freedom comes from embracing that which it is given one to do. The 'secret of man,' writes Havel, 'is the secret of his responsibility.' This responsibility consists, in part, in knowing rejection of God-likeness and mastery. For when man takes on this hubristic role he becomes the sole source of meaning in a world rendered dead and meaningless. Man exceeds his strength and he becomes a destructive Titan ruining himself and others. We are not perched on top of the earth as sovereigns; rather, we are invited into companionship with the earth as the torn and paradoxical creatures that we are."

[9]See Václav Havel's commencement speech at Harvard, June 8, 1995:

> The main task in the coming era is . . . a radical renewal of human responsibility. Our conscience must catch up with our reason, otherwise we are lost. It is my profound belief that there is only one way to achieve this: we must divest ourselves of our egoistic anthropocentrism, our habit of seeing ourselves as masters of the universe who can do whatever occurs to us. We must develop a new attitude and find respect for what transcends us immensely: for the Universe, for the Earth, for nature, for life and for reality. Our respect for other people, for other nations, and for other cultures, can only grow from a humble reverence of the cosmic order and from an awareness that we are a part of it, that we share in it and that nothing of what we do is lost, but rather recorded in the eternal memory of Being, where it is judged. A better alternative for the future of humanity, therefore, clearly lies in imbuing our civilization with a spiritual dimension. It will certainly not be easy to awaken in people a new sense of responsibility for the world, an ability to conduct themselves as if they were to live on this earth forever, and to be held accountable for its condition one day. Who knows how many cataclysms humanity may have to go through before such a sense of responsibility is generally accepted. But this does not mean that those who wish to work for it cannot begin at once. It is a great task for teachers, educators, intellectuals, the clergy, artists, entrepreneurs, journalists, people active in all forms of public life.

[10]One of the most horrible of national disasters is now known as "9/11."

After years of self-examination, the 9/11 Commission report, according to the *Washington Post*, "chronicles US failures" and "faults two administrations" (Dan Eggen, "9/11 Panel Chronicles US Failures," *The Washington Post*, July 23, 2004). Politically complex, personally wrenching, the issues explored by the commission are embedded in the responsibility of knowledge, i.e., who knew what when? Why didn't someone *know* more fully? How could brilliant, able people in organizations and institutions like the CIA and the White House not have *known* more? The assumption is that "someone" should have, because we must hold someone responsible. Someone somewhere has to be held responsible.

[11]See chapter 8, where Polanyi's thinking is more fully addressed.

[12]Over thirty years ago, I heard Os Guinness reflect on this theme, and offer a variation on this formulation. His words lit a candle in my mind and have been a light in the path of my thinking and rethinking its meaning over the years. I am very grateful, deeply grateful, to him for many gifts over many years.

[13]See John Calvin, *Commentaries on the First Book of Moses, Called Genesis*, trans. John King (Grand Rapids: Eerdmans, 1948), 1:124-25.

Moses now teaches, that man was the governor of the world, with this exception, that he should, nevertheless, be subject to God. A law is imposed upon him in token of his subjection; for it would have made no difference to God, if he had eaten indiscriminately of any fruit he pleased. Therefore the prohibition of one tree was a test of obedience. And in this mode, God designed that the whole human race should be accustomed from the beginning to reverence his Deity; as, doubtless, it was necessary that man, adorned and enriched with so many excellent gifts, should be held under restraint, lest he should break forth into licentiousness. There was, indeed, another special reason, to which we have before alluded, lest Adam should desire to be wise above measure; but this is to be kept in mind as God's general design, that he would have men subject to his authority. Therefore, abstinence from the fruit of one tree was a kind of first lesson in obedience, that man might know he had a Director and Lord of his life, on whose will he ought to depend, and in whose commands he ought to acquiesce. And this, truly, is the only rule of living well and rationally, that men should exercise themselves in obeying God. . . . What I have before said, since it is of far greater moment, is to be frequently recalled to memory, namely, that our life will then be rightly ordered, if we obey God, and if his will be the regulator of all our affections.

[14]Vos, *Biblical Theology*, 30-31. "The name would then really mean 'the tree of the choice of good and evil.' Some keep this in the general form of 'the tree by means of which man was to make his choice of good or evil.' This would be equivalent to 'the probation-tree.' Others give a peculiar sinister sense to the word 'knowing,' making it to mean 'the independent autonomous choice over against God's direction of what was good and what was evil for man.' This makes the name of the tree one of evil omen anticipating the disastrous result. . . . An objection, however, lies in this, that an arbitrary twist is thus given to the verb 'to know,' when it is made to mean to 'to choose' in general, with a neutral connotation, but particularly 'to choose presumptuously,' for which no evidence can be quoted."

[15]See Steven Garber, *The Fabric of Faithfulness: Weaving Together Belief and Behavior During the University Years* (Downers Grove, IL: InterVarsity Press, 1996). In chapter 4, "Making Sense of It All," I have argued that worldviews are a complex of the history of ideas, the sociology of knowledge and the ethic of character.

[16]Hal Hinson, "Weapons of the Spirit," *The Washington Post,* January 19, 1990, www.washingtonpost.com/wp-srv/style/longterm/movies/videos/weaponsofthespiritnrhinson_a0a92f.htm.

[17]The best source of information on this story is Phillip Hallie, *Lest Innocent Blood Be Shed: The Story of the Village of Le Chambon and How Goodness Happened There* (New York: Random House, 1970).

[18]In the words of Jeanette Rosenfeld in her speech for the Elie Wiesel Prize for Ethics in 1996, "While he lived in Le Chambon, Albert Camus observed the people of the village and was a witness to their courageous choice. In *The Plague*, Camus recognizes the clear-sightedness which compelled the Chambonnais to fight against evil. Though Camus never mentions Le Chambon explicitly, the allusion to the story of the village is too powerful to be ignored." Rosenfeld, "'Love Your Neighbor as Yourself': Nonviolent Resistance in Le Chambon," speech given at Barnard College, New York, New York. Full text available at http://ewflive.ctt-inc.com/cm_Images/UploadedImages/WinnersEssays/Jeanette_Rosenfeld.pdf.

[19]Pierre Sauvage, "Ten Questions," in *Courage to Care*, ed. Carol Rittner and Sondra Myers (New York: New York University Press, 1989), 135.

[20]Albert Camus, *The Plague*, trans. Stuart Gilbert (New York: Vintage Books, 1991), 124.

CHAPTER 5: COME AND SEE

[1]Jay Tolson, *Pilgrim in the Ruins: A Life of Walker Percy* (New York: Simon & Schuster, 2007).

[2]I have already written about the story of Jesus with Lazarus (chapter 1), but allow me to place it within this vision of the covenantal epistemology in the Gospel of John.

[3]Dave Matthews Band, "Tripping Billies" by Dave Matthews, on *Crash* (Nashville: RCA Records, 1996).

[4]Wendell Berry, *What Are People For?* (Berkeley, CA: Counterpoint, 2010), 197-200.

CHAPTER 6: VOCATION AS IMPLICATION

[1]Wendell Berry, *That Distant Land: The Collected Stories* (Berkeley, CA: Counterpoint, 2005), 356.

[2]The following excerpts are from *That Distant Land*, 145-63.

[3]Several years ago a foundation drew me into its work, identifying me as "a public teacher," describing what they knew of my work as they observed it. For many years I have had a classroom in Washington, but over time in many places among many people. Their language made sense of the life I have had. Through the rest of this chapter I will tell the stories of people that I have known as students, in a wide variety of contexts over many years. When the story is of a couple it is because both have been students in some way, and when not, I have included their spouses, integral to the story as they are. These men and women have been in my classroom in many different kinds of ways in many different settings. Come and see.

[4]See Lesslie Newbigin, *The Gospel in a Pluralist Society* (Grand Rapids: Eerdmans, 1989), 222-23.

[5]See the end of chapter 4, "Knowing Is Doing," 109-10.

[6]Thomas à Kempis, *The Imitation of Christ*, bk. 1, ch. 16.4.

[7]C. S. Lewis, *The Abolition of Man* (New York: HarperCollins, 2009), 26.

[8]Wendell Berry, "To Tanya, on My Sixtieth Birthday," *Given: New Poems* (Washington, DC: Shoemaker & Hoard, 2005), 6.

[9]Iris Murdoch, "The Idea of Perfection," in *The Sovereignty of Good* (New York: Schocken, 1971), 36-37.

CHAPTER 7: THE GREAT TEMPTATIONS

[1]It is for this reason that Rowan Williams, the archbishop of Canterbury, summed up centuries of Christian spirituality by titling his study, *The Wound of Knowledge.*

[2]Steve Turner, "History Lesson," in *Nice and Nasty* (London: Marshall, Morgan & Scott, 1980).

[3]Tom Wolfe, *A Man in Full* (New York: Farrar, Straus and Giroux, 1998).

[4]The same vision that drew Todd Deatherage into the neighborhood several years later.

[5]J. I. Packer, "Knowing and Being Known," in *Knowing God* (Downers Grove, IL: InterVarsity Press, 1993).

[6]Over several years, each has been the chairman of the board of our work.

CHAPTER 8: LEARNING TO LIVE PROXIMATELY

[1]See N. T. Wright, *Reflecting the Glory: Meditations for Living Christ's Life in the World* (Minneapolis: Augsburg, 1998).

[2]The literature on this is rich, and growing more so. One of the best is Oliver O'Donovan, *Resurrection and Moral Order: An Outline for Evangelical Ethics* (Grand Rapids: Eerdmans, 1986). Others that have contributed to this are Albert Wolters, *Creation Regained,* 2nd ed. (Grand Rapids: Eerdmans, 2005); John Stott, *Issues Facing Christians Today,* 4th ed. (Grand Rapids: Zondervan, 2006); and Michael Williams, *Far as the Curse Is Found* (Phillipsburg, NJ: P & R Publishing, 2005).

[3]Wendell Berry, "Word and Flesh," in *What Are People For?* (New York: Farrar, Straus & Giroux, 1990), 200.

[4]For two examples, see "A Wedding Sermon for Nathan and Sandie," in *Get Up Off Your Knees: Preaching the U2 Catalog,* ed. Raewynne J. Whitely and Beth Maynard (Boston: Cowley Publications, 2003); and "A Wedding Homily" in *Critique,* no. 4 (2009): 12-16.

[5]Stanley Hauerwas, *Reformed Journal* 36 (November 1986): 12-16.

[6]Madeleine L'Engle, "To a Long-Loved Love: 7," in *The Weather of the Heart* (New York: Crosswicks, 1978).

[7]See *Tacit Knowing, Truthful Knowing: The Thought and Life of Michael Polanyi* (Charlottesville, VA: Mars Hill Audio, 1999). I have also men-

tioned him in chapters 4 and 6, as well as the epilogue.

[8]In Lesslie Newbigin's *Proper Confidence: Faith, Doubt and Certainty in Christian Discipleship* (Grand Rapids: Eerdmans, 1995), he takes up Polanyi's work with great skill, showing that the Enlightenment assumptions about the nature of knowledge do not account for the way that human beings know and live.

[9]Marx himself never advocated violence, but his intellectual heirs Lenin, Stalin and Mao saw the genocide of their own peoples as necessary for the revolution of consciousness required for their utopian visions.

[10]Rohinton Mistry, *Family Matters* (Toronto: McLelland and Stewart, 2002), 334.

[11]See chapter 4, "Knowing Is Doing," where the vision of a covenantal cosmos and the dynamic interaction of relationship, revelation and responsibility is set forth.

[12]U2, "Grace," on *All that You Can't Leave Behind* (London: Island Records, 2001).

[13]Michka Assayas, *Bono: In Conversation with Michka Assayas* (New York: Riverhead, 2005).

[14]B. F. Skinner, *Beyond Freedom and Dignity* (New York: Knopf, 1971).

[15]Lesslie Newbigin, *The Gospel in a Pluralist Society* (Grand Rapids: Eerdmans, 1994), 89.

[16]This threefold vision is the heart of the covenantal epistemology set forth in chapter 4: revelation, relationship and responsibility.

EPILOGUE

[1]For more on Francis Bacon, see www.guardian.co.uk/culture/2005/aug/09/edinburghfestival2005.edinburghfestival1 and http://nymag.com/arts/art/profiles/56786/.

[2]Theodore Roszak, *Where the Wasteland Ends* (New York: Doubleday, 1973).

[3]Francis Bacon (1561–1626) was an English lawyer, statesman, essayist, historian, intellectual reformer, philosopher and champion of modern science; the author of *The New Atlantis, The Great Instauration* and *Novum Organon;* and the forebear of the twentieth-century painter of the same name.

[4]Francis Bacon, *The Great Instauration* (Calgary: Theophania Publishing, 2011).

[5]See chapter 8, "Learning to Live Proximately."

6Theodore Roszak, *Where the Wasteland Ends* (New York: Doubleday, 1973), 131.

7Os Guinness, "The Striptease of Humanism," in *The Dust of Death: The Sixties Counterculture and How It Changed America Forever* (Wheaton, IL: Crossway Books, 1994).

8Steve Turner, "The Conclusion," *Up to Date: Poems 1968–1982* (London: Hodder & Stoughton, 1982), 24.

9"Sigh No More," by Mumford and Sons on *Sigh No More* (London: Gentlemen of the Road / Island Records, 2009).

About the Author

Steven Garber is the principal of The Washington Institute for Faith, Vocation & Culture, which is focused on reframing the way people understand life, especially the meaning of vocation and the common good. A consultant to foundations, corporations and schools, he is a teacher of many people in many places. The author of *The Fabric of Faithfulness*, he is also a contributor to the books *Faith Goes to Work: Reflections from the Marketplace* and *Get Up Off Your Knees: Preaching the U2 Catalogue*. He lives with his wife, Meg, in Virginia.